THE ILLUSTRATED
COUNTIES OF ENGLAND

THE ILLUSTRATED
COUNTIES
— OF —
ENGLAND

Edited by
JAMES BISHOP

and published in association with
THE ILLUSTRATED LONDON NEWS

GEORGE ALLEN & UNWIN
London · Sydney

CONTENTS

EAST ANGLIA

THE NORTH

Text copyright © 1980, 1981, 1982,
1983, 1984, 1985 by the authors.

Illustrations copyright © 1980,
1981, 1982, 1983, 1984, 1985, by
The Illustrated London News.

First published in Great Britain by
George Allen & Unwin 1985.

George Allen & Unwin (Publishers) Ltd
40 Museum Street, London WC1A 1LU, UK

George Allen & Unwin (Publishers) Ltd
Park Lane, Hemel Hempstead,
Herts HP2 4TE, UK

George Allen & Unwin Australia Pty Ltd
8 Napier Street, North Sydney,
NSW 2060, Australia.

ISBN 0 04 9140606

Printed in Hong Kong by
Colorcraft Ltd.

Half title Burford Church, Oxfordshire
Title page Derbyshire hills
Contents page Autumn in the Wylye valley
Page vii Brown Clee Hill, Shropshire
Page 248 Estuary scene in Cornwall

INTRODUCTION by the Editor

Ask an Englishman where he comes from and he will give you the name of a county. It may not be where he is now living. It may be where he was born, but has not lived for many years, or it may be somewhere he has come to know in later life. It may even be a county that no longer officially exists. But so powerful is the Englishman's sense of identity with his county that a loyalty towards it can persist throughout his life.

This book is about that sense of identity. Its genesis was a series of articles which are being published separately in THE ILLUSTRATED LONDON NEWS. Thirty-nine English men and women have written about their counties, and photographers have followed in their footsteps. Those who read the very personal pieces in this collection will quickly appreciate the remarkable difference in character between each county, even those which share a common boundary, and the fierce pride which each can generate among those who are, by birth or by habitation, firmly tied to it.

Such loyalty is most evident, in this book and elsewhere, among those whose counties have recently been mucked up by bureaucracy. Until a decade ago there were thirty-nine counties in England. Today that number has been increased to forty-six; but not all of the thirty-nine survive, some having been exterminated, or redesignated, by the Local Government Act of 1972, whose changes came into force on 1 April 1974. That these changes have yet to be comfortably accepted will be readily discerned from the contributions to this book; and since it is a personal and not an official volume its contents have been determined by the logic of loyalties rather than the preference of planners. Thus Huntingdonshire, Middlesex and Rutland are included, and Herefordshire and Worcestershire remain separate, because the people who live there still think and speak of these counties, which no longer officially exist, as their homes. On the other hand some of the new official counties, such as Avon, Cleveland and Humberside, are omitted because they have yet to establish themselves as anything more than administrative units. They neither command the allegiance nor inspire the imagination in the way of the older counties. Perhaps this is not surprising, since many of them had their boundaries established in the old Saxon shires.

There are two exceptions to this reactionary rule. The Isle of Wight, now the smallest English county, has long had an identity of its own, and Cumbria has the logic of its history and the geography of the Lake District to justify its creation. Both are therefore included.

The historian Sir Arthur Bryant, who has written regularly for THE ILLUSTRATED LONDON NEWS for nearly half a century, once began an article on the English counties with the words: "England has thirty-nine counties – and I do not know which is the loveliest." He went on to note that there was not one of them which had not some claim to be beautiful, and "whose sons and daughters would not be ready to champion her above her thirty-eight sister shires." His immediate predecessor as author of the ILN's Notebook, G. K. Chesterton, wrote that memorable poem about the rolling English drunkard making the rolling English road – "the reeling road, the rolling road, that rambles around the shire" – which

seems an equally admirable description of the shape of the county boundaries as they have long existed.

There are thirty-nine counties in this book, with thirty-nine eager champions, and it would be foolhardy for an editor to show any preferences – though, under another hat, as a contributor, he makes a case for that least glamorous of counties, Middlesex. From the well-castled coastline, rich pasturelands and the Roman Wall of Northumberland in the north-east, to the great rocky scrolls of granite, the fuchsia and tamarisk hedges and the rolling seas of Cornwall in the south-west; from the chalk deposits, weather-boarded houses, farms and man-made landscapes of Kent in the south-east to the lakes, fells and old mine works of Cumbria in the north-west; from the bridleways, fortified hills and lush valleys of the Wye in Herefordshire in the west across the belt of England to the flat fenlands, acres of cornfields and great churches of Norfolk and Suffolk in the east – every part of England has something to be said in its favour, and a good deal of it will be found here. The reader may judge for himself which county he prefers, though I suspect he will already have a view that will not be changed by anything anyone can write. What is surely unchallengeable is that we are fortunate to have so many riches and so much variety crammed within the erratic boundaries of what we call our English counties.

James Bishop *London, June 1984*

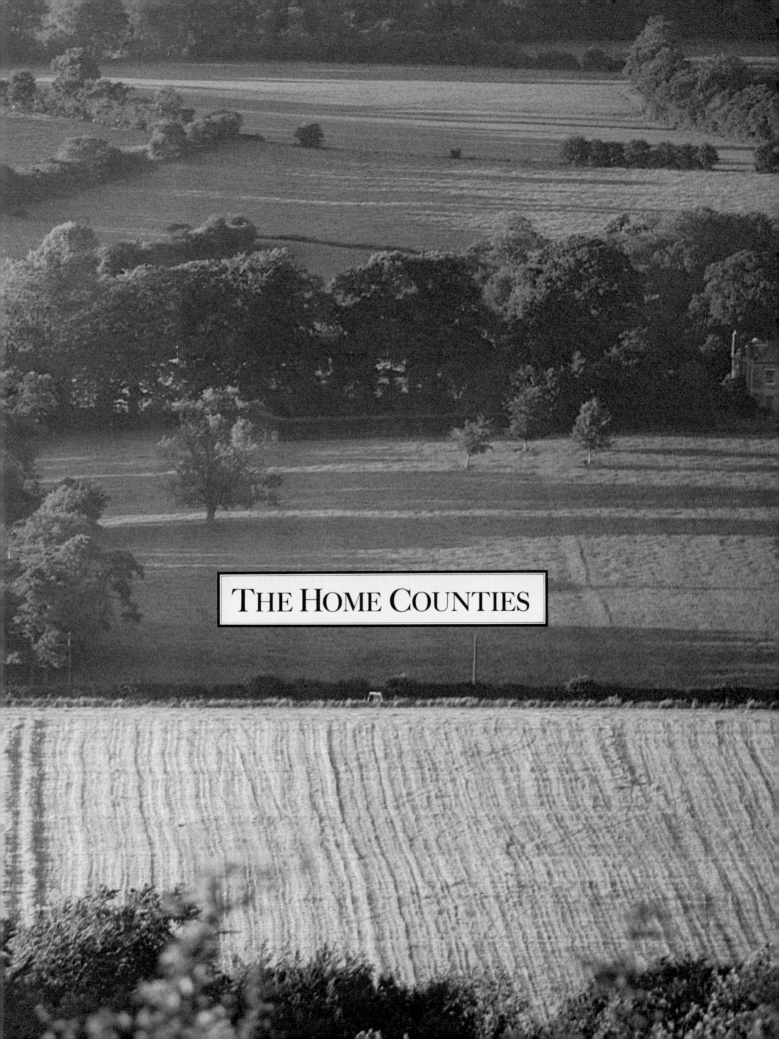

THE HOME COUNTIES

JAMES DYER'S
Bedfordshire

Photographs by David Gallant

The happiest days of my childhood were spent in the tiny hamlet of Higham Gobion, where from a small cottage beside a brook we looked south across the cornfields to the rounded ridge of the Chilterns above Barton-in-the-Clay. The cottage, one of three built in 1877, was tiny, two rooms up and two down, with an outside privy. It was linked by internal doors to its neighbours and formed a doss-house for the coproliters who worked across the adjoining fields in the 1870s, digging out the phosphatic nodules to be crushed in the mill behind the Musgrave Arms at Apsley End, Shillington. By my time the industry was long forgotten and the cottages provided homes for two farm labourers and a gamekeeper.

St Margaret's Church was where my aunt, Grace Ingram, did her share of the cleaning, polishing and flower arranging during the week, and took her place regularly every Sunday. Too small to take part, I sat on the hard wooden bench while she and the half-dozen parishioners knelt at the communion rail. My eyes wandered around that little church built early in the 14th century, with its tiny north aisle, up to the beam above the chancel arch carved with the date of the Armada and the letters H.B. The Victorians had restored the church, but the mixture of greenstone and Totternhoe stone of its exterior blended with its ancient gravestones, set among green trees and making it a delightful place of simple mystery. I longed to know something of its former worshippers, particularly Edmund Castell, rector from 1665, whose monument above the chancel door is written in Arabic, recalling that he was a professor of that language at Cambridge and author of the great *Lexicon Heptaglotton*, a dictionary in seven languages, many copies of which were destroyed in the Great Fire of London or eaten by rats.

For a time I travelled the two miles each way to Shillington School. Although it was beautifully situated beside the church with a wide view from the playground, I hated the large classroom, a hall with at least three classes all being taught at once and the headmaster sitting at one end on a raised platform. The only relief from boredom came when, during air raids, we were ushered into a smaller room with bricked-up windows, where someone read us the *Just So Stories*. I have loved them ever since. For lunch I walked round the corner to "Aunt" Polly Welch's cottage, facing the churchyard wall, to eat my sandwiches. It was cosy but minute, with plants on every conceivable ledge. School over, I walked down the churchyard path to the Richardsons' store where I met Aunt Grace, and helped carry the week's rations back along "The Baulk" to Higham.

From the cottage we looked out to the chalk escarpment. Along its summit ran the Icknield Way, the pre-historic track that was to influence enormously my later life as an archaeologist. From my bedroom window I could see the trees growing on the Iron Age fort of Ravensburgh Castle, whose ramparts straddled the county boundary. In the 1970s my excavations showed that Ravensburgh was likely to have been the head-quarters of the Catuvellaunian chieftain, Cassivellaunus, who was attacked there by Caesar in 54 BC.

The Icknield Way had formed the main east-west route across the county for thousands of years. A small Roman settlement grew up close to the gravel ridge by which the track crossed the River Lea marshes at Leagrave, and it was here that Luton

The Iron Age fort of Ravensburgh Castle, seen from the village of Higham Gobion.

ABOVE: Shillington Church. LEFT: The view to the east from Sharpenhoe Clapper. BELOW: The Dovecote at Willington. BELOW CENTRE: Oakley Bridge, which has been recently restored and crosses the River Ouse. BELOW LEFT: The ruins of Houghton House.

was to start its long, slow growth southwards to become the largest town in the county.

I explored Bedfordshire on a bicycle, which meant that the north was largely out of reach, but I investigated the centre and south quite thoroughly. Though the chalk hills constantly called me, I travelled north to the Ouse valley, to Odell with its chestnut trees lining the path to the church, and its ancient memories of woad growing.

At Willington I explored the dovecote with its stepped gables and 1,400 holes for pigeons, built as part of Sir John Gostwick's 16th-century manor house, and across the road I ate strawberries and cream in his stables, now administered by the National Trust. In later years aerial photographs revealed the outlines of circular ditches on the banks of the river, and I excavated the interior of one of these to reveal the stone footings of a rectangular building containing much burnt peat and human bones, apparently an Iron Age crematorium.

Farther down river the 17 arches of Great Barford bridge are typical of most of the Ouse bridges in Bedfordshire, leaving ample room for flooding. Three hundred years ago coal barges sailed to the wharf nearby and the river provided a major thoroughfare. Earlier, in 1323, its only Bedfordshire tributary, the Ivel, enabled boats to sail up to Shefford and collect 20 oaks from Chicksands Priory for the construction of the lantern of Ely Cathedral.

At Sutton I rode with my companions through the ford beside the rust-coloured pack-horse bridge. In the church I found box-pews, and graffiti scratched by a bored schoolboy centuries past. Most intriguing was the Sacred Barrel Organ, restored 15 years ago, with three barrels playing 30 different hymn tunes ranging from "Lord Mornington's Chant" to "Sicilian Mariners". Somehow it seemed in keeping with the Reverend Edward Drax Free (1808–30) who was prosecuted for lewdness, indecency and immorality, kept cattle, pigs and horses in the churchyard and fodder in the porch, fought with his clerk during a service and had three illegitimate children.

A visit to Ampthill always gave me much pleasure. The neat Georgian streets, today unhappily bursting with traffic, led me very soon to St Andrew's Church. As a schoolboy I was fascinated by the monument to Richard Nicolls which carries the actual cannon ball that killed him during the battle with the Dutch off Sole Bay, Suffolk, in 1672. To the west of the town is Ampthill Park with its cross in memory of Catherine of Aragon, set up by Lord Upper Ossory at the instigation of Horace Walpole.

It was at the base of the cross that Kit Williams, author of *Masquerade*, buried his golden hare. From here the view north-west is one of the most dramatic in mid-Bedfordshire. The pool at the bottom of the gorse-covered hill leads one's eyes through the trees to Ampthill Park House, and the rolling countryside beyond. But here there is conflict, for the scene is interrupted by the chimneys and clay pits of the brick-works that dominate this part of central Bedfordshire. There can be few counties in Britain that do not contain bricks of our local clay. Millions of tons have been excavated, leaving great pits, some of which are now flooded and provide aquatic pleasures, while others are being filled with rubbish brought daily in container trains from London. Of the tall chimneys which dominated the landscape, and whose fumes carried as far as Scandinavia, some have recently been demolished, and this can only be for the good of conservation.

On the eastern side of Ampthill Park lie the ruins of Houghton House. Built about 1615 for Mary Countess of Pembroke, it was later occupied by the Ailesbury family. In 1738 it was bought by the Duke of Bedford for his son the Marquis of Tavistock, who fell from his horse and died at the house in 1767. Houghton House was a splendid building commanding enormous views to the north. It had a great dining room, smoking room and withdrawing room. In the cedar closet were 140 books and in the boarded hall were 24 muskets. There were numerous bedrooms and a chapel, as well as the servants' quarters. Peacocks strutted on the terraces outside, and apricots and peaches grew in the orchard. Today the house stands empty and forsaken. There are stone pillars and carvings, and fireplaces high above our heads, reminding us of rooms once warm and alive with activity.

It has long been a custom for the children of Toddington to lie with their ears to the ground on top of Conger Hill, a medieval castle mound, at midday on Shrove Tuesday. As the church clock strikes it is recorded on good authority that a witch can be heard frying her pancakes. Toddington is one of Bedfordshire's finest villages. There has been lots of fringe growth in recent years, but this has done little to detract from the ancient core around St George's Church and the large and pleasant green which dates back to the 16th century. A map by Ralph Agas is preserved in the British Museum, dated 1581, and a remarkably large number of the properties shown in detail on it still survive, although they may have been refronted. There used to be a market day on Thursdays and three annual fairs, but these have long since disappeared to be replaced by an annual show. It seems strange seeing the village today to think that there were once 16 butchers' stalls on the green. Even the present population would have difficulty in providing them with trade. Another sight long since vanished is that of skaters on the village pond, now a memorial garden to Sir Frederick Mander, a past president of the National Union of Teachers and World Federation of Educational Associations.

I began with the chalk hills and I will finish with them. I am conscious that I have omitted much, not least the county town, today a thriving cosmopolitan community that has had little influence on my life. For me the chalk hills make Bedfordshire. They have been desecrated by cement manufacturers and the conurbation of Luton and Dunstable, but enough remains to sample their pleasures: Deacon Hill above Pegsdon, the Warden and Galley Hills at Streatley and the Dunstable Downs stretching across to Whipsnade Zoo. Beside Bison Hill is a broad stretch of the Downs belonging to the National Trust, wild and beautiful and under-visited. In contrast, at Streatley, is the outstanding beech-clad spur of Sharpenhoe Clapper. Views both from and to it are among the finest in the county. The National Trust has constructed a tiny car park, but the queues of parked cars stretching back into Streatley village on summer weekends shriek loudly that this is not enough. Sadly the popularity of the spot is wearing away the soil and plants that the Trust would like to protect. Few people realize that the Markham Hills on the west side of the road, stretching away towards Sundon, are equally beautiful, and also open to the public. But for me, and for hundreds of others, Sharpenhoe *is* Bedfordshire, and long may it remain unspoilt.

RICHARD ADAMS'
Berkshire

Photographs by Trevor Wood

Everyone feels that his own county has a claim to be of major historical importance, but if the Berkshireman has no strong case, no one has. I emphasize that I am talking about the true, not the despicably truncated, Berkshire — the Berkshire where I was born, the entire northern boundary of which was formed by the Thames. Precious little of importance has taken place in English history without Berkshire having something to say to it. There is far too much history and there are far too many interesting and beautiful places for me to hope to squeeze everything into an article like this, so I have selected what means most to me.

We start very strongly, with one of the oldest known burial sites in England — Wayland's Smithy, so-called, which lies a little north of the Ridgeway, the oldest road in England, about a mile west of the White Horse on the Lambourn Downs. Wayland was a Scandinavian folk hero whose story is told in one of the oldest songs of the Edda; *Beowulf* also alludes to him. When I was a boy the "smithy" (see Kipling's *Puck of Pook's Hill*) was nothing more than a cromlech — a pile of tumbled stones in a spinney, the remains of some ancient construction. Since the Second World War it has been excavated and restored, proving to comprise two Neolithic and Bronze Age barrows, dating from about 3700 and 3400 BC.

The White Horse of Uffington has long been the emblem of Berkshire. The oldest of the white horses of the chalkland scarps, it is 374 feet long and was probably created some time about the first century AD as a territorial landmark of the Dobunni tribe. The strange, stylized shape was kept pristine through the centuries by the villagers of Uffington. Traditionally, the annual "scouring fair" was the occasion for weeding and cleaning up the horse; now the job is done by the Department of the Environment.

> "The owld White Horse wants zetten to rights
> And the squire hev promised good cheer,
> Zo we'll gie un a scrape for to kip un in zhape,
> And a'll last for many a year."
>
> (Tom Hughes, *Scouring of the White Horse*, 1859.)

Michael Drayton (1563–1631) evidently liked the White Horse, too:

The view from White Horse Hill, the highest point on the Berkshire Downs.

> "And but that Evesham is so opulent and great
> That thereby she holds herself in the sovereign seat,
> This White Horse all the vales of Britain would overbear
> And absolutely sit in the imperial chair."
>
> *(Polyolbion.)*

It is said that if you stand in the eye of the White Horse and wish (or pray), your wish will be granted — once. It certainly worked for me, in a matter of vital importance.

In Anglo-Saxon times Berkshire formed part of the kingdom of Wessex and there are many relics of Saxon occupation, including the burial grounds at Long Wittenham and Frilford. King Alfred the Great was born about 848 at Wantage in the White Horse Vale, and fought the Danes up and down Berkshire in the 870s. In days gone by, people believed Alfred created the White Horse as a sign of victory, but even though he didn't, he deserves to be associated with it as the greatest of all Berkshiremen.

In 1066 Berkshire was part of the earldom of Harold, and a local force supported him strongly at Hastings. This loyalty was punished by the Conqueror with sweeping confiscations, and the first Domesday survey of 1086 shows no estates of importance in the hands of Englishmen.

There are not many early Norman churches remaining structurally unaltered since they were built in the late 11th century, but Berkshire has at least one: at Avington, a hamlet with a farm and a great house on the left bank of the Kennet a few miles east of Hungerford. It is well worth a visit (the key is available from a cottage). Here, with the Kennet weirs pouring near by, you can really form some idea at first hand of just how bleak, meagre and basic life must have been 900 years ago. The rectangular stone shed is about as bare and twilit as it could be; movingly spare and beautiful. The south door has a fine, zig-zag Norman arch. The beak-headed chancel arch (orginally round, too, of course) has sunk inward, so that now it is getting on for horizontal. There is an arcaded Norman font with 12 bays containing 13 figures, but I am not altogether sure whether these represent Christ and the apostles. Certainly one figure has a key, but some of the others seem more cryptic. In the floor of the choir are some beautiful, early 18th-century gravestones of the James family, complete with coats of arms and their splendid punning motto "J'aime à jamais".

I am a Newburian and, although Newbury is no longer the rural market town where my father was a surgeon of the hospital and doctor in attendance at the race meetings (we all used to get free passes to the members' enclosure, to say nothing of

tips from grateful jockeys), I retain a deep affection for it. Its most famous citizen was John Winchcombe (sometimes called John Smalwode), known as Jack of Newbury. Jack's historical significance lies in his rise to wealth and influence at the turn of the 15th century, although born a nobody and never raised to the nobility. He exemplifies the contemporary rise of the middle classes and the growing prosperity of England through wool. He was an early capitalist and employer of mass labour. When Jack was young his master died and he married the widow, overcoming several rivals to do so.

> "Who flocked to see her, young and old,
> In part for love, in part for gold.
> But this was a gallant Cloathier sure,
> Whose fame for ever shall endure."

Jack did so well as a clothier (nothing like him had hitherto been seen in England) that he was able to rebuild St Nicholas's Church, the parish church of Newbury, a fine example of Perpendicular, with a beautiful tower (and the addition of some excellent 19th-century stained glass). When the Scots invaded the north in 1513, in the absence of Henry VIII in France, and Queen Catherine was desperate for troops, Jack, so it is said, equipped and led 30 bowmen to Flodden at his own expense. The story goes that he knelt to the Queen, who said, "Rise, gentleman." Jack answered, "Your Majesty, I am no gentleman, for my rentes come from the backes of little sheepes, but we are here to serve our Queen." An old ballad runs:

> "The Chesshyre Laddes were bryske and brave
> And the Kendall Laddes as free,
> But none surpassed, or I'm a Knave,
> The Laddes of Newberrie."

LEFT: Wayland's Smithy, ancient burial site. BELOW: The Church of St Mark and St Luke at Avington, which is entirely Norman and still has nearly all its original windows. RIGHT: Combe Gibbet, site of a 17th-century hanging.

Jack died in 1519 and has a rather modest brass in the church.

Jack's "manager" was William Dolman, whose son Thomas proved a worthy successor. He, too, became rich and began the building of Shaw House, the fine Elizabethan dwelling still standing north of the town. A contemporary local comment ran, "Lord, have mercy on us miserable sinners. Tommy Dolman hath builded a new house and turned away all his spinners." Dolman's retort was, "Edentulus vescentium dentibus invidet et caprearu oculos talpa contemnit." (The toothless man envies the teeth of those who gnaw and the mole has no use for the eyes of the doe.)

In the Civil War Berkshire was a veritable cockpit. I was born and grew up very near the field of the first battle of Newbury (September 20, 1643), where Viscount Falkland, one of the most attractive and able of King Charles's supporters, was almost suicidally killed. It has often been suggested that if the king had won this battle he would probably have won the war. The Parliamentary army, under the Earl of Essex, was returning from Gloucester, desperate to get back to London. It aimed to pass just south of Newbury, where Charles and Rupert barred its way. At the end of the day Essex had still not broken through, but the Royalist army retired into Newbury and did not renew the engagement; Essex marched on, by way of Greenham Common, to London.

More than a year later Cromwell himself was involved in a second battle with Charles at the other end of Newbury. The aim was to prevent Charles's retreat to Oxford and if possible destroy his army. The king's headquarters were none other than Tommy Dolman's Shaw House, now occupied by his descendant Humphrey. It was hardly damaged, but there is a tradition that a Parliamentary bullet just missed Charles standing in a window of the library, and also that both Charles and Dolman fought hand-to-hand with the rebels in the garden. If this is true, Charles was the last English king to engage in personal fight. Owing to a certain lack of aggressive spirit on the part of Lord Manchester, commanding the Parliamentary side, the Royalist army was able to slip away towards Oxford that night.

In the extreme south-west of the county, between Inkpen Beacon and Walbury Hill, stands Combe Gibbet. It is kept in repair, and renewed as often as necessary, by the terms of the lease of the tenants of a neighbouring farm. The present gibbet, however, was erected by the Hon John Astor. (In 1895 the Berkshire-Hampshire boundary was moved south to include Combe; so the gibbet, formerly in Hampshire, has been in Berkshire for nearly a century.) The story is grim, though we really know no details. In 1676 George Broomham and Dorothy Newman were convicted at Winchester of the murder, on Inkpen Down, of Broomham's wife and son "with a staff". The crime excited so much local horror that they were sentenced to be hanged *à la carte*, as it were, on the highest point in the county. A double gallows was erected and it has never been used again. The story was adapted by the film director John Schlesinger, himself a Berkshireman, for his first film, *Black Legend*, made on the spot with a local amateur cast in 1947.

I was at school at Bradfield, and I cannot end without mentioning that beautiful place. Its glory is the famous Greek amphitheatre, unique in Great Britain. In 1890 Dr H. B. Gray (Bradfield's equivalent of Arnold of Rugby) began its construction, entirely with local labour, in an old chalk pit. In 1898 he enlarged it to its present

The River Kennet at Thatcham, possibly the oldest village in the county, with Chamberhouse Farm in the background.

capacity of about 1,600 to 2,000. A Greek play in original Greek has been performed triennially at Bradfield for the past century (excluding the wars). In the bye years they do Shakespeare. The theatre, embowered by surrounding trees, has wonderful charm and atmosphere, and I have been happier there than in any other single place in my life. Thanks to "Greeker", as it is called, I have seen most of the surviving Greek plays produced in a theatre similar to those for which their authors wrote, and understand thoroughly the difference between ancient Greek and Shakespearian drama. In Greeker, I saw my first performances of *Twelfth Night, A Midsummer Night's Dream, Romeo and Juliet* and *The Taming of the Shrew*.

Its rural setting makes Bradfield a pleasant place for a boarding school. In summer we used to roam the countryside freely. I well recall Bucklebury Church (which also has a fine Norman south door) with its Jacobean pulpit and famous painted glass sundial window, complete with a *trompe l'oeil* fly.

What an inadequate piece! Nothing about Windsor, Ascot, Reading and much more. Berkshire is like a great sponge of history. It needs but squeezing and the past comes pouring out. This, perforce, has had to be only a gentle squeeze. If my ghost ever walks, it will be by the Kennet at, say, Chamberhouse Farm on a June evening, with the trout rising to the mayfly and the swallows skimming and splashing over the sunset-reddened water.

Buckinghamshire

Photographs by Tim Graham

If some fellow European, with only a weekend to spare and wishing to understand our rural England, were to ask me to demonstrate very shortly the essence of what we cherish and why we cherish it, I should take him on a quick tour of Buckinghamshire. Yet "an insipid county" Horace Walpole called it, and it was a lot less insipid in his day than in ours. But I see what he meant. It has neither moors nor mountains nor coast, not even the superb sweep of our grassy downland unless one counts little Quainton Hill. It is tranquil with the calm and delicacy of an old lady whose unbroken memories unite our agricultural past and present.

Buckinghamshire starts with a flourish that it cannot keep up. Suddenly the soggy flats of Middlesex and the outer suburbs of London give way to the range of the Chilterns and its glorious beech woods. Up from the valleys followed by road, rail and the many levels of the Grand Canal — and it is rail which offers the best view of the typical scenery — rich 200 acre fields climb to the forested skyline between bands of copses. On the high ground it is a region of prosperous villages, of farms carefully manicured and white-railed, of leafy lanes leading into the "ends" and "bottoms" so common in Chiltern place-names. To the south are some of the most spectacular reaches of the Thames and on the way to the river, in dips and dells, such perfect villages as Frieth, Fingest and Turville. The northern slopes hide the five great country houses of the Rothschild brothers and cousins, all of whom had appalling taste in architecture but a wonderful eye for a site.

It was their pleasure to look across the Vale of Aylesbury, which is the right way to appreciate it. The Vale reminds me when I am down in it of a wide estuary with, instead of sea, field and hedgerow, nothing much but field and hedgerow, stretching between the sharp escarpment of the Chilterns and the line of low hills which are the beginning of the true Buckinghamshire and the Midlands.

The Vale of Aylesbury should be looked at from these hills, preferably from the mound where stood Bolebec Castle. That is the view painted by Rex Whistler which did so much to save us when we seemed doomed to the third London Airport and were reprieved when already on the steps of the scaffold. The wonder of this view is that the eye is subject to a time warp, inspecting a more ancient England. Those hedgerows

ABOVE: The forest of Burnham Beeches with its huge, pollarded trees, covers 600 acres. BELOW: Bledlow in the thickly wooded Chilterns.

are — or were until disease felled the elms — dappled with trees so that the impression is of temperate forest with here and there the clearings of the yeoman farmer offering privacy and silence to men and cattle, and perhaps a glimpse of his chimneys and the thatch of his roof. The Chiltern range, the opposite wall of the Vale, is so steep and dark that it seems a home more proper to wolves than to Rothschilds.

Walk ¼ mile from the castle mound to the north-western slope of these miniature hills and there below is the gently rolling plain of the Midlands with the blue line of the Cotswolds visible on a clear day. The effect in summer is that of the Vale of Aylesbury on a grander scale, mile after mile of trees, though little of it is actually woodland except for a strip running along the Oxfordshire border where remnants of original forest are close enough together for the roe deer to pass safely from cover to

cover in a short June night. In fact the trees are springing from innumerable boundaries and hedges. Our farmers, encouraged by the grain subsidies of the EEC, tend to plough up the rich grassland of their ancestors, but for the most part have kept the hawthorn hedges.

The northern peninsula of Buckinghamshire which thrusts into Northamptonshire is very different country, rather bare, with handsome villages far apart and cut by the windings of the Ouse, its tributaries and the standing water of floods. Olney, the market town, was the home of William Cowper, the pastoral poet better known today for his hymns. The power of Olney church, a miniature cathedral with its splendid chancel and towering, windowed spire standing above the river and bridge, is enough to make anyone have a shot at a hymn.

The agricultural population of the countryside has, of course, fallen. How many farm-hands are displaced by a combine harvester? But some idea of how thickly inhabited the manors were in days before the call of urban industry can be guessed from the size and number of the churches. For example, within three miles of the parish of Whitchurch there are six more churches. All are of some distinction and to keep them in repair costs far more than any village can raise by fêtes and fairs and jumble sales; but it would be disloyalty to our past to let them fall down.

It has always been a religious county — still is, to judge by the scatter of godly chapels which carry on in the little towns. Oldest of all sanctuaries is the 7th-century crypt of Wing, probably built on the site of a pagan temple which, according to some, was itself built on a High Place of immemorial age. We have mysterious Creslow, once a priory of the Knights Templar and now only a farm where human bones may be turned up by the plough; for when the Pope placed all England under interdict and no church services could be held, the Templars were exempt, so that the dead for miles around were brought in for Christian burial. There is also a well attested story that in the crypt beneath the farmhouse were found skeletons in chains, but who imprisoned them and why is beyond conjecture.

In contrast to the Templars with their occult heresies we have the lovely simplicity of the Quakers. Around the Chalfonts, where now the last of London meets the Chilterns, was a famous community of Friends in and out of Aylesbury gaol, including Thomas Ellwood who read to the blind Milton in London, later establishing him in a cottage at Chalfont St Giles, and William Penn, the founder of Pennsylvania.

ABOVE: Walkers beside the River Misbourne, Amersham. RIGHT: The church at Olney—a market town on the River Ouse—has a 14th-century spire rising 185 feet.

Both are buried in the graveyard at Jordans. Four hundred years earlier Buckinghamshire had its local saint, Sir John Shorne, whose church at North Marston became a place of pilgrimage since he bestowed upon the village well the power of healing; it is still there and still visited discreetly. He also caged the devil in a boot, a firmly believed legend which suggests that one of our small and mischievous Buckinghamshire elves was understandably mistaken by Sir John for the devil. Another of our less conforming clerics, more suited to modern California than his own 17th century, was the vicar of Stony Stratford who claimed to be Elias and persuaded mobs of dancing villagers that within three days of his death they would behold him resurrected.

When the Civil War broke out the county was a natural breeding ground of Puritans and sectarians and became a minor but continuous battlefield, dividing the Parliamentarians of the eastern counties from the king at Oxford. The great houses withstood sieges until they were burned or surrendered. Families were divided in their sympathies, son against father and brother against brother. All across this perfect cavalry country Prince Rupert's raiding parties collected cattle and horses for the king while the towns were pretty solidly for the Parliament, their musketeers behind the hedges playing the part of today's anti-tank weapons. One bloody engagement was fought at the bridge over the Thame just outside Aylesbury. The dead were buried where they fell and their bones, when discovered in 1818, were laid in a common tomb at Hardwick.

Now that I have shown my foreigner this pastoral England which was and to some extent still is, he may admit — provided we have lunched at some inn where the cooking is more honest than the bits of brass on the walls of the Tudor dining-room — that our villages can beat his for beauty. But what of the towns? Can we compete with his at all? Well, try Amersham for its broad street, its central market hall, its taverns and houses of all dates from the 16th century on.

A main street wide enough to hold along both sides fairs, market stalls, and live-

The Church of St Bartholomew at Fingest, whose rare Norman tower is topped by twin gables.

stock is typical of Buckinghamshire towns. High Wycombe has market hall and street but has allowed commerce to ruin its effect. Marlow's street leads down to the bridge over the Thames and has a touch of ancient dignity. Buckingham has the widest street of all, divided into two levels, the upper for the market, the lower carrying the traffic and ending up against the 18th-century town hall with a fine gilded specimen of the county's heraldic swan on top, and three narrow corners which are the terror of drivers of heavy, long vehicles and of pedestrians. Stony Stratford is unique in remaining a proud thoroughfare ever since the legions marched along Watling Street to Rome's northern garrisons. It needs little imagination to recapture the age of the mail coaches galloping through or pulling up for a change of horses at the stately hostelries, and the carrier carts stopping for beer and a straw mattress at still quaint ale-houses.

And what of Aylesbury? Twenty years ago it preserved many picturesque corners and an unspoilt market square with such inviting inns around it that the author of a county history could declare: "We leave Aylesbury with reluctance." It is hard to believe that he would repeat that today. The fault is that of the GLC and an ambitious town council which accepted the London overflow and built for it some 6 square miles of cheap housing remarkable for the planners' avoidance of straight lines, so that the car driver, searching for a street and finally appealing to a policeman or milkman who himself is not too sure, feels like an untrained rat in a maze. But let us give the city fathers full marks for not compelling their fellow Englishmen and English-women to live in high-rise flats; if they have a house they have a fairly generous strip of garden. The centre of the town, of course, became too small for the needs of its new population, so it was demolished and handed over to architects who were encouraged to experiment and, unfortunately, did.

The last and now the most famous town of the county is Milton Keynes which has swallowed in one gulp the cluster of villages south of a line between Stony Stratford and Newport Pagnell. It is formed at present of little colonies of crowded houses — some destined, I fear, to become slums — separated by open spaces of grass, by a wood, by the streams of the Ouse. It is easy to make fun of it, especially of the group of plastic life-size cows set in a meadow, but one must not forget that every road, field, sports complex and public building is lined with young trees. With luck it can become as good a breeding ground for healthy youth as the villages it has displaced.

The culmination of all this is the vast shopping centre set under one glassed roof, avenued, decorated with fountains, colonnades and exotic plants and providing a variety of shops equal to that of Oxford Street. The centre, the library and the admin-istrative buildings can, however, be reached only by bus which is as well for the inhabitants of the outer colonies who, if retired old people, may not have a car. The effect of all this is that of a luxurious airport terminal. The place is Wellsian and I do not know what to make of it. I feel that I am in an entirely foreign civilization and am uneasy until I remind myself that when those thousands upon thousands of trees have grown, hiding the low-built factories and the errors of taste, the whole town could be an indistinguishable part of that apparent forest of Buckinghamshire.

JOHN ARLOTT'S

Hampshire

Photographs by Richard Cooke

Hampshire is a far more complex county than the casual tripper or the through traveller appreciates. Geographically and topographically it is remarkably varied for its size. Its most striking major feature, the high chalk hills, turn in on the south-east from the South Downs in Sussex, divide and link with the North Downs running in from Surrey by the Hog's Back. Through the valleys of those hills run small but well-known rivers, the Test, Itchen, Wiltshire Avon, and Meon — famous for angling and watercress; the sailing estuaries of Beaulieu and Boldre in the New Forest, and Hamble and Ems farther east, flow south to the Solent seaboard. On the other side of the watershed the Loddon, Lyde, Blackwater, Whitewater, Wey and Enborne run north to the Thames. A total of 165 watermills have been recorded in the county.

There is the New Forest, private country but in immense public demand; in the south-east the narrow, fertile strip of strawberry country, and north-east the Aldershot scrub and commons suitable for housing estates, military exercises and rhododendrons.

If that seems a complex pattern within so small an area, the character of Hampshire is far more involved and defiant of definition. Indeed, it is unique among English counties, and that is by no means the insular opinion of a native. Britain is a country of varied but generally stable characteristics. Most large towns in England are typical of their counties in habits, customs, attitudes, accent, roots and loyalties. After all, it was only in the post-First World War period that the majority of the population of Great Britain became mobile, prepared to move freely and widely and settle in different districts. Even then, unless there was a strong economic or emotional reason, a considerable majority preferred to remain in their native district, the environment they knew, among friends and relatives. Thus it is true to say that, in their different ways, Sheffield, Huddersfield, Bradford, Leeds, Richmond, York and Scarborough are all essentially, profoundly and proudly Yorkshire towns. Despite — and indeed largely emphasized by — the insensitive decisions of boundary-changing bureaucrats, the same is true of Manchester, Liverpool, Preston, Lancaster, Barrow and Fleetwood in Lancashire. It is, though, quite strikingly not the case in — almost alone among English counties — Hampshire.

There, an area of some ancient habitation and history, the dilution of indigenous population began more widely and earlier than elsewhere. So now the main towns which, not quite by coincidence, ring the county look outwards for their populations who, in their turn, look outside for their futures. Thus the true heart of Hampshire does lie, in fact, at its physical heart.

Its main towns form a ring round Hampshire. By the 17th century Portsmouth and its related neighbours like Haslar and Gosport had become "Pompey", the headquarters of the Royal Navy, the base of sailors, the terrace housing of their wives and the dockyard workers, all recruited from far beyond Hampshire and in many cases moving out of it when their working days were done. Meanwhile Southsea, formerly the villa residential area for naval officers, had become a typical seaside resort with a shifting population. Even the cutback in the Navy and dockyard has not yet divorced people of Portsmouth, the only island city in England, or their vast overflow onto the mainland, from their outward outlook.

By the mid 19th century Southampton had become the most important passenger shipping port in the country; Cunard and White Star liners carried the name Liverpool on their sterns as port of origin, but they plied in and out of Southampton and there the shipping companies sent their staffs, from London as well as Liverpool. The container, cruise and ferry firms maintain the town's dominant — outward-looking — merchant shipping tradition.

The wide, sweeping landscape reflects today's mechanized methods of farming.

Soon after the Crimean War it was decided to make a base for the Army not too far
from, but not too near to, London on a large available stretch of land too poor for
farming. Aldershot accordingly became the home of the peripatetic British Army and
in due course spread outwards over Farnborough. In 1909 the London and South
Western Railway moved its main carriage depot from Nine Elms to Eastleigh
with a London workforce and London loyalties. The 19th-century mushroom growth
of Bournemouth, though no longer officially part of the county, emphasized the
isolation of most of Hampshire's population.

Then, in the second half of this century, Fleet and Crondall became retirement
centres for Army officers from Aldershot, and the Hartley Wintney district a Surrey-
type stockbroker belt for commuters. Suddenly, too, Basingstoke and Andover,
within recent memory mellow market towns of some 12,000 people, decided of their
own volition to become London overspill areas, whereupon they multiplied four
times in size, with populations which still look back to London and constantly return
there for their amusements and social occasions. Meanwhile the coastal strip from
Emsworth to Lymington, to an increasing depth inland, has become a retirement
zone for people from all over Britain.

Those towns account for the greater part of the population of Hampshire —
three-quarters of its people living in a third of its area. Winchester, capital of Wessex
and of England under William the Conqueror and for several reigns afterwards, is a
place of impressive dignity. It is still essentially the medieval city, small enough to be

encompassed on foot and crowded with history, full of pleasing buildings and maintaining a mild tempo of life. Its true centre is not the county council offices but the Cathedral (12 English kings lie there) with the fine and mellow houses of its Close, and the College, most intellectual and influential of British public schools and, in its turn, architecturally mature and in sympathetic setting. The city cannot avoid being a tourist attraction yet, despite the volume of visitors, it contrives to maintain its own life.

About it lies the least changed, least populated and least disturbed part of Hampshire: the region of empty roads. Early in history the rivers attracted Saxon and Jutish invaders down from their hill-top fort-villages into the fertile valleys. The tracks they established were, because of their situation, necessarily narrow, far too narrow for the motor cars that were to come, and in many cases could not be widened. Today the main roads in Hampshire, following roughly the same lines as the railways, are essentially through-routes, ending in the docks or going on to the west, and they are busy. Indeed, outside the main towns about 95 per cent of the traffic travels over 8 per cent of the roads. The rest, over the hills or twisting between banks or hedgerows, are lonely, many barely affording passing space, and they link villages quieter, or at least less busy, now than for centuries. Hampshire has always been a basically agricultural county with its specialist crops like strawberries, watercress and hops and mixed arable and dairy farming. Much of the agricultural land in the central area is the most expensive in Britain and there are some very large and valuable holdings indeed, many of them parts of great estates. Present-day methods are reflected in the landscape. Tractors can work at speed over wide spaces but

John Arlott's favourite Hampshire view is over the South Downs.

Inset on an aerial view of the New Forest are pictures of its native ponies; Winchester Cathedral; and the villages of Long Sutton and Upton Grey.

hedge-trimming is slow work and regarded as wasteful of labour, so many of the hedges have been grubbed up, leaving wide and generous sweeps of landscape but leading to the virtual extermination of many hedgerow flowers, plants, herbs, birds and insects. There is little use now in village children plodding round the hedges — where they exist — of the expertly managed farms in search of medlars, crab-apples, nuts, blackberries, violets or even, in far fewer cases these days, birds' nests.

The reduction in the farm labour force through mechanization, rationalization, amalgamation of farms, labour and machine rotas has altered village life almost beyond recognition. The cottages which used to house the large number of farm labourers who moved on foot and worked by hand are no longer needed. The farm hand, now rated and paid as a skilled worker, does not want a small, thatched cottage. He prefers a semi-detached, or even detached, house with modern conveniences indoors and a garage out. The farmers found to their delight that their former tied cottages, whose upkeep seemed a financial handicap or a questionable asset, make enough on the housing market as retirement or week-end homes to provide the tractorized ploughman with the solid, up-to-date, brick house of his desire. Meanwhile the newcomers to the cottages maintain them more smartly than ever before, so well that thatching has become a profitable craft and reproduction carriage lamps are a saleable commodity. Competition for the county's "Best Kept Village" is intense and the entries impressively prosperous in appearance. So the countryside is trimmer, more efficient than before, but country life has altered. Village hall entertainments tend to be smarter than formerly; the average age of the population is higher, and it is less easy to raise a cricket team.

Up on the chalk hills life is different. A lark or a hawk hovers; a pigeon tumbles in the sunlit quietness. The top layer of fine soil is so shallow that it nurtures only the short, sheep-grazing turf; given a little more earth you will find the slender juniper, above all others the tree of the chalk downs.

Typical of the down country — indeed, of upland Hampshire — is the short track where the wheel ruts have cut through to the bare chalk and powdered it, leading off a road to a lichen-covered gate with a juniper leaning, wraith-like, over it. Farther down in the valley, where the clay pockets are deeper, you will find the yew — "the Hampshire weed" — which lives to an immense age in so many churchyards.

Hampshire is said to be the most richly wooded English county; almost a sixth of its area is covered by trees. Much, but by no means all, of it is accounted for by the New Forest. The slopes of Stoner Hill, known as "little Switzerland", the massive beeches of Monkwood and the avenue of yews at Preston Candover are outstanding in their own right. The most famous of the beech hangers on the south-eastern slopes is that at Selborne, above Gilbert White's house. Development has, however, bitten deeply into Woolmer, Pamber, Alice Holt and Bere Forests.

The New Forest is the largest stretch of woodland in England. Its soil is on the whole poor and often acid, but it affords a great variety of terrain and scenery from rolling heath, through the Forestry Commission's regimented pines, the fine Douglas firs of Bolderwood, the ageing beeches of Mark Ash and the dramatic oaks of Whitley Wood, to the lush, well-watered woods of the Lymington Valley. It has long been in need of protection. William the Conqueror preserved it, after his fashion, as his personal hunting ground, through savage legislation against anyone who dared to take game there. There is, though, no evidence at all to support Henry of Huntington's allegation in 1135, often repeated since, that he "caused churches and villages to be destroyed and drove out the people and made it a habitation for deer".

Leave the main roads and avoid the towns and villages; there are few enough of them in the Forest anyway and most of the places marked are little more than hamlets. Simply walk into the Forest, stand still and look; no need to move. You will find it peopled by several different kinds of deer (statuesque so that you do not even see them until your eyes have become accustomed to the light); pigs which have been there almost as long as the Forest; ponies; grey squirrels; snakes; a wide range of both common and rare birds, and splendid butterflies and moths. That is the measure of its richness.

For many, though, the best of Hampshire lies in its small towns and villages. Of course Winchester is hoary with history and Southampton and Portsmouth are full of interest, modern as well as antiquarian. The villages, though, are as good as any England affords and as varied. The classic village shape survives in the grouping of the church, manor house, vicarage and 19th-century school, with a garage or petrol pumps where the blacksmith's shop used to be, a green or pond, sometimes both, near the centre, and farmland running away into the open country.

The wide main streets or squares, broad enough to turn a coach and six, are a great feature of the county; you may see them at Wickham, Botley, New Alresford, Stockbridge and Petersfield. Some villages have suffered from infilling or other vandalistic development, but there remains a glorious variety of small country places which have grown slowly under the influence of unhurried life. Their attractions are exceedingly diverse. To name all those worth visiting would be impossible, but the curious should be happy to pull off the main road for Long Sutton, Upton Grey, East Meon, Longparish, Ovington, East Stratton, Longstock, Easton, New Alresford, Romsey, that part of Porchester which lies remote from the main road to Portsmouth, Cheriton, Tichborne, and Rockbourne. For the church fancier the county is a treasure chest, from Saxon to modern. There are some fine, great houses like The Vyne, Hackwood and Broadlands, but the wealth of domestic building lies in the manor houses and farmhouses, and there are mighty examples of barns at Damerham, Silkstead, Odiham, Old Basing and Minstead.

There were always fine vistas; the new roads have opened up many which were not to be seen before. One aspect of country life and especially of Hampshire too rarely appreciated is the aspect of well farmed land, ideally displayed in a rolling countryside, where pasture, cornfields, grazing cattle, farm buildings, hedgerows and trees form a pattern at once rich and ancient and which can be seen constantly changing — not merely day by day but minute by minute under the natural cloud-shutter of light and shade.

Hertfordshire

Photographs by Anne Cardale

I t came as something of a shock when I found out that most of the important bits of my growing-up had not happened in my home county at all, but just outside its boundary. I was born and brought up in Hertfordshire. But my own contributions to the business were, as it belatedly turned out, played out a few hundred yards over the border, in Buckinghamshire — all those fiercely defended childhood camps in holly thickets, those teenage trysting grounds, those private shrines and hideaways too daft to list, all separated from the motherlode by a stream that managed to struggle above ground about once every 10 years. It surprised me when I learnt the truth, but I cannot say that I was hurt. The only dented pride was in my map-reading abilities.

That is the problem with Hertfordshire. It has a low profile and earns low loyalties. There is no such thing as a quintessential Herts landscape, no great range of hills or heaths. There is no Hertfordshire cheese, sheep, hot-pot or pudding (though there is Hertfordshire Puddingstone, a unique glacial hotchpotch which consists, as you might expect, of all kinds of rough stones held together with natural cement). You will need to find a life-long inhabitant for first-hand memories of a genuine regional industry or a team of sporting giants. Hertfordshire persons do not even have any reputed oddball qualities, for people to make jokes about. The nearest thing to a piece of county mythology I have heard is Bernard Miles's laconic tale of the family tombstone that was "the finest piece of sharpening stone in all Hertfordshire", which he would relate in a dry and measured accent exactly halfway between Wessex round and Norfolk flat.

Having no clearly defined character of its own, Herts is apt to take on the contours and hues of its more distinct neighbours. Much of the south of the county, for instance, seems little more than a dense and busy carapace for north London. But here all edges are blurred. Drive down from the more rural north, along the old Great North Road through Stevenage, or the A10 through Hoddesdon, and Herts appears as a long, low industrial estate, a working suburbia of compact electronics factories, garden centres, office complexes and gravel pits landscaped for anglers and weekend sailors. Wind your way westwards from the North Circular, through Bushey and Chorleywood, and it is a vista of beechwoods and gorse-covered commons.

LEFT: The Grand Union Canal, one of the county's many links with London. BELOW: A post mill near Cromer currently being renovated by Hertfordshire's Building Preservation Trust.

If you actually live here you may not have any view of the countryside as such. It is hardly firm enough ground to grow roots in. Herts is more a kind of temporary mooring, a place to commute from, to pause in on the way to somewhere else, to leave behind at the end of a working life. Through-traffic has been one of its burdens since prehistoric times. The county's oldest road, the Icknield Way, was in use as the main route between Wessex and the Wash 4,000 years ago. It was deliberately taken along the chalk ridge on the extreme north-west edge of the county to bypass the densely wooded claylands that covered its centre. Since then Herts has been criss-crossed by the Grand Union Canal, four main railway lines and bits of five motorways. Most of the proposed sites for the third London Airport have been just a few miles one side or other of its boundary.

All these facilities for hectic toing and froing reflect the looming presence of the capital, which has been the major force in shaping Hertfordshire's character for more than 1,000 years. With nothing particular to act as a counterbalance (a coastline, for instance, as have Essex and Kent), London exerts its influence in much the same way

as a magnet affects iron filings, giving a slant, a kind of metropolitan restlessness, to everything from house prices to insect life. The very first memory of my life is of watching the local searchlights playing about the night sky during the war, looking for German bombers bound for London. The morning after a raid I would toddle out on to the lawn to gather the thin strips of metal foil they had dropped to confuse our radar defences. They lay among the daisies and dew like gossamer, Hertfordshire's ambivalent fall-out from the bigger war in the city.

ABOVE: A snowy landscape close to the county's border with London.

Such odd and incongruous mixtures are the style of things here. Much of the countryside has an unsettled feel, as if it had other plans for itself. The towns seem always on the point of fraying at the edges. Herts is the county where, in the 1920s, a fig tree sprouted out of a tomb in Watford cemetery, and where, with a pattern of growth scarcely less remarkable, the first Garden Cities of Letchworth and Welwyn were created.

But I am making it sound like so much puddingstone, all quirky lumps set in rather bland dough. Drive into Hemel Hempstead New Town on the A41 in mid May and look at the golden blaze of Boxmoor's buttercup meadows wedged between

road and railway. Or leave Baldock on a winter's afternoon, up the graciously broad medieval market street, east into the Icknield Way, past the Victorian maltings on your left, to find yourself, suddenly and unexpectedly, in a vast East Anglian vista of limitless chalky fields, shining as the low sun is reflected off flints and furrows.

This point is one of the gateways through Hertfordshire's chief internal boundary, that between the light, chalky soils of the north and east, and the heavier clays of the south and west. The arable fields that stretch for miles around Royston and Bunting-ford and into Cambridgeshire and Essex, with scarcely a hedge or bank between them, are the latest developments in a pattern of agriculture that was set by neolithic settlers. The forest being easier to clear on the light soils than on the clay, this is where most of the major early settlements clustered and grew. By Domesday the pattern was fixed: "woodlands with swine" are concentrated in the west and "ploughteams" in the north and east. If the woodland settlements meant a pastoral economy with a multitude of scattered self-sufficient smallholdings, the cornlands were the strongholds of the open field system and of highly organized and co-operative nucleated villages. These, sadly, were all too vulnerable to human disease and crop failure, and to the bureaucratic "improvements" of Parliamentary Enclosure during the 18th and 19th centuries. The rationalized landscape of rectangular fields and dead straight roads that resulted led inevitably to the huge, hedgeless prairies and similarly huge machines that are the current fashion in arable organization.

As a landscape it is too airy to be oppressive, but I find it lonely as well as featureless, and full of melancholy echoes. This is not the first time these now very open fields have been drained of people. The region is littered with the sites of deserted medieval villages, abandoned during prolonged periods of bad harvest or plague. On an inside wall of the great tower of St Mary's Church in Ashwell an anonymous reporter (probably the priest) has scratched a bleak graffito about the march of the Black Death. It is as chilling a cry out of the past as I have ever

RIGHT: The "almost too perfect" village of Aldbury in the grip of a hard winter.

A cottage in the hamlet of Moor Green.

read: "1350, wretched, wild, distracted. The dregs of the mob alone survive to tell the tale. At the end of the second [outbreak of plague] was a mighty wind. St Maurus thunders in all the world."

Many villages survive in the north and east, but they do not quite have that anciently rooted feel of those in East Anglia proper. Despite all the flints in the fields the cottages are mostly bright red brick or plaster and lath. They are pretty enough, if that is important: Much Hadham like a miniaturized Long Melford; Barkway, tall and businesslike and slightly Dutch in feel.

But I confess my own tastes are for untidier, less explicable, eccentric settlements that were not part of that depressingly logical progress between two sorts of open field. Between Walkern and Buntingford and Cottered in the north, for example, there is a stretch of territory quite out of keeping with the arable plain. A hotch-potch of scattered Ends and Greens, solitary moated farmsteads, queerly shaped fields, green lanes and ditches, it suggests a landscape that was carved out piece by piece.

The most outlandish story of village redeployment during the changes of the 18th and 19th centuries concerns Ayot St Lawrence, probably Hertfordshire's best-known village because of its associations with Bernard Shaw. In 1778 Sir Lionel Lyte, director of the Bank of England, London tobacconist and local squire, decided to pull down the village's modest medieval church and build something more in keeping with the spirit of the age. The Bishop stopped him before he had finished demolishing old St Lawrence, but Lyte continued with his other plans and as a result there now stands on the edge of this tiny village a large and stunning Palladian Temple. It was — and is — a working folly, used for worship, though "the villagers had to make a wide detour, approaching the building from the back and entering by a side door so as not to spoil the view from the House".

Shaw himself regarded it as a monstrosity, though his own piece of early 20th-century detached, Shaw's Corner, is hardly an architectural jewel. Shaw's churlish tastes, however, were to receive their come-uppance at the hands of Hertfordshire's capricious *genius loci*. In 1931 he began an acrimonious correspondence with Islington Council over their refuse tip at Wheathampstead, which was just 1 mile, as the wind blew, from Ayot. He quoted Exodus 8 on plagues of flies, and compared the smoking tip to the volcano of Stromboli. The Council denied his charges. The tip, meanwhile, taking Judges 14 — "out of the strong came forth sweetness" — as its retaliatory text, prepared a more substantial reply. The following year an apple tree of prolific blossom and unknown pedigree grew out of Islington's rubbish. In 1936 it produced one single, gigantic fruit weighing 1½lb, and Shaw was tricked into consuming it in a stew.

Ayot, strictly, is over the Hitchin-Hertford line and in the county's western woodland zone. This is my own patch of Herts, especially where the claylands merge with the Chilterns in the extreme west. I find it an agreeable landscape, compact, manageable, but always surprising in its sudden small dips and folds and groups of straggling commons that have probably never been enclosed since they were first grazed in the Iron Age. Above all there are the woods. Too many have become uniform smudges of conifer for my taste, but there are not many high places where you cannot stand among trees and look at a continuous line of woodland on the next scarp. In autumn they are as colourful as the woods of the Weald. Beech is native on the plateaux and extensively planted on the slopes, but there is wild cherry, field maple and hornbeam in abundance as well, mottling the beeches' rusts and coppers with crimson, orange and lemon.

One of the most striking woods, and by now one of the most familiar in Britain, is the beech hanger that sweeps down the hill behind the much-filmed and almost too perfect village of Aldbury, with its commuters' cottages clustered round pond and green and stocks. There is also a mansion called Stocks in the village, where the Playboy Club's Bunny Girls used to be trained. Unfortunately, perhaps, given the house's recent occupation, it is not named after the instrument of correction, but after the old word for an area of stumps, or cleared wood.

And this is really the key to the landscape of west Herts. It was cleared and enclosed by individual effort and it is the mosaic of clearing and wood that gives it its character. Hence the many odd-shaped fields, the triangular greens (as at Aldbury) that once served as night-time refuges for cattle, the idiosyncratic pattern of every village.

It was this personalized mixture that so moved Cobbett when, in 1822, he rode between Redbourn and Hemel Hempstead: " . . . the sort of corn, the sort of under-woodland timber, the shape and size of the fields, the height of the hedgerows, the height of the trees, all continually varying. Talk of *pleasure-grounds* indeed! What that man ever invented, under the name of pleasure-grounds, can equal these fields in Hertfordshire?" So close were these do-it-yourself landscapes to the ideal of pastoral wilderness that when Capability Brown came to create "landskip" parks, he remarked of one, "Nature has done so much, little was wanting, but enlarging the River."

I suspect both Brown and Cobbett would be shocked at the degree to which the variety that so impressed them has been levelled down. Yet a streak of wildness still plays across these western frontier lands. At the beginning of this century much of the western protuberance of Herts was owned by the Rothschilds. They bought Tring Park in 1786, and many of the villages round about are graced by the distinctive gabled cottages they built for their workers. But the Rothschilds were eccentric explorers and animal collectors as well as farmers and financiers. One was famous for riding about Tring in a cart drawn by zebras, and dotting the Park with enclosures full of exotic animals. Happily the enclosures were not quite secure enough. Rothschilds' edible dormice, the glis-glis, now spend the winter snoozing in many a local loft. Rothschilds' giant catfish, introduced from central Europe, still haunt the depths of Tring Reservoirs.

Even the capital of the region, the demure cathedral city of St Albans, has pagan leanings. Although it is best known as the site of the Roman town of Verulamium, it was before that the stronghold of a tribe of Belgic Celts called the Catuvellauni. They lived in Prae Wood, about a mile west of the present city, and by all accounts were wealthy, artistic and pioneers of benign and alternative technologies. They fought off the Roman chariots with some astonishing and still surviving 40 foot deep ditches, but were finally beaten in 54 BC. It is encouraging to see that their descendants are gaining ground against the last vestiges of Roman authoritarianism. "Snorbens", as the new Herts Celts, with a proper respect for their pre-Christian roots, call their city, is a bright and enterprising community, full of theatre groups, poets, pubs with live music, and all manner of modern friends of the earth. It was the birthplace of the wood-burning stove revival and the Campaign for Real Ale. It even has a resurrected Catuvellaunian in the shape of Ginger Mills, the wildman of St Albans who lives in a tent on the edge of the city and amazes the tourists in the summer.

It was an earlier wave of natural longings and environmental consciousness among the urban middle-class that led to the saving of much of west Hertfordshire's commonland. Parliamentary Enclosure put paid to many commons at Watford, Elstree, Bushey, Barnet and Wigginton. But by the middle of the 19th century it was becoming clear that the remaining lowland commons had a vital role to play as places for the recreation of the new urban multitudes. When Lord Brownlow rather dubiously fenced off 400 acres of Berkhamsted Common it was not so much the dispossessed graziers who fought back as the new commuters, led by Augustus Smith, Lord of the Scilly Isles. In March 1866, he imported a gang of 130 London navvies, who marched up from the station and tore down the 3 miles of iron railings. There followed a great open-air celebration by the townspeople, a 15-verse ballad in *Punch*, a law suit for damages by Brownlow, and an immediate and successful counter-suit for illegal enclosure by Smith. It was a famous and decisive victory and it subsequently became increasingly difficult to enclose commons near towns. Hertfordshire now has 186 registered commons and village greens, of extraordinary variety: Berkhamsted (one of the biggest in the home counties) with its ancient pollard beeches and sweeps of birch and gorse; Chipperfield, with a cricket pitch set in a holly wood; Roughdown and Sheethanger at Hemel Hempstead, where in a tangle of golf courses and bungalows Soay sheep graze among orchids within sight of John Dickinson's paper factory.

So many of Hertfordshire's commons have golf courses that this sociable activity might be reckoned the county sport — if it were not for the fact that many villages now support more ponies than people. Even more have houses buried among the woods, in random patterns that echo the piecemeal medieval settlement of these wastes.

All these developments are a kind of apotheosis of the Hertfordshire paradox. A split-level house among the trees near a fairway, a pony and a suburban paddock for the children and a good motorway or rail link with London — this, for an increasing number of people, is the recipe for the Good Life.

It had all been anticipated, of course, even by the railway companies who bought up housing development land along their extending lines and created the first generation of commuters. "The song of the nightingales for which the neighbourhood is renowned . . ." ran a Metropolitan Railway Company advertisement in 1920, "the network of translucent rivers traversing the peaceful valley render Rickmansworth a Mecca to the city man pining for the country and pure air."

Ebenezer Howard's Garden Cities at Letchworth and Welwyn were based on the same notion; and if they seem unexceptional now it is partly because their curving, tree-lined roads and wide verges are routine features of up-market suburban development; and partly because they gave birth in their turn to the feckless, artificially grafted and unhappy New Towns at Hemel Hempstead, Hatfield and Stevenage.

Still, even these can have moments of improbable magic. The woodlands, as I have said, are my patch. But for Hertfordshire itself, for that elusive, amorphous county spirit, I love these fringelands, neither one thing nor another. E. M. Forster called the county "England meditative". In modern jargon I suppose we might say that it was "soft", low on definition, open to impression. So you may move about on the edge of things, inventing your own landscape as you go. Hertfordshire for me is eating fresh clams in a *trattoria* overlooking the Municipal Water Gardens in Hemel; listening to medieval carols in Watford's pedestrian precinct; and watching a deer scuttle out of a bungalow's back garden. It is the animal that gave the county its name, after all, though now it is not the royal beast that abounds but the little muntjac that once escaped from Knebworth, where they have an annual rock festival next to the deer park.

DUDLEY FISHBURN'S

Isle of Wight

Photographs by John Robert Young

The Isle of Wight is the same size and shape as Singapore: a diamond 13 miles deep and 23 miles wide. So similar is the geography of the two that in the last war British troops were issued with maps of the Isle of Wight when stationed in Singapore. In the 19th century the two islands had the same population: 30,000. But today Singapore boasts 2.3 million while the Island (as it is known by all who live on it) seems overcrowded with 110,000. The diamond of the Orient is a hive of industry; the diamond of the Solent is one of the most gentle, polite, tidy, cohesive, leisurely, picturesque places in the United Kingdom.

The Island is Britain's smallest county, a proud position once held by Rutland. It was the same Whitehall merry-go-round that abolished Rutland and severed the Island from its administrative tie with Hampshire and made it an independent county. Complete with three councils, almost 100 councillors and two tiers of local government, this community is the most over-governed in the country. Not that our population of retired people, hotel keepers, small businessmen and farmers are the sort who need keeping in line.

Nonetheless it is right that the Island should be its own county. Few other places, though they may be as diverse, have a stronger sense of community. There are clubs, fêtes, charities, dinners, societies for everything; and nowhere could the man from Mars land better to discover a slice of Britain. It is the feeling of identification, of being "an Islander", that does it — that concentrates things and provides a common link. To be "an Islander" is a phrase with a strong, if self-conscious ring, employed most frequently by those most recently arrived. Its validity is shared experience: the half-hour ferry ride to the mainland; the two weekly newspapers that get into a remarkable 95 per cent of the homes, and are full of earnest detail; the single Westminster constituency which gives the Island a political focus; the Governor, an ancient title and a position diligently held by Lord Mountbatten until his murder; and that primitive, but reassuring, feeling of knowing one's own territorial boundaries — the sea.

In many ways this "Island" attitude is nonsense; occasionally it is insufferable. Nine-tenths of the Island's concerns are identical to those of the south coast; but

Shanklin is renowned
for its fine sheltered sands.

BELOW: The Island's high chalk downs, rising to a
height of 787 feet at St Boniface Down, are
excellent country for walkers. There are 1,200 acres
of National Trust Land on the Isle of Wight.

Looking across Alum Bay towards the Needles in the late afternoon.

the one-tenth difference is a catalyst to the community. There are, in fact, very few islanders proper. The old accent has all but gone, so have the old Island names — Joliffe, Cotton, Oglander, Dawes. Probably less than a fifth of the population can trace their Island connexions back to the 19th century, the time my own grand-parents moved there.

Paradoxically local history thrives best in places of depopulation. The Island, which has more than doubled in population since the war, has had its past buried in newcomers. But its history is there for all to imagine, for the Island has been thrust into events by two unchanging factors: its mild climate and its position of strategic importance for the defence of southern England.

The Romans were attracted to the Island for both these reasons. Their colonial landlords built large villas there, grew vineyards, and must have imagined themselves, on those balmy, sunny days that the Island so brilliantly produces, as being almost in Italy, recreating a corner of the civilized Mediterranean amid the barbarians. They called the island Vectis: a name that still survives stamped on the side of the county's buses.

King Harold was the first of England's defenders to realize the Island's importance for keeping watch on the Channel. He stationed the bulk of his forces there during the long and fruitless wait for William's invasion from Normandy. In 1588 those same high downs from which Harold's Anglo-Saxons looked anxiously out provided the best seats for the rout of the Armada. In 1939 they were look-out posts again, for hidden in the Boniface Downs, which climb sheer from the southern tip of the Island, were those most secret of weapons, the first radars.

The Island has been a royal seat only twice, and in very different circumstances. For King Charles I it was a most unwelcome prison: he was mewed up in Carisbrooke Castle, in the centre of the Island, for the long months before his execution. It is a fine castle, with all the things a self-respecting castle should have, yet it is set in such a sea of green, looking out over gentle downs, and so domestic a village, that there is little foreboding about it.

The second royal visitor came of her own accord and left an impact on the Island that is still everywhere to be seen. Queen Victoria's country palace of Osborne, where she long held court and finally died, brought the world to the Isle of Wight. The fashion set by the Queen made it the Victorians' Riviera. That "change of air" recommended by 19th-century doctors, for everything from a broken leg to a broken heart, meant a visit to the Island. And the thousands who came endowed it with some of Britain's best Victorian architecture: the villas of Ventnor and The Undercliff are vast, sturdy, magnificent homes around which an already romantic landscape was preened to fit a picture-book ideal.

Piers were built at every seaside town — Sandown, Ventnor, Shanklin, Ryde — resplendent with wrought iron, receiving a ceaseless flow of ferries, those "penny-sicks" that would carry you around the Island for a single penny. They still stand, dilapidated monuments to a vanished jollity of crinoline and beach-huts, energy, modesty and confidence. And finally there is Osborne itself, outside East Cowes, with its Italian campanile, Victorian clutter and labyrinthine corridors — imposing but not oppressive. Every visitor to the Island should make the trip there as well as to Queen Victoria's church at Whippingham, perhaps the most perfect, purely Victorian chapel in England. You leave each place impressed by the Queen's personal and certain taste.

Those were the Island's great years, a period when it was, without exaggeration, one of the centres of the world, political, literary, international. Then it saw the

BELOW LEFT: Victorian villas at Ventnor, which lies under and is sheltered by St Boniface Down.
BELOW: One of the Island's six piers is at Shanklin.

German princes sporting themselves at Cowes; Marx and Dickens holidaying at Ventnor; Swinburne versifying at Bonchurch; Julia Cameron with her early camera at Freshwater, photographing that giant of the Island, Alfred Lord Tennyson.

This literary tradition, begun with Keats at Shanklin, continued into the 20th century with D. H. Lawrence, with J. B. Priestley, and with the poet who, in his late 70s, taught me to swim off the Island, Alfred Noyes. All these men chose the Island not merely as a refuge, but as an inspiration to their work. The octogenarian Tennyson, for example, wrote "Crossing the Bar" after the journey across the Solent to Yarmouth, where the bar still moans "when that which drew from out the boundless deep, turns again home".

The end began with Victoria's death. The Edwardians, spurning the things that had delighted their parents, made for the south of France. The villas became boarding houses; the promenades crumbled. The warm and gentle climate that had attracted bohemians and courtiers, artists and politicians, was found in Europe instead. The buildings and the palm trees remain; so does much of the picture-postcard beauty, but as a place of distinction the Island's days are gone. Today it has many qualities but it is no longer an inspiration or an escape; it is rather a neat and well-ordered corner of calm.

The Island has two particular miracles, the downs and the sea. I have often heard tell of the existence of an ancient Islander who had never seen the sea. Doubly unfortunate man, for he could not have known the downs either. The downs run in a spine east to west along the middle of the Island and reappear to the south in a burst above Ventnor. Walk along them towards the east and you see in the folds of the valley to either side the towns and suburban centres of the Island where two-thirds of the population live, and across the Solent, the sprawl of Portsmouth and Southampton. The contrast between country and town, seen from this hawk's eye view, is evocative of those early 19th-century prints in which field and factory abut one onto another.

Walk to the west, starting at the lovely thatched village of Shorwell, and across Tennyson Downs and the lands of the National Trust, and from one particular spot you can see the entire Island, all four points of the diamond. It is a walk I have done a hundred times, gazing over towards Yarmouth, tiny to the north-west, or back to St Catherine's Point, the high headland to the south. To the one side lies the open Channel, always busy with cargo-ships, to the other the protected waters of the Solent, filled with sails. The Island is veined with such bridle paths along cliffs and valleys and landfalls; it is a walker's paradise. Yet up on these downs, on a fine afternoon, you will seldom meet a soul.

From the downs one is overwhelmingly aware of the close encircling sea; but from the sea the downs do not loom. The Island's coast seems low and gentle, everywhere are welcoming familiar harbours: Bembridge, Fishbourne, Cowes, Newtown, Yarmouth, Totland. And long stretches of the coastline are, miraculously, unspoilt, with hardly a modern development to be seen. This water from the Spithead to The Needles, marked each end by an active lifeboat station, must be the best sailed stretch of England's coast; even on a blustery January day you will see some stouthearted sailor enjoying himself.

The centre of all this activity is Cowes, and the river Medina that splits the town in two, cleaving the Island right to its capital, Newport. At its mouth on the west bank is the Royal Yacht Squadron and the sailing side of Cowes: yacht chandlers, boatyards, slipways, clubs. On the east bank are some of the Island's larger factories; between them plies a chain ferry, joining the two worlds. For that first week in August — Cowes Week — the town is packed with sailors from every nation; every other year, when the Admiral's Cup is raced, teams come from as far away as Brazil and Hong Kong.

Every summer the floods of tourists come, with standing room only on the ferries. There are those who come to sail; those who make for Bembridge, where rows of nannies in uniform watch over their wards on the long, flat sands; those who stay at the hotels and boarding houses of Sandown and Shanklin. These visitors, mocked during the winter, are awaited in the summer as swallows of good fortune. They block the roads, dirty the streets, crowd the shops but they are the Island's biggest industry, its economic lifeblood. And yet they get their money's worth without ever touching the real Island unless they decide, as so many do, to retire here.

Only Bournemouth has a higher concentration of elderly people. You see them clambering the hills of the seaside towns, looking ruddy and healthy, entering the community, living long, becoming Islanders, having a second grasp at life. Island cynics scorn these invaders. Yet there can be few better places to grow old: the good climate, the fecund gardens, the impeccable social services, the sense of community are all there. But then there are few better places to be young, messing around in boats, lolling on the beaches, strolling along the downs. The Victorians were right — broken arm or broken heart, make for the Isle of Wight.

MICHAEL McNAY'S
Kent

Photographs by Richard Davies

The winding gear dominates the village, its iron skeleton towering over the pithead baths, the heaps of shale and slag, the rows of little trucks on narrow gauge rails, the rampant weeds growing through gravel and cement, the flood-light stanchions. Outside the concrete and wire perimeter rail are the miners' canteen, the medical centre, the club. The village shop looks as institutional as the National Coal Board buildings, one window all frosted glass, the other clear glass but empty of goods; the paintwork, which might once have been green, peeling and darkened.

There are two or three streets of functional brick-built cottages, all in need of repainting, some in need of restuccoing or fresh pebble-dashing. You can be out of the pit village in a minute, into the fields of spring wheat, turnips, and Brussels sprouts. And over the brow of the next hill are the hop gardens and the oasts and kilns with white cowls crisp and clear against the loam as dew drops on a leaf. For this is not the Durham coalfield, or the Rhondda, Orwell's Wigan or Lawrence's Eastfield. It is the Garden of England.

When the first Kent coal mines started production in 1913 people saw it as the end of the Kent of old. In truth it was a new beginning. The Romans had mined iron ore in Kent and Sussex, and the Wealden iron smelting industry existed when Consett was simply a green sward in the Derwent valley of County Durham and before the Duke of Bridgewater built the Worsley canal to halve the price of Manchester coal or Stephenson launched England into a new age with his *Rocket*.

For Kent is not the Garden of England in any indolent sense: true, the motoring organizations signpost the blossom routes every spring, but blossom to fruit farmers is what steel is to Dagenham and Cowley and Longbridge, the raw material of their trade. However pretty, if it is not useful it is dispensed with, which is why the Kent that the intrepid 17th-century traveller Celia Fiennes saw — "from Rochester that night I went to Gravesend which is all by the side of Cherry grounds that are of severall acres of ground and runs quite down to the Thames" — and Dickens's Mr Jingle recorded — "apples, cherries, hops, and women" — has changed. Apples, hops and women remain, but the cherry acreage, pretty blossom and all, has shrunk because cherries are hard to protect against the successive ravages of frost and rapacious birds.

ABOVE: The pithead gear of Snowdown and Betteshanger, two of Kent's three collieries that together employ 3,060 men and produce 810,000 tonnes of coal per annum.
LEFT: A hopfield near Brenchley.

The garden-factory of England, then. From at least the 16th century the market gardens around Margate and the hops and fruit of Maidstone were grown, not just to subsistence level for the locals, but for exports to London. London swallows great tracts of Kent now, up to Bromley and Beckenham and Orpington; but Kent had always impinged on London's doorstep. Rotherhithe and Deptford, John Evelyn's home and the royal dockyard of Henry VIII, were Kent. Henry himself and his greater daughter Elizabeth were Kentish people, born at Greenwich.

A native of the northern littoral of Kent as far out as Gravesend talks of going "up the road" to denote a journey to London. So Kent's proximity to London — or as a true Kentishman would say, London's proximity to Kent — has shaped her destiny. While other parts of the country carried on agriculture for the direct subsistence of the village or the manor, Kent made a living by selling fruit and corn and hops to the London markets, ragstone and timber for building and shipping, fuller's earth for the wool industry of East Anglia. Fuller's earth surplus to requirements, that is, for Kent's own cloth industry was formidable, nurtured by the great flocks of sheep on Romney Marsh, cultivated in the clearings in the forest of the Weald, the "dens" and "hursts" and "leys": Marden, Smarden, Bethersden, Tenterden; Hawkhurst, Lamberhurst, Goudhurst, Sissinghurst; Tudeley, Brenchley, Langley.

So Kent is a prime case of a man-made landscape: shaped by man, that is, on the basis of nature's gigantic handiwork — the chalk deposits laid down beneath the ocean up to 120 million years ago, the North Downs, the Weald, the ragstone ridge forced up above the waves in the colossal Alpine upheaval around 60 million years later. Those movements of earth and sea left Kent with a landscape as various as any in these varied islands: intimate river valley and wide estuary, tiny sunken lanes and sweeping panoramas of 20 miles and more, deep green forest and chalky-green down.

South of the chalk 4,000 years ago was unremitting marsh and forest, so Neolithic man settled and farmed the North Downs and the Medway valley. He left his implements by the banks of the river and his burial chambers at Kits Coty above Aylesford, at Addington, at Trottiscliffe (pronounced Trosley). The names of these settlements come to us from the Saxons and Jutes, but the county name itself is British, Cantium. Yet its principal city (not Maidstone, its county

LEFT: Rochester harbour, situated at the mouth of the Medway. FAR LEFT: The Royal Military Canal that runs from Hythe to Rye along the northern edge of Romney Marsh defining the ancient southern coastline.

RIGHT: A hop garden and oast house near the village of Brenchley. FAR RIGHT: A lichened gravestone and salty marshland in Snave in the heart of Romney Marsh.

town) is Old English: Cantwara burh, the citadel of the people of Kent. The Roman name, Durovernum, was closer to the original British Darovernon. Whatever the Romans found in this fortification, they left it a centre of Christianity.

Many parish churches in the county incorporate in their structure those narrow bricks from long-lost Roman buildings, but whole sections of the south wall of the little church of St Martin's, sitting above Canterbury on a small hill east of the city wall, are built of Roman brick. And here, it is supposed, Christian worship was continuous from the time of Constantine, through the dark ages after the retreat of the Roman Empire from the shores of Kent in 410 until the time of Bertha, the Frankish queen of Kent's heathen king, Ethelbert, when Augustine arrived from Rome with his 40 missionaries in 597. As the Venerable Bede put it:

"On the east side of the city stood an old church, built in honour of St Martin during the Roman occupation of Britain, where the Christian queen of whom I have spoken went to pray. Here they (Augustine and his missionaries) first assembled to sing the psalms, to pray, to say Mass, to preach, and to baptise, until the king's own conversion to the Faith gave them greater freedom to preach and to build and restore churches everywhere."

The building and restoring included the cathedral church of Christ on the site of a former Roman Christian church and the Saxon church of St Mary-in-Castro in Dover: Saxon, that is, in the brickwork of the arches of its blocked up south doorway and the arches of chancel and transept crossing, a movingly authentic witness to the rude faith of our forebears that has survived the worst excesses of Victorian restoring zeal; whoever coined the phrase lavatory Gothic must have been thinking of Butterfield's mosaic tiles in St Mary's.

Not that everything new in the churches of Kent is bad. Marc Chagall's stained-glass window in the little parish church by a barnyard at Tudeley is one of the most beautiful in England, in the direct tradition of the marvellous Romanesque carving over the south door of the little Norman church in a wooded valley at Barfreston, though the stonemasons of Barfreston were bound to the Christian faith and Chagall is a wandering Jew. The Barfreston masons may have been the same as those who worked on the cathedral of Rochester, which with the massive castle keep also designed by Bishop Gundulf commands the mouth of the Medway as it spills into the Thames estuary. But who made the windows at Canterbury, the only medieval glass in England to rival the glory of Chartres?

For some people Canterbury can never be a favourite cathedral. It has not the spectacular buttressed solemnity of Durham on its rock above the Wear, nor the length of Winchester's nave. It does not dominate the city as Ely dominates the fens for miles around. And the stone reredos at the east end of the nave blocks the view through to the choir, though there is a blue glimpse of stained glass in the distant apse. For all that, the richness of overlaid effects in the building by Lanfranc and Anselm and William of Sens and William the Englishman is unmatched, and the proportions of the exterior beneath that noble central tower, Bell Harry, are one of the world's sublime sights.

But parish churches and great cathedrals alone do not make the county: Kent to most people is the vernacular of its countryside, the brick and tile and half-timbering of yeomen's long houses and Wealden hall houses, the weatherboarding of its humble cottages, the functional dignity of the hop kilns, known popularly and erroneously as oasts (which are the whole complex of hop building). Even a great house like Knole is more vernacular building than fine architecture, for all the grandeur of its total effect, of its gables and multiple classical allusions. And Penshurst is essentially a medieval nobleman's house with its great hall and central hearth in which an open fire once burned.

Penshurst, though massive, represents the first stage of civilization after the fortified castle, for Dover itself and Leeds and Allington and Hever and Rochester remind us of Kent's military past. Farther back yet, there is the Iron Age fortification on Oldbury Hill and at Richborough are the extensive fortifications of the Roman base built after the invasion by the legions of Claudius.

A hundred years earlier Julius Caesar had landed for his exploratory mission at Deal, and at Deal Henry VIII was to build one of his extraordinarily modern-looking squat fortresses as proof against invasion: Martello towers and Second World War machine-gun pill boxes are its clear descendants.

But it is the ploughshare, not the sword, that has marked this ancient landscape. The blood of King Alfred's men and their opponents soaked away into the soil and drained into the Medway at Aylesford, the rebels Wat Tyler and Jack Cade and the insurrectionist army of Cromwell passed over the land and left no trace except in the history books and the folk consciousness, bombs and rockets and falling fighter planes plunged deep into the earth and buried themselves. On the other hand the farmers' plough and his hawthorn hedgerow have scored the earth and defined its areas since the Romans and beyond. One theory holds that the Romans adopted Celtic enclosed fields so that the basic pattern has remained much the same for two millennia: at any rate maps of parishes and manors show the same field patterns surviving since Tudor days.

In east Kent arable farming has succumbed to the wide open prairie systems increasingly common in the rest of England, but in hop gardens and orchards the only changes have been the evolution of crop varieties and yields and the mechanical revolution that cut back the number of regular farmhands and ended the annual invasion of hop pickers from the East End of London.

The revolution at the hopping season was timely, for a generation brought up on an annual fortnight in Majorca would not have taken so readily to harvesting hops, just as changing holiday habits have ended the high prosperity of Folkestone, Deal and Kent's most elegant town, Tunbridge Wells. Deal's pebble beach is picturesque with fishing boats but prettiness is not enough to ensure popularity in a seaside town for otherwise Deal's narrow streets lined by colour-washed 18th- and early 19th-century cottages must surely have been overrun. Instead, Sandwich, whose own prominence declined as she was isolated from the sea and as Deal took over as a safe anchorage for ships, now finds her medieval gate and streets jammed by modern tourist traffic in and often out of season.

Gravesend, too, was once a resort as well as home port for Thames pilots but the high and handsome houses of Rosherville are a seedily run-down enclave now on the road between industrial Northfleet and the down-at-heel town centre, which itself is the unlikely burial place of Princess Pocahontas. And Gravesend's otherwise dim High Street is distinguished by its sharp dip down to the Thames where the street's northern vista is often blocked by ocean-going liners and massive cargo ships from Tilbury on the Essex bank.

Folkestone had a mini-renaissance as a focus of flower power in the 60s but there, too, the only reminder of the turn-of-the-century days of florid prosperity when this little fishing harbour became the cousin of Normandy's elegant sisters across the water, Trouville and Deauville, is the grand sweep of the Leas with below it a vegetation-carpeted cliff, in effect a park reaching down to the sea like a lady's crinoline. The hinterland of Folkestone, cropped by sheep and swelling with strange tumuli, is a dropping-off place from England as decisive in its way as Land's End. Approaching through this strange, terminal landscape still induces that sense of impending loss so poignantly caught in Ford Madox Brown's painting of a departure from Folkestone, *The Last of England*.

The first of England, too, for many Europeans. Some come to Dover and Folkestone only for *le Marks et Spencer*, but those who travel farther do so along the Roman Watling Street and its parallel highways, the M2 and the A20, where notices warn trilingually right through to mid Kent, Keep Left, *Tenez la Gauche*, *Links Fahren*. East of Canterbury, farm-gate shops advertise *apfels* and *pommes*, and at Harrietsham a blackboard outside a transport café announces Roast Dinner 90p beside an enamelled Relais Routier sign, which in any language means to the long-distance lorry driver what the *Michelin Red Guide* means to the tourist.

The Last of England has one other modern connotation. Those lorry drivers enter the country in swelling numbers driving bigger trucks and heavier loads. More motorways despoil more land and a Channel Tunnel will bring yet more and service industries too. In 20 years Kent could turn from a green and pleasant land to an anonymous morass of bricks and mortar and expressways set with jewelled beauty spots.

JAMES BISHOP'S
Middlesex

Photographs by Clive Boursnell

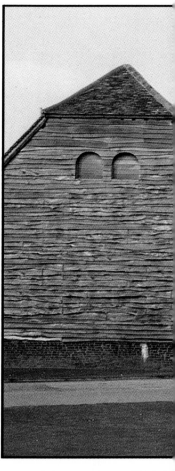

ABOVE: 17th-century barn at Headston
Manor, with the moat and manor hous
beyond.
ABOVE RIGHT: The Loudon monument
in Pinner churchyard.
RIGHT: The view today from Byron's s
at St Mary's, Harrow-on-the-Hill.

O fficially Middlesex should no longer exist. It lost a large proportion of its inhabitants and a good chunk of its land to the county of London under the Local Government Act of 1888, and the remains were swallowed up 75 years later to satisfy the insatiable appetite, and to meet the administrative convenience, of the Greater London Council. But a bureaucratic death sentence has not so far succeeded in exterminating the individual character of the area, which is suburban rather than urban, and very different from the city which in many ways has been dependent upon it — first for food and water, then for manufactured goods, and now, as always, for people.

Today people are Middlesex's most obvious characteristic. The county is London's densest dormitory. There is no obvious break between the houses and streets of London and the inner ring where Middlesex begins — Chiswick and Acton, Highgate and Wembley, Hornsey and Finchley, Tottenham and Edmonton — but the people who live in these places will still tell you that they live in Middlesex. The rows of semi-detached and terraced houses in which they live, and which have spread from the arterial roads and the underground railways almost to the limits of the county's borders with Essex, Hertfordshire and Bucks, are undeniably monotonous, though perhaps they seem more so from the train or to the passing motorist than they do to those who live inside them. But they provide reasonable comfort, patches of land on which to grow grass, flowers and vegetables, and an element of privacy.

To those who previously lacked them the acquisition of such advantages must have seemed akin to gaining a smallholding in paradise. Macaulay may have had something different in mind when he pronounced that an acre in Middlesex was better than a principality in Utopia, and certainly he cannot have imagined the county as it is today, but as a historian he would have recognized that suburbia, for all its unattractions and disadvantages, meets the needs, albeit inadequately, of many of those who have to work in or near the centre of London. Critics who note the ugliness and uniformity of the suburbs, and conclude that life within them must be equally drab and standardized, are wrong. Architects may certainly be condemned for

lack of inspiration in designing them, in Middlesex as elsewhere, and local authorities can be criticized, perhaps particularly in Middlesex, for insisting that small suburban areas be renamed and integrated to form part of larger groups instead of preserving their individuality, originality and eccentricity.

But there is romance in the suburbs, and it shows in small ways — such as the decoration of houses and the design of gardens, in the custom of naming houses Ivanhoe or The Poplars rather than numbering, and in the abandonment of the city word "street" in favour of "avenue", "way" or "close" — as well as in some grander gestures of personality. As a boy living near Pinner I used to enjoy visiting that attractive little town, where I would sneak into the churchyard to gaze at the tomb put up by J. C. Loudon, the Victorian horticulturalist who is credited with the spreading of plane trees in so many London squares. He erected an extraordinary obelisk, from which two ends of sarcophagi stick out at either side 10 feet above the ground, in memory of his parents. Another local eccentric I used to enjoy hearing about was Daniel Dancer, who was born in Pinner in 1716. He lived a life of almost total seclusion, eating only one meal a day, which always comprised baked meat and a dumpling, and wearing hay round his feet instead of boots. Though he inherited a sizeable estate in Harrow Weald his lands lay fallow to save the cost of cultivation. Dancer has an entry in the *Dictionary of National Biography* in which he is

ABOVE and RIGHT: Middlesex housing —the same only different.

RIGHT: Grim's Dyke near Old Redding. BELOW: Exterior of Syon House, which gives no hint of the Adam magnificences within. BELOW RIGHT: Letchford House as it is in use as offices today.

described simply as "miser". I have no doubt there are many equally engaging individualists living happily in Middlesex today.

Though I was not born in the county I lived there as a child in the 1930s and throughout the war years. We rented a 17th-century farmhouse which at that time lay in an enclave of fields between Headstone Lane and Hatch End, two modern villages well served both by the bustling red electric trains of the Bakerloo line and by the more stately brown ones of the LMS from Euston and Broad Street, and inevitably destined, like two blobs of mercury, to spread and join in an indissoluble mass of housing, as they now have. The old farm buildings have been swept away by this growth, but the house remains. Known as Letchford House, it is used as offices, with the garden turned into a car park. The mulberry tree at the front has survived and is bearing fruit, though I doubt that the birds have the leisure and the peace now to gorge themselves until they collapse upon the lawn, well beyond take-off weight.

The house also retains its cellar, from which it was alleged there was an underground passage leading to Headstone Manor, more than half a mile away. The manor is a small, well preserved, two-storeyed house, dating from the 15th and 16th centuries, and surrounded by a brick-banked moat. It once formed part of the medieval estates of the Archbishop of Canterbury, and it is believed that Wolsey, when rector of Harrow, lived here. Outside the moat is a fine barn with 10 bays, dating from about 1600, used now for concerts and other entertainments. If there is a hidden escape route from the manor it may date from the Civil War, when it was occupied by Sir Francis Rouse, one of the many influential men of Middlesex who supported the King's party.

Headstone Manor lies within a park and recreation ground, carefully tended and jealously protected, as such small areas of open space have to be in Middlesex, though even today the explorer prepared to leave his car will find, towards the outer rim of the county, pleasant woods and fields of sufficient size and number to illustrate what it was once like. It is possible to get lost in the country beyond Ruislip, and from Headstone Lane station it is only a few minutes' walk across the fields to Pinner Park Farm. There is another farm up Oxhey Lane, and if you turn into Old Redding towards Harrow Weald you will come to the viewpoint marked in the Ordnance Survey map of west London (by which is meant mostly Middlesex), from which opens up a wide panorama across to Harrow-on-the-Hill, and thence out westwards in the direction Byron used to view from his perch on the Peachey Stone in the churchyard of St Mary's on the Hill. The stone is now protected by iron casing, and the view is very different, with a prominent gas-holder marked for the identification of aircraft making for Northolt and almost uninterrupted housing spreading out to Hayes, with Heathrow beyond. Byron would no doubt have known of Hayes. Michael Robbins, in his excellent survey of the county published 30 years ago, noted that Hayes in the 18th and 19th centuries was reputed to be a neighbourhood of peculiar uncouthness and barbarism. Twentieth-century Hayes, an area of factories and housing estates, is more subdued, the dullness of its architecture redeemed only by the prettiness of its girls.

Behind the view from Old Redding lies Grim's Dyke House (now a hotel), a

Norman Shaw confection of heavy timbering, overhanging gables, incongruous chimneys and leaded glass windows designed for the painter Frederick Goodall. Later it became the home of W. S. Gilbert, who died there in 1911 of heart failure after saving a girl from drowning in the lake. Just up the road is a pub called The Case is Altered, where as children we used to be revived from our walks up the Weald with a glass of ginger beer and a Bath Oliver.

It has to be conceded that there is not much of ancient or medieval interest in Middlesex. Dr Nikolaus Pevsner has suggested that a history of art and architecture in England before Henry VIII might omit the county altogether, and it would be presumptuous to argue with him. There are plenty of later treasures to concentrate on – Syon House and Osterley Park for Robert Adam, Swakeleys at Ickenham for Inigo Jones, Chiswick House and garden for William Kent, Strawberry Hill in Twickenham for Horace Walpole's adventure in Gothic, Harrow school for Victorian worthiness, Bedford Park and Hampstead Garden Suburb for the first and most memorable experiments in this form of modern living, Charles Holden's underground stations and a good many striking new churches all over the county for examples of acceptable modern architecture. Crowning all, and the reason why Pevsner stopped short at Henry VIII, is Hampton Court, the grandest house of its time, made even grander by the later work of Christopher Wren, and certainly the most important surviving house in Middlesex.

Nonetheless I would not want to end this personal memoir of a part of Middlesex with a flourish of trumpets that might seem too close to a lament for things past. We can regret, particularly when we see rare glimpses of old rural Middlesex, the passing of Sir John Betjeman's lost Elysium, and the loss of some of the finest agricultural land in England, but in contemplating the county as it is today we should also recognize that given the economic conditions of the 19th and 20th centuries, the development of the county for more and more people to live in was inevitable. Perhaps it was also inevitable, given the nature of the people, most of whom want houses and gardens of their own and are prepared to travel considerable distance from their work to get them, that development should have been along the lines it was.

Above all, I believe it should be recognized that Middlesex is an entity worth preserving. It is more than a name, more than a postal address and a highly successful cricket team, and to assume that it is London is to misunderstand the history and nature of both the city and the county and to do justice to neither.

STANLEY BARON'S·
Surrey

Photographs by Richard Newton

For a small boy living in bricks-and-mortar Fulham, Surrey began at Putney and Putney was paradise. Across the River Thames, visible from our one green oasis of Bishop's Park, were the famous boathouses. The parish church of St Mary the Virgin beyond the bridge had its magic, too. Had it not sprung triumphant on the spot where the Devil flung a thunderbolt? And was it not there that the heroes of my youth, the Levellers, were laid low by country gentlemen who supported a revolution but would not pay the price? Best of all were the rumours that at the top of Putney Hill, wild, untamed country started. At the age of four I set out to walk there and was fetched home howling, but not before I had seen the green promise of the two great commons spread beyond The Green Man, and the little wooden-fenced cattle pound where the old Portsmouth Road widens out. The road, which is approximately the A3 of today, crosses the county from Esher in the north-east to Hindhead and the Hampshire border in the south-west.

Putney is not officially in Surrey now, having long since vanished into the bureaucratic maw of London. By some quirk, however, Putney Heath and Wimbledon Common are administratively joined and are beyond the GLC's clutches. There have been changes, of course. Mr Tibbet, of Tibbet's Corner, would find it hard today to recognize the whereabouts of the gatehouse where he touched his cap to Capability Brown, then engaged in creating "one of the finest parks in England" for Lord Spencer. The park has gone and so, except for the name, has the Corner, obliterated by a roundabout for the A3 dual carriageway. Yet much remains the same: the winding paths that lead to the Windmill on Wimbledon Common, once famous for the bread-and-jam-and-slabcake teas served on trestle tables in its yard; the little meres and occasional swamps attracting minuscule wildlife, grateful birds and shimmering dragonflies; and the trees, perhaps more plentiful now than ever. The sense of mystery which can still be felt here, within 7 or 8 miles of Hyde Park Corner, is not peculiar to the Putney-cum-Wimbledon commons, for Surrey has many such places, each with its own character. As gifts of the past, when cattle and sheep-grazing were common rights and the heaths were no-man's-lands, they give this county a special flavour.

ABOVE: The Norman Keep of Guildford Castle.
ABOVE RIGHT: Farnham Castle, founded in the 12th century, former seat of the bishops of Winchester and of Guildford.
RIGHT: View from Leith Hill, the highest point in South-east England, across the Weald to the South Downs.
BELOW: The clock of Abinger Hammer, an old iron-forging village; the figure of the blacksmith strikes the bell on the hour.

Away from the Thames great houses and parks have never seemed at home in Surrey's small-scale landscapes and such as there were have long since crumbled. Henry VIII's Nonsuch Palace near Ewell was demolished in 1628 and Richmond Palace is now reduced to a few ruins. Richmond Park, with its ancient oaks and deer herds, still has the atmosphere of a pleasance rather than a chase. The poor, uncoveted soils of Surrey's commons which elsewhere might have been enclosed, perhaps as a warning not to build too close to jealous monarchs, may explain why there have been no Chatsworths, Blenheims or Burghleys. On the other hand, to see how well the medium-sized country house fits in you have only to drive through traffic-battered Kingston upon Thames (so unsure of its identity these days that even its Coronation Stone has been pushed around) and on past The Angel at Ditton to Esher. We are heading for Claremont House and lake, in which I declare an interest for I lived near them for 27 years.

The history of Claremont and its demesne is typical of many of the properties of this kind which once ringed London. Sir John Vanbrugh built the first house, and having lived there for about seven years sold it with the estate to Thomas Pelham, the Earl of Clare, who named it Claremont. He asked Vanbrugh to add to it in a manner befitting his subsequent dukedom (he became Duke of Newcastle). Some 50 years later Claremont changed hands again. The new owner, Lord Clive of India, finding it unmanageable, pulled it down. Capability Brown designed the new house in 1772 aided by his partner Henry Holland and the young John Soane. In the high-handed fashion of the time, they diverted the Portsmouth Road from the lakeside by slicing a gap (still called Clive's Cutting) through a neighbouring hill.

Ripley's charm still smacks of the stage coach. Its chief inns are the Georgian-fronted Talbot and the rambling old half-timbered Anchor, just before St Mary's Church. There is a curious link between The Anchor and the church, where a window is dedicated to Annie and Harriet Dibble who ran the inn and who died in 1895 and 1896, and to the racing cyclist, Herbert Liddell Cortis, a hero of the Ripley Road. He was one of the scores of Sunday morning "scorchers" riders who, having gathered at The Angel, Ditton, would race the 10 miles to The Anchor and on to St Mary's for the morning service. In days before the invention of tarmac, this road, like all others, was kept in repair by semi-skilled roadmen whose job was to hammer their piles of stones down to a fine mash. Mixed with sand and water, this was spread into road holes and flattened into a patch indistinguishable from the rest of the surface. I can just remember one of the last of these men squatting by the roadside, his eyes protected by wire-mesh goggles while his chip pile grew. It was badly paid work and thankless, except for the appreciation of the "Ripley Roaders", who treated the men to an annual feast.

Such lowly history underlying present Surrey has an echo in Guildford High Street, whose ancient cobbles give a textured setting appropriate to its fine old houses. Although the old parts are now modified by pseudo-restoration, the steep curve of the street, overhung by the great Guildhall clock, offers the best urban views in Surrey, save possibly Farnham's Castle Street.

Guildford is quintessentially a county town, full of cheerful bustle, with a ruined castle founded in Saxon times to attest to its history, and a Jacobean hospital for the old and needy, given by the Guildfordian George Abbot, Archbishop of Canterbury, to express his love for his birthplace.

Guildford lies very much at a crossroads. The old Portsmouth Road carries on south-westwards to its summit at Hindhead; eastwards lie the North Downs where, from Newlands Corner, a famous beauty spot, there is a splendid view over the Tillingbourne valley; northwards the downs take the shape of the Hog's Back and the road leads to Farnham.

Here is an anachronism, for Farnham, the most individual of all Surrey towns outside Guildford, is today no more than a postal address. There is a society actively involved in the protection of the town but there is no local authority with which it can confer. Ridiculously Farnham, once a seat of the bishops of Winchester, the birthplace of that doughty individualist, William Cobbett, is now, thanks to Whitehall, a part of a nonentity called Waverley, named after the scanty ruins of the Cistercian abbey a couple of miles away. This might just be bearable to local romantics but what of distant Godalming and far-off Haslemere, yoked under the same name? And what, too, of historic Chertsey, ruled from upstart Addlestone, or Esher, mysteriously detached from its own River Mole to be part of Emberbrook?

Much of Farnham as we see it today is the work of three men who were answerable only to themselves. Charles Borelli, Harold Falkner and Maxwell Aylwin had been pupils together at Farnham Grammar School early this century. Falkner and Aylwin were the architects and Borelli the business brain behind almost a complete facelift of the streets they loved. One now regrets the passing of some of the Victorian buildings removed in their enthusiastic rediscovery of the Georgian idiom. They opened up Castle Street, with its extremes of 12th-century grandeur in the episcopal castle at the top end and the early 17th-century almshouses for "eight poor, honest, old and impotent persons" halfway down, and restored its wide, lower end with a new Town Hall and Bailiffs' Hall. Falkner, an idiosyncratic anti-bureaucrat with a determined contempt for building bylaws, was as happy with a mortar-and-trowel as with a drawing board. He died battling with the then urban district council, leaving his memorials all around him.

The do-it-yourself mentality of the Borelli-Falkner-Aylwin era is still strong in Farnham. The Farnham School of Art has become the West Surrey College of Art and Design in a new home of its own thanks in large part to its former Art School principal, James Hockey. The Maltings, a fine 18th- to 19th-century industrial complex on the banks of the River Wey, echoes to the sound of young voices. Volunteers from local youth clubs, led by a former army engineer, substantially adapted it into a now thriving social centre.

At Frensham Common on the way to Hindhead we can still trace remnants of Farnham's history. The Great Pond there was dammed to increase its size and was a source of fish for the Castle and the Abbey. Downstream from its outlet is one of the prettiest short walks in Surrey. But Bernard Shaw, walking on a damp day from Farnham to stay with his old friend of the Humanitarian League, Henry S. Salt, thought the rest of the journey to Hindhead dismal. Villages like Tilford and Thursley are pretty but this is primarily Thelwell pony country from which the realities of country life have long since drained away.

It would be better for the serious walker to take a giant leap eastwards to the

ABOVE LEFT: Dominating Guildford High Street is the gilded clock of 1863, outside the Guildhall. ABOVE: The alms-houses in Farnham's Castle Street. LEFT: Frensham Common's Great Pond, rich haunt of bird life.

North Downs, landing perhaps at the hilltop chapel of St Martha, between the River Wey and the Tillingbourne stream, and walk along any of the tracks claiming to be the Pilgrims' Way. Connecting Winchester and Canterbury, it is a route certainly older than Christianity and is not so much a single path as a skein. As early pilgrims would have varied their route according to weather and danger, so can we, stopping off at valley villages like Shere, through which the Tillingbourne meanders prettily.

Since the Pilgrims' Way also belongs to Hampshire and Kent, it can only be said that Surrey embraces it as it might a stranger. The sense of county is stronger with the approach to John Evelyn's woods at Wotton. As a boy, learning my journalist's trade on *The Middlesex County Times* at Ealing, I would put my pen down at the end of press day and cycle across the width of Surrey to swim in a pool nestling on Leith Hill's slopes. The adjoining hamlet was Archbishop Stephen Langton's birthplace. Lucky man to be young in such countryside and lucky Evelyn to have the raw material for his great work *Sylva* all around him. And we are lucky to inherit so much of the forestry practice he preached. This is the very best part of rural Surrey and it reaches its peak, literally, at Leith Hill. Approached by a maze of paths through a wealth of woods, it is just short of 1,000 feet high but the tower on top makes up the difference. From the foot of the tower the South Downs are in sight.

Box Hill, Leith Hill's neighbour and its rival in popularity, hides behind the great tide of trees reaching nearly all the way to Dorking. For the vigorous, the best way to climb up it, through the boxwood, is by the stepping stones near Burford Bridge. The best way down is across the open slopes of Zig Zag Hill past George Meredith's old home at Flint Cottage, where he lived for 30 years. Nowadays even its enormous box hedges would scarcely have protected him from prying eyes on the hill above. Opposite the Zig Zags, across the River Mole, is a steep, wooded escarpment topped by Ranmore and its common. This long green strip offers the start of a good walk to Polesden Lacey, another of Surrey's modest mansions and once much favoured by European royalty who could also visit Epsom nearby. Stroll the length of the Long Walk, sniff the air for postprandial cigar smoke and you will be back in Edwardian times. The scene has changed very little.

PATRICK MOORE'S
Sussex

Photographs by Colin Curwood

Sussex by the sea . . . once a proud, independent kingdom, now one of the best-loved of England's counties. Appropriately it has been left untouched by the recent bureaucratic atrocities which have obliterated Rutland and Westmorland, created such hideous newcomers as Cleveland and Avon, and mercilessly shifted whole towns from one county to another. Not even the most revolutionary chieftain of Westminster would dare to touch Sussex; Sussex simply would not permit it. It even raised its eyebrows at being divided into West and East.

It has never had one overriding characteristic — at least not since its days as a Saxon kingdom. It is not the Garden of England, as neighbouring Kent is; it is not dominated by coalmines or tranquil lakes, and it is neither particularly hilly nor particularly flat. In this, surely, lies its charm. It is a county of many landscapes and many moods, and it is sufficiently far from London not to be swamped by the ever-spreading metropolitan octopus, in the manner of parts of Surrey, Essex and even Kent. There are some Sussex regions which may be called commuter country, but there are others which are too far out — particularly since only a few of its towns, such as Brighton, are really well served by British Rail.

It has a major airport, Gatwick, which is fast rivalling Heathrow. It also has a new town, Crawley. I remember Crawley in the 1930s as a tiny, placid village; there was the little main street, with the ancient George Hotel, and very little else. When the planners moved in, Crawley was transformed into what it is today, but at least it is still more or less confined; open country still separates it, for instance, from East Grinstead, one of the old coaching-stops between London and the coast.

East Grinstead, too, has been transformed to some extent, partly by deliberate intent and partly by Hitler's bombers. The black-and-white buildings in the upper High Street remain, but the road has become busier and busier — something which has affected many other Sussex towns as well. True, they have lost something of their charm — the weekly markets have faded into obscurity, overshadowed by the super-markets and the huge departmental stores — but on the whole Sussex has been able to save most of its population centres from being changed into concrete jungles.

There is rich history in Sussex. Chichester, a Roman town, retains its atmosphere

LEFT: The village of Poynings with its Norman church tower seen from the Devil's Dyke, a neolithic hill-fort on the South Downs. BELOW: The sea-front at Brighton, whose holiday resort popularity is enhanced by the romantic quality of its narrow back streets.

ABOVE: An early spring pastoral near the village of Colworth. RIGHT: Bodiam Castle, the last of England's military castles, was built in 1385 and is surrounded by a moat. Though it looks complete, it is in fact a roofless ruin.

despite what is almost certainly the most confusing one-way traffic system in the whole of south England; unquestionably it was designed by a committee. The famous Cross may be a hazard to motorists, but as it comes into view when you walk down South Street it is both dignified and distinctive. Parts of the Roman walls remain; but if you are really interested in the Occupation, you have only to go a few miles down the road and visit Fishbourne, where you can see the remains of the palace once ruled by King Cogidubnus. There is not much vertical structure, but the colourful mosaic is a reminder of those bygone days. Moreover, it is excellently arranged and organized, a credit to its county. Go also to Bignor, some way inland, where there is another Roman villa — and Roman roads are to be found everywhere.

More recently there has been the greatest of all Sussex battles, perhaps the most significant in the whole story of our island. There can be nobody who does not remember the date 1066, when Saxon England came to its dramatic end, not actually at Hastings but at Battle. You can walk where King Harold walked (or, rather, rode); you can see the lovely old Abbey; and you can go on to Rye, one of the most peaceful and beautiful of all the smaller Sussex towns even though it is no longer on the coast (but Camber Sands are nearby, if you feel inclined to go for a swim).

Inevitably much of the coast of Sussex has been built up, and during summertime crowds flock there, enjoying the sunshine in one of the sunniest parts of England, and the beaches. For sheer size Brighton is unrivalled, and here, too, there is history, because it still has its Regency Pavilion and much else to remind us of the man who reigned over the country for 10 years before he became officially King George IV. Brighton is a town of two moods. It is a holiday resort, with ice-cream parlours, funfairs and hotels; but I wonder how many of its visitors take the trouble to explore its narrow, romantic back streets, which seem to hide themselves from the public eye? Eastbourne is more overtly dignified; Hastings, I always feel, comes somewhere between the two in its outlook. To the casual visitor Brighton's rock-and-roll contrasts sharply with Eastbourne's symphonies and concerts.

Then there is Bognor, which became Bognor Regis in the earlier part of our century, when King George V was sent there to recuperate. Perhaps it is rather unfortunate that the town is always associated with the famous last comment by the dying monarch when told that he was almost ready to go back there. "Bother Bognor" is a bowdlerized version of what he is alleged to have said. Bognor Regis today has its Butlin's and its holiday atmosphere; frankly I have a great affection for it, if only because I lived there until I was six years old, and to me it seems a home town. I prefer it to Littlehampton or Worthing or Bexhill, but I admit to being prejudiced. I suppose the time will come when the whole coast between Bognor Regis and Brighton is built up, but I hope that it will not be yet.

Sailors of all kinds have a great love of Sussex, which is not surprising; there can be few lovelier sights than Chichester Yacht Basin on a sunny day. Selsey Bill sticks out into the sea, and there can be trouble offshore; I wonder how many lives have been saved by the famous lifeboat? I live in Selsey, which prides itself on being older than Chichester, and I would not leave it even though it has grown so much during the past decades; mercifully all roads to it end in the sea and the planners have no chance to spoil the village by building a through road, as they have done at Wittering and Bracklesham. Erosion has taken its toll. The sea has edged in, and one can still meet old men who remember fields and houses where the ocean now rolls. Years ago — it must have been in or before 1927 — I talked to a very senior citizen who told me that he could recall hearing the bell of the old church which has long since been swallowed up. Nowadays the erosion has more or less stopped, partly naturally and partly through the construction of a massive sea wall. Farther east the situation has been reversed; there is now land where there used to be water, and Winchelsea belies its name.

But do not forget what lies inland; there is often too much concentration on the Sussex coast, glorious though it is (and the view from Beachy Head is as magnificent as anything in Britain). Arundel is dominated by its Castle; Lewes retains much of its

ABOVE: Typical Sussex pubs like The Cricketers outside Petworth have managed to retain their individuality. LEFT: The shingle beach and pier at Hastings, William the Conqueror's base before he set out to defeat Harold II at Battle in 1066.

The 500 foot high cliffs of Beachy Head.

old-world atmosphere. Other towns like Horsham and Haywards Heath are perhaps less distinctive, but hardly less pleasant; I would never speak against them.

All in all, it is perhaps in its villages that Sussex shines most brightly. There are endless numbers of them, some hidden in the hills, others doing their best to forget the existence of main roads passing by them. Slindon, Newick, West Hoathly (pronounced with a long ȳ), Chelwood Gate, Robertsbridge, Wisborough Green . . . one could go on and on, and each has something of its own to offer. Most of them have their ponds, their narrow streets and their village greens where cricket is played during the summer. Their bowlers do not hurl down Lillee-like thunderbolts, and their batsmen do not wear crash-helmets and armour plating; yet without village cricket there would be no Test Matches, and Sussex is one of the cradles of this most noble of all games.

Then there are the pubs, some of them ultra-modern and sophisticated, others remaining very much as they have always been. At Chidham there is even a brewery — I believe it is the smallest in Europe, but it certainly provides excellent beer. Somehow the typical Sussex village pub has retained its integrity; long may it continue to do so.

There are flat parts of the county, but there are also the Downs, which may not be Himalayan in altitude but which have a gentle beauty which is irresistible. Naturalists love Sussex, and so do bird-watchers. I am not a bird-watcher (the only feathered birds I can recognize with absolute certainty are the robin and the hen), but there is always the chance of finding something unexpected. Not long ago, at an inlet near Sidlesham, I spied a curious bird which I later found to be a flamingo, though I doubt if it could be regarded as indigenous.

Sussex is a large county. To the east lies Kent; to the west, Hampshire, to the north, Surrey and the beginnings of London. Despite its variety, Sussex seems, to me at least, to be different from its neighbours. Drive across the border to Tunbridge Wells, or Petersfield, or Dorking, and you are at once aware that Sussex has been left behind — I do not know why; and when I return to Sussex I am always glad.

I have left until last something which is of special importance to me. The English have always been a seafaring nation; the centre of all navigation and timekeeping was the Royal Greenwich Observatory, set up in the Park by direct command of King Charles II (who, typically, paid for it by selling "old and decayed gunpowder" to the French, way back in the 1670s). In our own time the lights and smog of London have cast a garish gloom over the Greenwich skies, and by the time of the war it had become painfully clear that the Observatory would have to move. But where to? There could be nowhere but Sussex; and the picturesque Castle at Herstmonceux, not far from Hailsham, became the new Greenwich. The Castle today looks outwardly just as it has always done, but inside it is the nerve-centre of British astronomy, and the grounds have sprouted domes in the manner of mushrooms. The largest of the telescopes, the Isaac Newton reflector, has been reluctantly shifted to a still better site in the Canary Islands, but plenty of other telescopes remain, and from here our scientists (and those of other countries) explore events taking place in star-systems so remote that the light from them now reaching our eyes started on its journey even before the Earth itself came into being.

Can one ever claim to a complete knowledge of the whole of Sussex? A few people can, I suppose, but not many; there is so much to see. There is something for everybody, whether you prefer the grandeur of the Downs, the charm of Lindfield, the bright lights of Brighton or the yellow beaches of King George's Bognor. Other counties have different merits, and no two are alike; but having seen most of them I say, emphatically, that Sussex will do for me.

THE WEST COUNTRY

BELOW: The scenic cliffs of Boscastle.
RIGHT: The village of Cadgwith.
FAR RIGHT: The remains of Cornish tin mines at Carnkie and Carn Brea, Redruth.

JOHN TREWIN'S
Cornwall

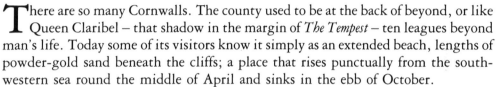

Photographs by Jerry Mason

There are so many Cornwalls. The county used to be at the back of beyond, or like Queen Claribel – that shadow in the margin of *The Tempest* – ten leagues beyond man's life. Today some of its visitors know it simply as an extended beach, lengths of powder-gold sand beneath the cliffs; a place that rises punctually from the south-western sea round the middle of April and sinks in the ebb of October.

For others, even in these days, it is a sea-coast of literary Bohemia, or a fantasy beleaguered by legend and myth. Piskies can multiply. Tregeagle weaves his ropes of sand. Arthur is with Merlin at Tintagel. From Dozmary Pool on Bodmin Moor and Loe Pool in the far south, hands reach for Excalibur.

That is not all. In fiction this has been an outlier of Cold Comfort. Zadkiel Polwhidden nightly seduces a Jennifer or Loveday under the lew of a cromlech. Plays – fewer of them than there were – used to be in the winding-sheet class, Hardy's "dire duresse that vexed the land of Lyonesse"; the key words were doom, gloom and tomb.

One more Cornwall, of many, from a guidebook just a century old: "The following objects are calculated to strike the attention by their novelty, viz: porphyry and granite houses; stone hedges, as they are called, though really stone walls so broad that footpaths run along their tops; teetotal inns." And the people? Well, observe their "love of excitement, and of preaching, or any sort of oratory" and their "utter absence of method in work or business". The helpful man did recognize the problem of local names – out of the West I am still irrevocably labelled "Truin" – and he avoided that most common mistake, the county of Cornwall muddled with the landed estate of the Duchy. A. L. Rowse, historian and scholar, explains: "The popular habit of referring to Cornwall as 'the Duchy' – in the 16th century they called it a 'shire' like any other English shire – is a modern error: it may be compared to what grammarians call 'the transferred epithet'."

For Anne Treneer, from Gorran, the peninsula was a "great rocky scroll, graved by the wind, Cut by the bright blades of the sea." Claude Berry, from Padstow, who edited the *West Briton*, saw it as shaped like Parson Hawker's sea-boot. The Launceston (or Lanson) poet, Charles Causley, imagines a time – "One day, friend and stranger, The granite beast will rise" – when Cornwall looses itself suddenly from the English mainland and floats away on the water. Always that Cornish sea.

Our only genuine archipelago is the Isles of Scilly, out among its flowers in the track of the sunset; but a West Country editor said to me years ago that Cornwall is itself an archipelago undivided, every village a potential islet, a self-contained republic.

First, as anyone must, I think of the sea and the villages. In childhood, on nights of "coarse weather", I would lie awake listening to the sea, separating and localizing the sounds it made: a furious explosive boom on the full face of the headland 300 yards away; a swoop and a despairing, baffled hiss among the cove's guardian reefs; and a sharp, steady drive along a more distant beach with the débris of a wreck among the surf. I hear the sounds yet. People round the coast, between Penwith and Morwenstow, Rame and The Lizard, have heard them for untold generations: the language of the sea, one of Cornwall's native tongues. It is emphatic in winter, gentler in summer when we used to scramble before breakfast over limpet-crusted slabs, by pools glistening with weed and starred with anemones, to a point where there was nothing to do but mark the curl and shimmer of the tide. That was in June. But eastward, round the corner, somebody had held me up against a glossily wet oilskin jacket to watch the great winter waves arch and tighten, and flotsam from a wrecked Scandinavian timber barque swirl below the cliff.

With the Cornish sea go the Cornish cliffs: West Penwith's granite, pinnacled and pillared; the southern serpentine and an agonizing sheer plummet-drop between the Rill and Mullion; Shipman Head, detached from Bryher out in the islands; the prospect from Cambeak, above Crackington Haven, like "the great blackness" in *The Arabian Nights* tale of Prince Agib.

My father, 45 years at sea and trained in sail, would walk on any extreme verge without a glance downward. Away from the cliffs he could be glum. Though for him that was reasonable enough, it is perverse to write off inland Cornwall in a few sour phrases. Fashion suggests that the place is just a grand coastline looped about a void, and I was glad when I got Ivor Brown, not the easiest Scot to persuade, to say how wrong fashion was. Yet he had not ventured far. He had never found the coil of lanes above the oak-shelved, heron-haunted shore of Helford River – my mother's world, Meneage – or penetrated the upper reaches of the Camel or Lynher; never known the by-road village of St Tudy, north of Bodmin; seen Altarnun, or St Germans, or the lands below Caradon; or traced the Fowey valley that "Q" celebrated.

There are so many Cornwalls. Some have always been an acquired taste. Still, whatever industry has done – and it has hardly spared itself – to the Mining Division round Carn Brea or to the White Country of the china-clay burrows, loyalists will stand firm. The Cornish are nothing if not loyal.

Most of the towns, wherever you look for them, are as strongly personal as the villages, and that says a lot: Falmouth, wedded to a harbour that matches Plymouth Sound; Truro, where the poised cathedral, young as cathedrals go, and much under-valued, seems to vanish like a mirage in mid-city; Helston of the "Furry" dance, the Georgian houses, and those lisping runnels down the slant of Coinage Hall Street; the sedate rumple of Bodmin; Lostwithiel that prompted Drinkwater's refrain, "Lostwithiel is found"; frontier Launceston of the castle and the church of St Mary Magdalene; Padstow and St Austell, Penzance and Penryn; Fowey, "Q"'s "Troy" – the names chime – clinging to its hill.

The Rill.

We are back with "Q", Arthur Quiller-Couch (not, he would insist, pronounced like a sofa), occasionally an unexpected realist but, far more abundantly, king of Cornish romantics; a man of an acute ear, fastidious allusiveness, leisurely relish. He began to write when Cornwall in literature was being freshly colonized.

Modern Cornish writers are helpfully diverse: the historian, A. L. Rowse, of All Souls and Trenarren; Charles Causley, the county laureate, faithful to Launceston on the relatively unfretted border; Jack Clemo, paladin of the claylands; Derek Tangye, chronicling in West Penwith; Daphne du Maurier, in the high romantic line. Clearly she was the writer to finish "Q"'s neo-Tristan fragment, *Castle Dor*, just as, long ago, he completed Stevenson's *St Ives*, a name misleadingly Cornish.

In an early book Daphne du Maurier described the central wilds of Bodmin Moor which on a rough night can be alpha and omega, the beginning and the end. Not, let me say, the moor alone: that tingle of isolation is endemic in Cornwall, at any hour or place: at the heart of winter or in the brisk seasonal chaos on the Costa del Newquay. True, it may not be generally noticed. Cornwall, anyway, is a Far End, a mystery that can never be solved too often; every summer visitors swarm across the broad gulf of the Hamoaze estuary, over Brunel's rail bridge to Saltash or on the Tamar road bridge beside it, with the shield of the 15 bezants midway. For the economy's sake, they are welcome. Yet, ungratefully, there must be a gentle sigh when autumn comes and Cornwall is itself again, still "undiscovered".

Probably we can say that of its natives. By now expertly hospitable – and, goodness knows, they have had enough practice – they can be as proud, clannish and

independent as their fathers were. Even in 1880 "an utter absence of method in business and work" was eccentric. But much in the old guidebook does hold. Cornishmen thrive on excitement; anyone must feel it after the sway and tumult, flash and outbreak, of a rugby crowd at Redruth. They are eloquent; anybody must agree after service in a village chapel: my pride was a nobly whiskered farmer, "the man with the halo", for whom an hour's sermon without notes was routine. And the theatrical side, "any kind of oratory"? Cornwall may have forgotten the tug between an impulse that created its medieval miracle plays, and the stern puritanism of later centuries; but I cannot forget a village elder, dramatic in voice and mien. He told me, an impressionable six-and-a-half, that if I listened to the "pomping folk" I would lie along with the deadly worm – "there, boy, down *there*, wriggling in the dust". It was a superb performance; and after an appreciable gap my guilt lingers.

Strolling players, "the night, the booth, the torches' flare", have not always been disregarded. Read Wilkie Collins, in the Cornwall of 1850, on the Sans Pareil fit-up at Redruth where "the beautiful drama of *The Curate's Daughter*" was announced by "the most talented company in England". These goings-on were a world away from the Minack Theatre, created by Miss Rowena Cade, terraced into a West Penwith cliff at Porthcurno, and used in summer by amateurs from near and far. Behind a crescent stage is the wide, restless plain of the Cornish sea, a backdrop perfect for Tristan and Iseult.

I think myself of a straight, dusty road in early April. A last hint of sunset; a "jingle", or pony trap, trots across an empty plateau towards the most southern Cornish village. The sea is invisible, but not far distant. It lies on three sides of us; the wind is quick and salt. If, at journey's end, the pony takes to the water, our next stop could be Brazil. In youth all appeared to be incapable of change. Now a naval air station has smothered the fields of my grandfather's farm; grotesque shapes against the sky have grown from science fiction. Not a jingle in sight.

What, in a few words, does the name evoke? Quickly and personally: gulls behind the plough; linchets on a hillside; fuchsia and tamarisk, sea-pink and mesembry-anthemum; a sheen of serpentine and a glint of mica; the vision of the "guarded Mount"; slate tombs of the Reskymers and the Nicolls at St Tudy; a font in Landewednack Church (*Ric. Bolham me fecit*); the round of Restormel Castle; Lemon Street in Truro, primly elegant; "Glorious things of thee are spoken" sung in evening chapel; names on the map, Constantine and Lanteglos and Portloe, Indian Queens and Zennor, St Endellion, St Mabyn, St Veep, Probus and Luxulyan; Trelowarren ilexes; daybreak at Kynance; the thrust of Tol-Pedn; an overwhelming sense of the past; the eager present; and always the encircling sea.

I can feel our awe as, soundlessly, the masts of the wrecked barque, *Queen Margaret*, Masefield's "frigate bird white", canted over in wreck on a hot morning in spring while we watched from a Lizard hedge. Secretly, I try to remember another occasion, a little before my time. That was when listeners on the Rill heard a mutter of guns as every galleon in the Spanish Armada fired a broadside and the sea castles of Medina Sidonia moved up the summer Channel to their doom. Let us call it double vision again; those ships are forever on my Cornish sea, ten leagues beyond man's life.

The Cornish sea: fishing off St Clement's Isle.

ARTHUR MARSHALL'S
Devon

Photographs by Jerry Mason

Atlantic rollers hurling me about, and the crunch of shingle, and seawater stinging my eyes and then being wrapped up and patted dry in a vast white bathtowel are among my earliest childhood memories and belong to bathing and learning to swim at Ilfracombe in north Devon. The sea there seemed never to be at rest. But in an establishment called The Tunnels the town had some large rock pools which were filled with fresh seawater at high tide and were reached by a dark and damp passage driven through the cliff, and here we could splash about in less tempestuous circumstances than in the sea. Not so much fun, but easier for mastering the breast stroke and, later, what we then knew as the "trudgeon".

My grandparents lived at Ilfracombe where my grandfather was a clergyman, and their garden had fuchsia hedges and fruit called wine-berries and a broad and rather muddy stream in which large trout swam lazily and undisturbed, save by clockwork liners whirring to and fro, bought at Twiss's magical toyshop in The Arcade. And also in the stream were two small islands rich with bamboo and reached by a rustic bridge and here I could fancy myself marooned and abandoned and as lonely as poor old Ben Gunn in *Treasure Island*.

My grandparents had a particular affection for Saunton, near neighbour of Woolacombe, both of them just round the corner from Ilfracombe, and every so often in those summers when the sun seemed always to shine they would hire a small coach (at that time referred to as a *char-à-banc*, shortened by some to charrer) and off we would set for those golden stretches of sand that provided good, safe bathing, though you had to walk quite a way to reach deep water. On clear days there was a view of Lundy Island 12 miles to the west, an inhospitable lump of granite rearing itself 400 feet out of the sea and originally – another link with *Treasure Island* – a favourite haunt of pirates. For bathing at Saunton we undressed, men to the right, ladies to the left, in the sand dunes and for days afterwards our clothes shed sand.

After being engaged to each other for four years (quite normal in those unhurried and decorous times), my parents were married in the parish church, Ilfracombe, and spent their honeymoon a few miles along that splendidly rugged Devon coast and in the Tors Hotel at Lynmouth, a hotel which escaped the terrible disaster of 1952 when the waters of the Lyn piled up at the head of that beautiful valley and then came roaring down, bringing with them appalling death and destruction. But in childhood, Lynton and the impressive Valley of the Rocks that leads down to a charming little beach made an agreeable expedition by motor, in those days a gallant old Metalergic in which we sat well up, the better to see over the high Devon hedges which, especially in summer, sometimes deny you a pleasing view: and all views in Devon are pleasing.

And so I gradually came to know well most of north Devon, for we often came from London, where we then lived, by the train which, after Barnstaple and that delightful stretch of the Taw estuary that leads past Instow to Bideford, had to chug its way up steep gradients (the steam engine saying, in imagination, "I-think-I-can, I-think-I-can") all the way to Mortehoe station, after which we got our first exciting sight of the sea sparkling below. And then, with the engine saying "Thought-I-could, thought-I-could", there came the final run down into Ilfracombe station, with a childish fear that the train might burst through the buffers, crash down through the town, demolishing the pierrot show and the Punch and Judy, and go plop into the harbour, a marvellously natural one where during the Great War a tramp steamer, holed by a U-boat, was beached. And at the station a horse-drawn cab was waiting for us and soon we would all be at the tea-table and eating what we called Devon

Bowerman's Nose, a rocky outcrop on Dartmoor near the village of Manaton.

TOP: Brentor, from which there are fine views of Dartmoor and Bodmin Moor in Cornwall, is 1,130 feet high and surmounted by the 13th-century church of St Michael. CENTRE LEFT: A full-scale and seaworthy replica of the Golden Hind, fitted out as a museum of Tudor times, moored in Brixham harbour. CENTRE RIGHT: A crab fisherman at Salcombe, a popular centre for fishing and yachting. BOTTOM: Dawlish, where the railway track runs right beside the sea.

cutrounds, delicious scones covered with strawberry jam (home-made, I need hardly say) and the cream than which there is no finer, though Cornish cream runs it pretty close.

By the end of the 1920s both my grandparents were dead, but that was far from being the end of our Devon holidays and it meant that we could go farther afield. Few excitements in life have been able to compare with boarding at Paddington the Cornish Riviera Express, as famous in its day as the Flying Scotsman, and, in the reserved seats that were then essential, flying westwards at the breakneck speed of 65 mph. I never knew exactly where the Somerset-Devon border lay but we always felt when we were coasting downhill after the long, steep tunnel 10 miles or so from Taunton that we were in Devon, and when we thundered through Tiverton we knew that we were. In all England there is no more beautiful road than the one that winds its way from Exeter along the Exe valley, through Stoke Canon and Rewe and Bickleigh and so to Tiverton and, if you need nowadays a purpose for the drive, the wonderful Knightshayes Court gardens there (as memorable in their way as those at Bodnant in Wales) provide it.

After leaving Exeter the line runs alongside the broad Exe estuary with, across the water, the picturesque gabled houses of the 17th-century Dutch settlers at Topsham, then the red sandstone tower of Lympstone church and, on the sandy promontory at the estuary's end, Exmouth, a favourite haunt of retired people and where two of history's most unhappy wives, Lady Nelson and Lady Byron, lie buried. High up above Exmouth is Woodbury Common with its marvellous views over Dartmoor and Exmoor, though lumping the two moors together, as one often does, it is easy to forget that a large part of the latter is in Somerset. And after our train had passed the sandy expanses of Dawlish Warren the line struck south-west in a long straight stretch to Dawlish and gave us our first proper sight of the sea.

Our holiday destination was often Yelverton. We changed trains at Plymouth and got into a far less august one which struggled nobly up the steep incline and at Yelverton we were within easy reach of Dartmoor. Sometimes we walked to the moor but quite often we took the GWR branch line to Princetown, a fascinating single track with great bends and loops and various "halts" on the way. A "halt" usually meant a wooden platform miles from anywhere, with an especially good one at Burrator near the immensely attractive wooded reservoir that looks like a perfectly natural stretch of water. Reservoirs on Dartmoor are a sore subject with preservationists but to me every new reservoir is an added attraction.

Princetown itself, the end of the line, is overshadowed by the grey prison. The name Dartmoor is a menacing one but the building is much less threatening when seen in bright sunlight and from a distance in its beautiful moorland surroundings. The railway exists no longer, but the moor itself is changeless, with its pools and streams and huge granite boulders and bright green bogs and friendly ponies. This is the place for walkers, provided they beware its frighteningly quick and bewildering mists. If caught unawares, a rough-and-ready rule for rescue is to walk downhill until you come upon one of the countless streams that rise on the moor and follow it downhill. If you are going far afield, strong shoes and a compass are essential.

We used to climb every tor within range and on our return to the hotel underline

RIGHT: The harbour at Ilfracombe.
BELOW LEFT: The nave of Exeter
Cathedral, which has the longest
unbroken stretch of Gothic vaulting in
the world. BELOW CENTRE: The east
gate-house in Totnes. BELOW RIGHT:
Overlooking the harbour at Salcombe.

these in red ink on our ordnance survey map. And for children it was a paradise of deep pools that could be bathed in, and fast-flowing streams that could be dammed, and you were ever conscious of the delicious picnic that was to come.

Devon is a fine county for picnickers, whether the food and drink be carried in those immensely heavy wicker-and-leather baskets, complete with glasses and cutlery (they used to be given as wedding-presents) which seem to demand and deserve such elaborations as game pie and salmon mayonnaise and terrines of pâté, and hock, or, much better, in a simple haversack with sandwiches and a Thermos or two. We have had wonderful picnics in Tor Bay on the sunny grass slopes of Berry Head, watching the fishing-boats putting in to Brixham harbour. We have had them on the banks of the Dart, that loveliest of rivers, where it flows through the woodlands behind Ashburton; and we have picnicked on the escarpment below Hay Tor from which you can see Newton Abbot and Teignmouth and its estuary and the hill that hides Torquay and sometimes, far to the east, the red cliffs of Budleigh Salterton near where Raleigh was born. We have picnicked on the beach at Sidmouth, a town with some pleasing 18th-century houses and to which Queen Victoria came as a child while her father, the impoverished Duke of Kent, was pursued by angry creditors. And we have wandered by car along the coast through Beer and Seaton to Lyme Regis, which always looks as though it ought to be in Devon but which, alas, is not.

And eventually, 36 happy years ago, I came actually to live in Devon in one of the many agreeable villages, such as Lustleigh and Lydford and Newton St Cyres, for which the county is so famous. We are in the Teign valley alongside that peaceful and unpretentious river that rises on the moor near Cranmere Pool where other rivers rise (the Dart, the Okement and the Taw), skirts Chagford, drops down to the waterfall at Steps Bridge near Dunsford and then obligingly turns south and comes down our valley, wild daffodils on its banks and trout and salmon in its waters.

I am lucky to have a 3 acre apple orchard in the middle of the village. There is a small stream in the orchard, complete with small trout and a heron who comes and breakfasts with us. And although relatively in the wilds, it is a bare half-hour to Exeter, with its excellent shops and its high-speed trains to London and elsewhere. And on the drive in who could ever grow tired of the breathtaking view of the superb cathedral, for many the finest in England, perched up on the hill which bore a church even before the Conquest and which Hitler's war-time bombs, though doing fearful and unforgivable damage in the city, could not destroy.

There is just so much else in the county – the Exeter Guildhall going back 600 years; the Atlantic lashing the rocks of Hartland Point; the steep and cobbled street of Clovelly that leads precipitately down to the sea; the fine rebuilding of the badly blitzed Plymouth; the romantic Hoe and Drake's Island and the ships of Devonport; the delicious and traditional Devon pot cake; the yachts at Salcombe and the wonderful walks round Bolt Head and Hope Cove; cider and its more lethal cousin scrumpie; the church on the summit of Brentor built 700 years ago by the monks of nearby Tavistock, and Tavistock itself with its fine medieval church and its statue of Drake, perhaps Devon's proudest son. And if you think that I have forgotten Widecombe and Uncle Tom Cobley and all – well, as you see, I haven't.

RACHEL BILLINGTON'S
Dorset

Photographs by Sarah King

Ten years ago I made a film about the village where I live in Dorset. I called it *A Country Dream*. More than a dream, it was an idyll. A celebration of a love affair that started one rainy afternoon.

The year before I had been married, inheriting with my husband a tiny top-floor flat in London. Almost at once I pointed out we would surely need a country home as well. My certainty was based on my own privileged childhood in which a London day school had been combined with country holidays. Just as marriage should start with the highest ideals, so, I felt, should the circumstances around it.

Our friends were sceptical, pointing out that although at present – young marrieds, film director and aspiring novelist, unburdened by children or an office schedule – we might manage, soon we would be returned to reality. Why waste time on what was only a fantasy? Since it was the fantasy that drew me, I ignored them. The question then arose, whither? The process of decision reminded me later on of that fascinating poker game known as "choosing a name for baby". Almost always husband and wife have a favourite, a trump card, kept secret until lesser alternatives are safely cleared away. In this case what neither of us knew was that we both had Dorset as our trump. My husband, it transpired, had come south from the verdureless streets of Warrington at the age of 13. He attended Bryanston School and had the happiest memories of long misty afternoons on the playing fields and punishment runs alongside the River Stour.

I had been brought up in Sussex, the wooded and cultivated area so far east that it looks over the shoulder of Kent into hop-fields and oast-houses. I loved it there but never thought of making it my adult choice. I can remember giving the reason to my slightly disconsolate mother. Sussex, I declared (grandly ignoring the existence of the Downs), was claustrophobic. Dorset, on the other hand, was like a painting by Gozzoli or some other early Italian master. All those little valleys and conical hills and mellow stone villages. It was an ancient landscape, suggestive of mysterious fictional pasts – my sister had just written a book about King Arthur. It was a westerly county making easy access from our W11 flat. And then there was Thomas Hardy. At the mention of Hardy my mother knew she was beaten. He had always been my most

TOP: Carved on a hillside in Cerne Abbas, the 180 foot high Cerne Giant. CENTRE: The strange stone Cross-in-Hand stands 1 mile east of Batcombe Church. BOTTOM LEFT: Monks from Batcombe Priory. BOTTOM RIGHT: Part of ruined Sherborne Old Castle which belonged to Raleigh and, beyond it, Sherborne Castle where he lived.

The view from Abbotsbury towards pebbly Chesil Beach.

beloved writer, novelist and poet. The possibility of actually inhabiting his land-scapes, meeting my own reddelman on Egdon Heath, coming face to face with my own gargoyle, was clearly irresistible. The search for an appropriate home was on.

What strikes me now about the whole search-and-find operation was the high element of good luck. For the truth was, I did not know Dorset proper at all. My physical experience totted up to occasional visits to friends who lived north of Bridport in a house which opened on to one of the swooping hill-sides that I so admired, and some vague childhood recollections of the glories of the coastal region.

Now I wonder that I was not more attracted to a house within the influence of the sea. Perhaps it seemed too exciting, the pounding of the waves too much competition for my own fledgling voice. It strikes me as I write this that the first "sin" in my new novel takes place in a little grassy field somewhere along the Dorset coast. And afterwards my heroine runs into Dorset's cold purifying waters . . . Perhaps I am, therefore, only recording a childhood conviction that a seaside house is a holiday house and a *home* is placed four square within settled land as far as the eye can see.

At any rate, estate agents sent alluring if untrustworthy slips ("secluded but not isolated" described a house on the main road to Dorchester) and we made two- and three-day sorties. It was the end of summer, really autumn, a green and rainy time, when the Ham stone in the north glowed an ever deeper gold and the grey flint of Purbeck had a distinctly mournful look. Estimating countryside through windscreen wipers is always a dismal experience. In the course of such journeys we came to the disquieting realization that both of us cherished ideas above our means. Our dream house, rather like a small child's drawing, was square with large regular windows and a long driveway and entirely surrounded by its own well stocked garden. This description perfectly fitted the elegant Georgian rectories with which Dorset is well supplied. But, others having the same dream, they were always well beyond our pocket.

To cut short a story that threatens to anti-climax, what we found on that rainy afternoon 14 years ago was a house billed, somewhat eccentrically, as "the oldest continuously inhabited house in Dorset". It was an early manor house built by William de Cheyne, a knight who lies in stone effigy in the church next door. (As I had spent the London part of my childhood in Cheyne Gardens this was an odd coincidence.) It was not square at all, having two jutting wings at the back and an irregular gabled piece at the side of the front. Moreover as its front and back door were both at the front it had the look of two cottages stuck together.

We bought the house from a majestic, white-haired widow of the sort that abounds in Dorset. Queen Motherly charm barely disguising a dynamo of energy, she inspired me to write a short story entitled *Last of the Empire*. The subject did not, however, suit the outlets for short stories in the 1960s. London editors always find it difficult to believe in country life. When the "Last of the Empire" passed over the house to me she left a list of recommended "tradesmen" in Sherborne. Until the neatly written list with "delivers" alongside nearly all (an era now past, alas) I had not appreciated the need for a country town – despite the obvious fact that our village had no shops. I certainly had not appreciated that by sheer chance we had chosen a village within bicycling distance of one of the least spoilt small towns of north Dorset, all built in my favourite golden stone and possessing the most ravishing abbey with positively exalted (and exalting) fan vaulting. This was Hardy's Sherton Abbas, with Sir Walter Raleigh's Sherborne Castle over the railway line and the remains of his original castle on the other side of the Capability Brown lake.

But that I learnt gradually, buying the house for the gargoyles on the stone tower of the church that shadowed the garden, for its position halfway up one side of my Gozzoli valley and for the *feeling* of ancient history. I knew no facts. Only lately I found a history of the village, written in 1928 by the then vicar, which linked us to Sherborne in the most satisfactory way. Apparently the monks from the abbey used our house as a "rest-house". They also planted our valley with delicious wine-producing vines – the patterns of the terraces are still visible to this day. Since I and my family are Catholics it is nice to think of this Catholic involvement.

Of course Dorset had a continuing Catholic history with the future Charles II hiding for 19 days in the beautiful old village of Trent before he sailed away from Brighton. And endless battles and skirmishes were fought all over it during that troubled period. Now, in these ecumenical days, I like the fact that there is an Anglican friary not many miles away at Hilfield and the monks still take constitutionals across the hill-sides. Farther south there survive a few of the old Catholic families. Recently the son of my friends above Bridport married into one of them and the service took place in the sort of private chapel that is generally supposed to have died out with *Brideshead Revisited*.

Catholicism apart, the churches of Dorset offer a mellow feast of variations on a stone tower. Even those spurned by the guide books for Victorian additions or clumsy restoration are usually in situations which make such architectural niceties hardly relevant. Sad though it is in one way, the obvious lack of clientele (the names on the flower rota recur with ever greater frequency) makes them all the more romantic. Yet someone usually cuts the grass and last thing at night turns the iron key in the heavy oak door.

Approach, of course, is everything. I now spend most summers car-less in Arcady. Choosing the mellowest days and times for my outings I thus imagine all Dorset villages bathed in a golden evening light. Batcombe is one of my favourites, set eccentrically under Batcombe Down so that its square tower arises against a sky of grassy green. Almost directly above it pokes up the strange stone "hand" where Hardy makes Tess swear she will never tempt Alec d'Urberville again. Last time I was there, having reassured myself of the way from a friendly, cigar-smoking farmer, I had barely started my literary communing when a helicopter rose from the field behind. It was an interesting conjunction of the romantic and the modern which I suspect Hardy himself could have used to effect. This is a very Hardyesque area, with the nearby church of Leigh sporting some of the best gargoyles.

My sun-gilt vision of churches does break for one sad but memorable afternoon at Powerstock Church. There Kenneth Allsop was buried. Julian Bream played the guitar and Henry Williamson spoke with sonorous majesty, while outside the rain fell in silver sheets over the green. Ken had lived in one of the most secret areas of Dorset behind the small town of Beaminster (with the only shopping centre I would consider a rival to Sherborne's). He owned an old mill and in front of his home rose one of those magic conical hills, turning back the landscape a few thousand years. From there he wrote about his beloved birds, fought oil pipe-lines (with the splendidly endowed Cerne Giant on the stickers) and celebrated all things country.

I have never wanted to dwell on the dark side of Dorset. Hardy's Egdon Heath no longer seems to me a place of terror. It is outside the (rather unenergetic) range of my foot or bicycle so I cross it, too quickly, too safely, by car. It lives best on the printed page. Even Portland, that grim grey place of rock, is gradually losing, with its prison hewers and toilers, its prison air. But my sanguine humour is threatened by a strange visitor we have in spring or early summer. Old houses have long histories, particularly when the house has a "court room". Judge Jeffreys, the dreaded hanging judge, certainly took his circulating court into this area. The visitor is a large black bird. Raven, crow, rook? At dawn he comes knocking at the court room window, tearing at the wistaria in his anxiety to get in. Nothing turns him away for good, not even a bluffing gun. Face bloodied by his battering, he merely retreats to better advance. Lost soul wrongfully convicted? Or the guilty judge himself? Either way, it seems a sinister act, unbecoming to my idyll. Lately I have found happier connotations. Maiden Castle, the great ringed and ancient fortress, is said to be the last home of the wild raven. And it is into one of these ravens that the soul of King Arthur is supposed to have flown. That is a black bird I would welcome to my home.

Happily Dorset gardens and hedgerows are frequented by many more charming winged creatures. In late August one year I counted 12 butterflies of four varieties basking with lazily flapping wings on a stone arch in my garden. An even odder sight was a Large Tortoiseshell sucking at a plum fallen ripely to the ground. The hedgerows beside tracks where the council cannot take its electric razor froth over with thorn, oak, wild rose, elderberry, blackberry and honeysuckle. When I take a walk up our hill I am often accompanied by a halo of butterflies, though they tend to lose enthusiasm after a mile or so. Just like children.

The truth is that Dorset is made up of at least four countries – geologists for example lecture about the land formation and nature of the soil. I found my dream in the far north of the county. If the truth were told my village was only removed from Somerset in 1896. But the feeling of that changing land spreading south and west and east is what makes it special. And if when we drive away to London a faithless fear of no return takes hold, I am reassured by the letters on our number-plate: DOR.

Gloucestershire

Photographs by Lucinda Lambton

I dare say each of us has a particular place with a remembered "feel" so vivid that it stirs the very beginnings of our consciousness. It is a remembrance that never goes away. It does not have to be a sumptuous secret garden; it could be a copse where you first heard the scrunch of boots on leaves, or a hillock out of which grew your first rainbow, or a deserted, tumbledown building which you felt, and still insist, nobody living knew but you. Whatever it is, it is the place to which, for no explicable reason, your adult mind darts back when you think of your first seasons of childhood.

Mine is a weatherbeaten, bottom-shined, thin-slatted iron bench that stands under an unfamous oak tree in which Charles II never hid. It is three-quarters of the way up a nondescript hill above Stonehouse in Gloucestershire. A family walk for us (unless the cowslips were waving in the water meadows down by the old neglected, green-slimed canal where we caught tiddlers in muslin flour bags and where sad, mad, old ladies committed suicide in Sunday hats) was invariably up the sharpest side of Doverow Hill. The bench was no more than a half-way house to pant for a minute or two, to exalt in the steepness of the climb. There was no dedication attached to the seat from either patron or parish council. It never occurred to me to ask who put it there, but somebody must have, an unknowing genius.

Well past our bedtime it was the place where lovers learnt their ropes, where knees were first touched and lips first puckered ("Gerroff! Or I'll tell our Mum!"). For us it was the saloon outside which we tied our imaginary horses after playing the sheriff's posse; or the place to examine, blue-fingered, which of us that day had basketed the most blackberries to sell to the Severn Valley Jam Factory; or to hold up in triumph and with nail-bitten, filthy fingers the most delicate bird's egg. In winter you pushed off from the bench with your gumboots to get a decent toboggan start. On Sundays it was the place to watch with wonder the Home Guard run around with rifles and with hedgerows in their helmets like Macduff's Birnam braves. It was the place to sit and smoke our illicit Craven A ("For Your Throat's Sake"!) for from that vantage we could see a grown-up coming.

Now I realize that had we children needed to look up as we gambolled we could have seen two-thirds of all Gloucestershire, and beyond it, Bristol, which some men

Stanway House, in the Cotswold village of the same name, has Elizabethan origins.

in suits and collars and ties say is not in Gloucestershire now but in Avon. How daft can you get! Why, it's still where "Glorse" plays cricket, innit? An' that's good enough for I.

It was from this iron seat of learning up Doverow Hill that our next-door neighbour, Jean Pearce, swore blind and crossed her heart that she had seen Bristol burn one night in the wartime blitz when all the rest of England was wearing blackout blinds. Swing back to the right today and a friendly city haze of smoke umbrellas over Gloucester, and right in the middle there pokes up the Norman tower of mellow perfection made of Painswick stone; eyes farther round and you can see the even more ancient, sea-monster humps of the Malvern Hills of Worcestershire.

Now here's something uncanny: if you put a tracing of a Union Jack on a map of Gloucestershire, the very cross-roads of St George – from, say, Tewkesbury in the north to Chipping Sodbury, and from St Briavels in the west to Lechlade – meet, as near as dammit, on my old bench on Doverow. The very heart of Gloucestershire!

Behind, eastwards up the hill and on the same ancient track where homesick Roman centurions might have pouted, deadpan, past cringing, sack-clothed drovers, the path rolls down a couple of miles through Randwick and into Stroud, a jaunty jumble of a hillside town, once noted as England's centre of the broadcloth industry.

87

In the last century there were over 150 mill factories here. Now they make green baize for billiard tables and white baize for tennis balls, and purple cloth for cardinals and scarlet coats for guardsmen, while sponsoring a thousand-and-one other tiny industries from combs to knitting needles.

I caught my first bus to Stroud. Its Gaumont was where I saw my first film (*Henry V*). Its Cadena café was where I first took a girl to tea (and sandwiches, 9d extra). Stroud was where I scored the HS of my career – 75 not out, for the Stroud Stragglers *v* Painswick. Stroud, I think, is where I want to die.

Apart from Stroud and its valleys, which some see anyway as a minor county on its own, there are three distinct Gloucestershires. You can see two of them from my Doverow eyrie, which itself is plonked on the very foothills of the third. Deep in the west is The Forest, a dark and solemn ancient tract between the Severn and the Wye; a place, we used to be told, where adders slunk in bluebell woods and witches brewed and giants bellowed; a place unvisited, but serenely loved by those who live there; a place where, it is said, men can still make and administer their own laws, and mine their own coal and ore. In 1001 the county of Gloucester became a "shire" in the Kingdom of Mercia, and 15 years later the Dane, Canute, named the Forest of Dean "the King's hunting ground for Royal chases".

At once, eastwards over the wide Severn, lies the plain where ancient Berkeley Castle guards the rich, lush vale of meadows and blossoms and growth in the various shades of greens and browns and yellows that take the farmers' fancy as the seasons come and go and come again. Then the clay gives way to limestone and in a line as straight and strict as parading soldiers stand erect the proud hills with my dear and modest little Doverow kneeling bashfully in the front row.

The great rolling glories of the Cotswolds (which tip their hat occasionally to Oxford and Wiltshire, Warwickshire and Worcester) are very much Gloucester-shire's. They can be bleak all right in the coffin-like days of midwinter when hedgerows are as stiff as corpses and only snowdrops smile. In a dreamy summer's haze they can be perfection – though even then, most say, not quite as perfect as when spring is silver-fresh or autumn gold.

When I was born, by chance 1,000 years of village life had just been topsy-turvey changed – when the infernal combustion engine replaced the horse. And even in my two score years this world has further changed. Yet has it all totally vanished? Don't shepherds still whistle, don't choirs still have choir outings? Don't vicars still bowl lobs after tea, and doesn't the squire still stand upright at slip? And aren't there quite a few blacksmiths left? Ah, the smell of a singeing hoof? I remember that from boyhood when the village smithy did his stuff behind the old Woolpack Inn in Stonehouse. They were great, patient, plodding Dobbins with hairy ankles and they used to pull the Co-op bread van. Last year, walking near Chipping Sodbury (we Stroudites ever referred to it as Soddin' Chipbury) I was led by the nose when I got the whiff again and, wearing the grin of a Bisto kid, I watched three smiths at work alongside three flanks, and each astride the fetlock of a sleek, liveried hunter.

That is horsey country. Sodbury is near Badminton, the Duke of Beaufort's sensational Palladian pile. In a little over 30 years Badminton has become as much a proper noun as the name of the game which was "invented" one wet afternoon in the

FAR LEFT: The stables of Berkeley Castle, where Edward II was murdered in 1327. LEFT: The spire of St Mary's Painswick and some of its 99 clipped yews.

1860s by two great aunts of the present Duke in the mansion's entrance hall. Badminton means the Three-Day Horse Event which, typically British, actually lasts four days. I went to the first Badminton in 1949, when Uncle John and I cycled to it up the long hill from Nailsworth. The jamboree had been dreamed up by the present Duke (who is now over 80 and has been called simply "Master" in these parts since he was a boy) during the showjumping at the 1948 Olympic Games. His friend, Colonel Trevor Horn, helped to organize. His first "office" was the piano top in the music room. The owner of the village shop typed the first entry forms. The Colonel spent the previous winter riding over ploughed fields with a mileometer on his bike. Within a year they had set up an institution. Many folk the world over, with straw in their hair and bow legs in jodhpurs, may not have a clue where Gloucestershire is but they all know what Badminton means.

The Duke is Master of the Queen's Horse. The Queen has not missed many Badmintons. Gloucestershire could indeed almost be called a County By Royal

Appointment these days. Princess Anne and her husband farm and breed horses at Gatcombe Park, near Minchinhampton, only a brisk morning's gallop from the mansion her brother bought for his bride.

The first monarch to enjoy regularly the charms of Gloucestershire – apart from Canute in the Forest's royal hunting grounds, or Edward III who granted separate county status to Bristol in 1373 – was "Farmer" George III, who made his first summer visit to take the waters at Cheltenham in 1788, organizing first an Act of Parliament "to pave and make more commodious the London road from Northleach".

Before 1716 Cheltenham had been a small market town with a population of about 1,500. Then it was noticed that pigeons were pecking at the saline deposits from a mineral spring. By the end of that century the town had mushroomed into one of the grandest spas in Europe, with the waters "especially rewarding for sufferers of liver and digestive complaint". On the King's first "walkabout" down Well Walk on July 12, 1788, the local wag remarked, "the people took their hats off as he passed and how surprised were folk to see that the King was only a man".

George loved Stroud and Painswick, and he stayed nights at Rodborough and Woodchester. One evening he went to Tewkesbury to see one of his son's lovers, Mrs Jordan, act in *She Would And She Would Not* at the theatre there. He was, apparently, not unimpressed by her charms himself. He attended the Three Choirs festival in Gloucester Cathedral, an annual choral binge held, in turn, also at Worcester and Hereford.

Another horseman, however, did not take to Gloucestershire at all. William Cobbett, rural rider and writer, went to the Three Choirs festival at Gloucester 34 years after King George. Listen to this: "Scandalous and beastly . . . those who founded the Cathedrals never dreamed that they would have been put to such uses as this . . . made use of as opera houses! . . . these assemblages of player-folks, half-rogues and half-fools . . ." The scribbling jockey quite liked Tewkesbury, "a good, substantial town", but, dearie me, Cheltenham's watering hole he found "a place to which East India plunderers, West India floggers, English tax gorgers, together with gluttons, drunkards and debauchees of all description, female as well as male, resort, at the suggestion of silently laughing quacks, in the hope of getting rid of the bodily consequence of their manifold sins . . . When I enter a place like this, I always feel disposed to squeeze up my nose with my fingers".

Gloucester is now a sprawling, even ugly, workaday city, a plain fact which makes its jewel shine out more brightly from Cathedral Close. To me as a sacrilegious schoolboy, the "real" cathedral was at Kingsholm, the rugby union ground where the cherry-and-whites played. There are not many places round the world that match the atmosphere in the city on the day of a big match. The burr and buzz of it represents my first memory in sport, my small hand enveloped in my father's as the auctioneers at the old Saturday morning cattle market (it is the bus station now) gabbled at even more than nineteen-to-the-dozen so as to shut up shop in time for "the game" at Kingsholm. Bill Hook was my first rugby hero, a full-back who played for England. He had a Brylcreemed middle parting, crisp white slicing jet black hair, as if it had been painted on each morning by a meticulous sign writer. One winter in the early 1950s I would spend hours staring at him through the window of his sports shop. But when England played Wales the whole county did not know where to look for weeks because Bill twice missed the flying scarlet sprinter, Jones, at Twickenham.

Cheltenham is still a spa town. It has high spires and is wide and handsome. It fancies itself (or rather, its Public Relations Officer does) as the Queen of the Cotswolds, but that to me will always be Cirencester of the warm and cosy, untrying elegance and the glorious medieval parish church. Cheltenham to me was always "the cricket". Three times a year Bristol used to allow the county to play on the college ground in August. What summers! We would catch the Western National from Stonehouse soon after dawn. A queue outside Woolworth's for the Cheltenham bus, then over the top past Painswick's 99 yews and mystery churchyard. At Prinknash we would crane to see if the monks were making pots and wonder how they were doing at building their own great abbey church. Then we would roll down the hill to Chelt, clutching our mum's sandwiches in greaseproof paper and forecasting what deeds would be done that day by our litany of saints: Tom Goddard, who kept a furniture shop in Gloucester, and only four men in the history of the game took more than his 2,979 wickets; his shy apprentice in wiles and guiles, Sam Cook, the Tetbury plumber; the "Siren" fishmonger, Charlie Barnett, who could hit like fury; George Emmett, with the feet of Astaire and the whipcord wrists; his solemn partner, Jack Crapp, a left-handed Buster Keaton; Andy Wilson, tiny-tot stumper who became the Farmers' Union organizer out towards the Forest; George Lambert, sleek of hair and action; and his new-ball mucker, Scott, a great trier who used to work at the Co-op; Graveney, the *nonpareil*; and our bestest favourite, a tubby ball of fun who was a Gloucester printing apprentice, the one and only Bomber Wells.

An eminent Victorian who left his mark on Gloucestershire was Isambard Kingdom Brunel who opened up the west by building his famous "billiard table" railway line from London (it is, to all intents, dead level for 85 miles from Paddington). The great terminus at Bristol Temple Meads and the magnificently zany Clifton Suspension Bridge remain monuments to his memory. Everything overlaps. When Brunel died in 1859, W. G. Grace was 11. The other day I came across a letter from Brunel written in the last year of his life. He was trying to persuade a Mr C. Richardson to become his engineer on his final project, the line north from Bristol through Ashley Down and Patchway. He offered £300 a year, rising to £450, and he wrote as bait: ". . . the country immediately north of the city I should think a delightful one to live in – beautiful country – good society near Bristol, Clifton etc. – I can't vouch for any cricketing, but I should think it highly probable . . ."

It was. He took the job and the 11-year-old WG more than likely watched Mr Richardson build his line; when he was not cricketing in his orchard, that is.

Only a mile or two away now is that breathtaking modern span of which Brunel would have mightily approved, the wondrous Severn Bridge. Mr Richardson's railway line runs on to Gloucester and just outside Stonehouse it is joined by the line from Stroud and Swindon. And alongside that railway now, in a kaleidoscope of sprayed-on colours, cars and lorries skim by on the great M5 motorway conveyor belt to north and south – and everywhere.

You can see it all from my slatted iron bench on Doverow Hill.

ABOVE: Wells Cathedral, begun in the 12th century. RIGHT: The Church of St Mary the Virgin in Upper Swainswick, where the author lives and the birthplace of the puritan William Prynne.

BEL MOONEY'S

Somerset

Photographs by Julian Calder

Somerset is my adopted county. I was brought up in Liverpool, and the landscape of my childhood was either that of the city river or of the north-west coast of England, with its wintry, corrugated beaches and razor-grassed dunes. My vision of ideal scenery was cast then – toughly – so that when my family moved to Wiltshire my teenage sensibility rebelled against the softness of southern fields and lanes. Devon, Dorset, Gloucestershire – I rejected them, finding the lines of the land too gentle, like the climate; in prejudice, you see, is rarely truth.

But then I discovered Somerset and I have returned to it. The county sits in the bend of England like a crusty croissant, and within its curve is all the variety of English landscape: rich agricultural land, yes, but the maw of Cheddar Gorge, too, the odd bleak coastline, and the poetic Quantocks. As for cities (and I am still a city lover) Somerset is dominated by two of the most beautiful small cities in Europe, Bath and Wells, which sit within its borders like twin representatives of the worldly and spiritual, the secular and the deeply religious.

Borders. Ah, that word forms a small hitch in this narrative. The praise must pause while I explain with great patience that Bath *is* Somerset. In 1974 one of those petty, unimaginative bureaucratic decisions that so characterize modern Britain lopped off the northernmost tip of Somerset, tackled it roughly on to the Bristol areas with all the skill of a demented surgeon, and called the Frankenstein monster thus created "Avon".

Now Avon is not a county. The Avon is a river and William Shakespeare is sometimes called the swan thereof. It is impossible to change in one clumsy move the habits of centuries, the sense of belonging, and the unconscious resentments against outsiders which is what the English counties mean to all those who inhabit them.

As you may have guessed, I live in the lopped off part of Somerset, on the edge of a valley just north of Bath. Bath has been written about so much that it would be superfluous to add more. All I will say is that it is the most perfect place to live for anyone who wants beauty as well as good shops, concerts, books, paintings, parks, jollity. I am only amazed and a little grateful that half the population of England does not immediately pack up and come here, as we did. Outside the town itself are

93

wonderful winding valleys like ours, distinguished by tiny villages which lack even the convenience of pub or shops. Our village is called Upper Swainswick, and for years our house was the Rectory. The Reverend John Earle, Professor of Anglo-Saxon at Oriel, lived here for 46 years until his death in 1903. In 1906 one of his sons wrote a poem, of which I have a copy:

"In a fair vale of Somerset
Facing where the Avon flows,
There is a lovely village set
Where life unnoticed goes."

The village church, St Mary the Virgin, has a lovely dogtooth Norman arch, a tiny medieval window over the pulpit showing St George and St Margaret, and one good brass (hidden under a rug in the sanctuary) showing a Mr Edmund Fforde who died in 1439. Our house and the church overlook one of the most beautiful views in Somerset. If it sounds exaggerated, remember that I am a relatively new convert, and they are the most zealous.

It is no accident that I start here, in my own parish church. Country churches are my passion and Somerset is the county for anyone who shares that passion. As John Betjeman points out in his guide to parish churches, no county comes up to Somerset for medieval churches, three-quarters of which are Perpendicular (14th-16th cen-

BELOW: The tower of St Mary Magdalene Church, Taunton. BELOW RIGHT: The Somerset Coast at East Quantoxhead.

The various buildings of Brymton d'Evercy, constructed of Ham Hill stone.

turies). Within a 25-minute pace of our house are the three churches of this parish – Swainswick, Woolley and Langridge – all very different, all pretty. Then in the next valley, hidden from the narrow lane is the tiny, secret church of Charlcombe. It is only about 50 feet long and very, very still, with the smell of damp and stone and flowers that magically brings to life the rectors' list, dating back to 1312. There is a monument inside the tower to Sarah, the sister of Henry Fielding, who was frequently a guest of Ralph Allen at Prior Park on the other side of Bath. Before I moved here from London I completely shared the uncomfortable, agnostic piety that made Philip Larkin remove his cycle clips "with awkward reverence". No longer. These churches around me, and the ones I have visited farther afield in Somerset, do not disconcert me any more; visiting them I feel rather like a recalcitrant teenager who after a long absence has returned to a familiar and comfortable home.

This valley is dominated by the broad back of Lansdown Hill, scene of one of the most crucial battles of the Civil War, for Somerset (except Taunton) remained staunchly Royalist until 1646. The heights of Lansdown, with such splendid views and strong historical associations, remind you yet again how monstrous it is to meddle with counties, their boundaries and names. For centuries phrases like "the men of Somerset" have had a deep tribal significance – and I believe it still exists. Bath, Wells, Glastonbury – nothing can remove or split up that triumvirate from this county's history, or reduce the pride of Somerset itself in its possessions. Avon has no history, and so no possessions – except on paper.

To travel south through Somerset, stopping at unfamiliar little churches along the way, is one of the most peaceful and (a deliberate paradox) stimulating ways of spending a day. And if you also take in the suburban sprawls of Taunton and Yeovil then so much the better, for no one who truly loves a particular county can be blind to

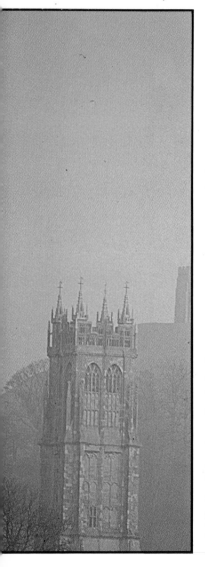

On Glastonbury Tor only the tower of a 13th-century church remains. In the foreground is the tower of St John's Church, built in the 15th century.

the real necessity not just for parish churches amid the waving grass of their graves but for factories, shops and housing estates as well.

In pursuit of the literary as well as the architectural I made a pilgrimage to Nether Stowey, where Samuel Taylor Coleridge was staying when he wrote "The Rime of the Ancient Mariner", and where his reverie of "Kubla Khan" was broken by the famously anonymous "person from Porlock", who made his hefty, uncalled-for walk from the coast. Nether Stowey is a typical Somerset village, neither distinguished nor ordinary, neither fodder for the indifferent tourist in search of the exclaimably picturesque, nor marred by development for the romantic enthusiast who wants to view the very (plain) church door where Coleridge's Mariner grasped with his skinny hand the unfortunate wedding guest. A little stream runs along the street between the pavement and the road, so that it has to be spanned by small bridges. Apart from Coleridge's cottage (disappointing), the church is all there is to see and, as is so often the case, you have to search for the memorable details. For me it was the memorial to Thomas Poole: ". . . a man not more distinguished for his masculine intellect than for integrity of life and inestimable qualities of heart. His originality and grasp of mind counter balanced the deficiences of early education and secured him the friendship of some of his most illustrious contemporaries. William Davy, Southey and Coleridge were his guests and conferred distinction by their visits to his native place. 8 Sept 1837 aged 72."

The sister-village, Over Stowey, lies at the foot of the Quantock hills. It must be because of these famous hills that the hamlets in this part of Somerset seem to be cut off, so untouched and still – you could not drive great motorways through the hills, even if there was somewhere for them to go, and the high land forms an obstacle to whatever profitable man-made developments might ruin the countryside. The church at Over Stowey had a couple of fine Burne-Jones windows, and memorials to Henry Labouchere (the great Victorian radical) and his daughter. A few miles away the dull little village of Stogursey is dominated by the enormous priory church of St Andrew, founded by Benedictine monks in the 12th century. It is an odd, vast, unhomogeneous place, at odds with the expensive bungalows with teak doors and bottle glass windows that surround it. It was something of this century that most moved me there – one of those memorial plaques you see in almost every church throughout the country, which commemorate those who died in the Great War. It always makes me feel bitter, somehow, to see it described as a "roll of honour"; the appalling slaughter took from this small parish six Nurtons, nine Chilcotts, five Graddons, six Gunninghams, seven Paynes, and members of other families, too – about 200 men, whose names are now riddled with woodworm.

It is easy to feel melancholy after that, on a bleak November day, when you drive to the top of the Quantocks and stand there, whipped by the wind, staring at Somerset in all directions and even seeing beyond to Devon and Wales. The Bristol Channel is very near, not wild enough to be romantic, too wide and flat and grey and tame to elicit more than a shiver, but lit by a low, wintry light for all that. Because you can see at once water, coast, hills, fields, towns and villages, you feel at the heart of England in a sense I have experienced nowhere else. The contrasts of that Somerset landscape, especially its unexpected harshness, always make me feel that this is *real*. For years I identified "reality" with city life – with people and their problems, and with politics, too. Reality dwelt on pavements; everything else was an escape.

Perhaps "escape" is the Cheddar Gorge on an August day, with thousands of people fantasizing for a few seconds that they are back beyond time, when the stalactites formed; it may also be the apricot elegance of the Royal Crescent. But reality is the roll of honour in Stogursey; it is the worn knights on tombs, with their feet on little faithful dogs; it is the climb up the Quantocks, which exposes you to the elements as ruthlessly as any northern hill. There you are forced to feel at one with all the successive generations who fought for a living from the land and the sea, who knelt in those carved pews; as vulnerable to love, fear and death as we are, and hoping for some sort of immortality, even if only through the generations who would follow.

This could easily become a catalogue of places to visit because, remember, I am still discovering Somerset. Go to Bruton, where the church tower is so fine it stands out even in a county rich in them, and where in the chapel at Hugh Sexey's hospital (a Tudor masterpiece) bored choirboys sat in the light of clear windows and carved their initials in the oak: "YG 1694, RC 1771". Where else in the west can you also wander into one of the finest art galleries in England, the Bruton Gallery, with its shows of Rodin? Crowcombe has the most wonderful bench-ends in the county; at Brympton d'Evercy the combination of great house, bellcote and tiny church, all built in golden Ham Hill stone, must be one of the most precious sights in England, let alone Somerset; Mells, Wells, Castle Cary, Montacute . . . the list grows. Walk to the weird volcanic coast at East Quantoxhead and you will forget you ever imagined Somerset a soft, cosy place.

I might just have moved to Somerset to be near the ghost of T. S. Eliot, whose ashes are buried at East Coker in the church where his ancestors worshipped and after which he named the second of the "Four Quartets". Eliot chose East Coker as the place for his permanence because it was there that his family originated before the leatherworker, Andrew Eliot, sailed for New England in the middle of the 17th century. St Michael's Church is unprepossessing, and it is fitting that the modest man who is arguably the greatest poet of this century should choose it. The opening section of "East Coker" celebrates the cycles that carry ordinary men and women into a form of immortality, or continuity at least; cycles of life and death which transform the life of the individual fitting him into the larger pattern. "Home is where one starts from" he says and Somerset has become my home.

ABOVE: The Wiltshire downs above the Vale of Pewsey. FAR LEFT: The ancient monument of Stonehenge. LEFT: Corsham Court.

ELSPETH HUXLEY'S
Wiltshire

Photographs by David Beatty

My childhood memories are not of Wiltshire; I was 30 when I came to live here but I have been here ever since – and that is 45 years – in north Wiltshire, that is almost on the Gloucestershire border. The distinction is important; a sort of chalk curtain separates the north from the south of the county. The word "Wiltshire" summons up for most people the great white Plain with its villages clustering along the shallow valleys of chalk streams; thatched lime-washed cottages; tank-tracks scarring hillsides; and the spire of Salisbury Cathedral rising from that ancient city at the foot of the Plain. All this is quite different from north Wilts which is less spectacular, generally flatter (the Marlborough downs excepted) and agriculturally richer. Industrially richer, too, for there is Swindon.

There is, indeed, Swindon; it swells and swells, peppering green fields with matchbox houses all alike and with hideous factories, and poised to gobble up pleasant little market towns like Wootton Bassett and Cricklade – a sort of boa-constrictor swallowing goats whole. I am told that this is unjust to Swindon, which is trying hard to be good by preserving as parks bits of the fields it has destroyed, by planting trees – 50,000 a year, it is claimed – and by restoring what is left of its past. Right in the heart of the sprawl is a hill, and on top lies The Lawn, where the Goddard family lived for nearly four centuries. Part of the grounds, laid out by Capability Brown, survives as a city park. One of my neighbours, now aged 82, has described to me her youth in service in the splendid Georgian mansion, now demolished, with its staff of 16, its private chapel, its stables full of hunters, and its gamekeepers in green velveteen breeches coming to report on the state of the pheasants. All this right in the middle of Swindon and within living memory.

Among the villages under threat from Swindon are Lydiard Millicent and Lydiard Tregoze. The latter has an 18th-century manor house built on the site of a much older one by John St John, second Viscount Bolingbroke. When I saw it first it was a wreck, half the roof caved in, handsome crimson wallpaper peeling from sodden walls. It had lain empty for years after the death of the fifth Viscount whose widow, with her numerous progeny, had pigged it in the kitchen while the mansion crumbled around them. The progeny, so the story goes, were all born out of wedlock except for the youngest who was made legitimate when the Viscount, then aged 76, married his lady secretly and soon after died, leaving nothing but debts, the lusty bastards and the small and weakling heir. After an interval the Swindon Corporation, now the Borough of Thamesdown, bought the place and started on a long, expensive process of regeneration. Here are the two faces of Swindon: careful restoration of the mansion, inside and out, and, on the very boundary of the Park, huge yellow machines grubbing up fertile fields for two new housing estates.

Heading south, you soon leave the sprawl behind you and climb the Marlborough Downs, which of all parts of Wiltshire and possibly of England, too, have the greatest wealth of visible remains of our ancient history. Visible, and unseen also; I defy anyone to visit Avebury without feeling the touch of mystery and the breath of wonder. Avebury is not just a ring of enormous sarsen stones standing on end, guarded by a ditch and muddled up with a village and two roads; it is a complex of stone circles and avenues, of man-made hills and burial chambers, covering a huge area. All these must have formed a great religious centre for our neolithic ancestors. They brought the first agriculture to Britain, the first domestic animals, the first stone and bone tools; and on these chalk uplands free of dense and dangerous forests, they built the first homes. Here we began. These downlands must have been much more densely populated then than is the case today; and such a massive deployment of communal labour as was needed to haul and put in place these great boulders cannot have been carried out without some central authority. So here, perhaps, government was born as well as religion.

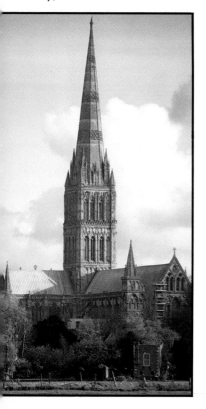

Salisbury Cathedral, built in the 13th century, seen from the water meadows.

It was the antiquary John Aubrey (a north Wiltshireman from Kington St Michael, near Chippenham) who discovered these long-buried stones. In 1649 he took Charles II and the Duke of York to see them. The Duke observed some snails "no bigger than small Pinnes-heads" on top of Silbury Hill and commanded Aubrey to collect some; next morning, "as He was in bed with his Duchess at Bath, he told Her of it, and sent to me to show Her as a Rareity". Silbury Hill is the most mysterious of these Stone Age remains, and the largest man-made mound in Europe, an almost perfect cone with a flattened top. What was its purpose? Assuming it to have been a burial chamber, three probes have been made, but not a bone or tunnel has been found, only blocks of stone and chalk arranged in terraces and covered over with earth. The Pyramids are built to a similar design, and about the same amount of material went to make Silbury as the smallest of the three Pyramids of Giza. A coincidence or a connexion? These Wiltshire downs tantalize the mind with mysteries.

Perhaps the greatest mystery of all, Stonehenge, lies about 25 crow-miles almost due south. There is something ineffably lonely and haunted about these circles and horse-shoes of sarsens standing all by themselves near the junction of the A344 and A303. Here they have stood, only a little weathered, for about 5,000 years. A totally erroneous theory that they formed a Druid temple has been exploded; now it is thought that they were a celestial observatory of a highly sophisticated kind. Without telescopes, logarithm tables, sextants and compasses, let alone computers, without (so far as we know) any system of recording observations, the builders of Stonehenge achieved a method of measuring the movements of sun and moon and the length of nights and days, of anticipating exactly the coming of winter and summer solstices, even of forecasting eclipses of the moon.

Now it is sad to see the stones fenced off by wire and guarded by dogs to keep the public at bay. "And each man kills the thing he loves" – never has Oscar Wilde's maxim seemed more true. There are too many of us, we are too mobile and too curious (or bored); our feet trample growing plants, our cars clutter up the landscape and we have to ban ourselves to keep our heritage.

If our feet do not do the damage, our ploughshares do. Only one thing saves the close-cropped turf and the birds and insects special to the chalk uplands of Salisbury Plain from becoming a sea of barley, and that is the Army. Areas marked "danger" on the map spell safety to the wildlife and natural flora. I shall never join a demo against military ranges and training grounds that deny the public access to about two-thirds of the Plain and so leave in peace the butterflies and birds – which get used to bangs – and the trees, plants and burial barrows. Stock doves have nested in derelict tanks, and wheatears in abandoned shell-cases. Hen harriers, hobbies, kestrels and buzzards may be seen swooping on their prey, stone curlews have been heard at dusk, nightingales sing by day in certain thickets. Even Porton, repository of horrible poison gases and germ warfare, may count for virtue the 10 acres it has set aside for greater bustards which ornithologists are trying to re-introduce.

Four main roads traverse the Plain to converge upon Salisbury, whose cathedral spire, the tallest in Britain, presents an unforgettable first glimpse of the city. One of these roads, following down the valley of the Salisbury Avon, passes through Amesbury, which legend links with the Arthurian saga. Here, after Arthur's death, Guinevere took the veil, and here came Lancelot to bear her body to Glastonbury to lie alongside the king. Today Amesbury is a rather undistinguished little town and Guinevere's convent has long since vanished.

Salisbury is a late cathedral as cathedrals go, since the original one, at Old Sarum, proved unsatisfactory and the current bishop got planning permission from the Pope to build a new one on a more watery and less windy site. With only 40 years between its inception and its consecration, and built to the design of one man and by one master builder, it is all of a piece except for the spire, which was added a century later, and lacks the heaviness and might of the Norman style. It is a place to lighten the spirit.

The water-meadows that once surrounded the cathedral seem now to have disappeared beneath a huge car-park and more modern temples such as Tesco's, but Salisbury's narrow streets, wide market place and old coaching inns remain. At the George, the oldest, Pepys lay "in a silk bed and very good diet", but the charges were so exorbitant that "I was mad and resolved to trouble the mistress about it and get something for the poor" – which he did, one shilling.

The Wylie and the Nadder rivers join at Wilton where the grand house of the Herberts, Earls of Pembroke, stands. And grand it is, the first part early Tudor, added on to by Inigo Jones and finally remodelled cumbrously by James Wyatt. So it is an architectural mix; but stuffed with treasures. The first Earl was one of those Welshmen who clustered round the Tudors and acquired many rich pickings. Now the 17th Earl in an unbroken line inhabits part of the mansion, and relays of sightseers are shepherded round with perfect tact and rigid timing by ladies with impeccable upper-class accents and well-pressed woollens. A couple of miles down-stream from Wilton is the village of Bemerton, where George Herbert's bones lie and where he wrote his imperishable poems.

Alone among the stately homes with which Wiltshire is so well endowed – Longleat, Stourhead with its marvellous gardens, Laycock, Bowood, Sheldon, Littlecote, South Wraxall, Stockton, Cole Park, many others – Corsham Court, the seat of Lord Methuen, has for me some personal connexion. An ancestor of mine called Thomas Smyth, a hosier, built its Elizabethan core, since much rebuilt and added on to. He made his way to London and acquired a fortune by marrying the Lord Mayor's daughter, and then by farming the customs for the Queen, a lucrative business which earned him the name of Customer Smyth. His portrait, with that of his sour-looking lady and several of their progeny, now hangs over my staircase.

South of the chalk curtain I found myself back in a remembered country, for my mother's home lay just over the Dorset border, and when I visited relations I came into Wiltshire to picnic with cousins on Great Ridge, high and cold and in spring carpeted with bluebells, and in the Fonthill woods surrounding William Beckford's fallen tower (designed by Wyatt) where a tiny little great-aunt lived all alone in a huge and hideous house and kept her coffin, so we understood, in readiness upstairs because she wanted to be buried in timber cut from her own much-loved trees.

Our chalk uplands seem to have offered an irresistible invitation to cut white horses in the turf, but only one of several dates back beyond the 18th century. This is on the northern scarp of the Plain above the little town of Westbury. Here, commanding a stupendous view across the vale to the Bristol Channel, is Bratton Castle, a large Iron Age fort; and here is the legendary site of the battle of Ethandune where King Alfred defeated the Danes after a struggle lasting nine days. To commemorate the victory Alfred (so the legend goes) had this white horse cut out of the turf. In the 18th century an appropriately named Mr Gee had its shape changed to that of a more modern-looking animal.

This part of Wessex is full of memories of Alfred, who granted to Malmesbury, my home town, the charter that justified its claim to be the oldest borough in England. The borough lasted for 2,000 years and then was swept away by the local government reforms of 1974 to become an insignificant part of the North Wiltshire District, governed by a sizeable bureaucracy in Chippenham. Alfred's grandson Athelstan had his court at Malmesbury and is commemorated in the names of a cinema, a garage and a bus company, and also by its famous Commoners. These are descendants of the men of Malmesbury who fought so valiantly at the battle of Brunanburgh in 937 that Athelstan gave to them and their heirs a common outside the town known as King's Heath. There are still over 200 of these Burgesses, who nowadays share out the rent of the land and preserve their Court and its ceremonies, shorn of the political power they formerly exercised. To be a Burgess in Malmesbury still carries prestige.

How backward-looking all this seems! Wiltshire really *has* moved on since Saxon times. Even Malmesbury has a factory making lighting fittings and another making stylish telephones. It is like an island, standing on a hilltop almost entirely surrounded by the Bristol Avon, which once had seven mills gristing away; and the

monks of the Abbey, whose splendid ruin crowns the hill, grew vines on the hillsides. The town is full of little twisting by-ways, flights of steps, and alleys through which you glimpse allotments running down to the curling river, with green fields beyond. Its most famous son is, I suppose, Thomas Hobbes, and in the garden of the house he is said to have lived in grows an acacia tree, one of six he planted. If so, it would be about 350 years old — it must be a descendant.

William Cobbett, writing in the 1820s, was nothing if not astringent in his comments. A ride through Cricklade, "that villainous hole", prompted him to exclaim: "This Wiltshire is a horrible county." But when he came to Malmesbury his opinions mellowed. He called it "a nice town, with a fine situation and a most pleasant place to live in". Its inhabitants, he added, looked well fed — according to Aubrey "chiefly on Milke meates, which cooles their brains too much, and hurts their inventions". I doubt whether Cobbett would change his opinion were he to visit the town today.

The White Horse at Westbury was first cut, according to legend, by Alfred the Great.

THE MIDLANDS

THE DUCHESS OF DEVONSHIRE'S
Derbyshire

Photographs by Richard Cooke

I was brought up on the borders of Oxfordshire and Gloucestershire and have the unassailable affection for that beautiful part of England that everyone who has had a happy childhood feels for their native heath. When I moved to Derbyshire in 1943 my husband was with his regiment in Italy, and I settled into our first proper home in Ashford in the Water with a baby, two dogs, a pony and cart and a pig.

I thought I should never get used to the scale of the Derbyshire countryside, to the size of the hills and valleys, to the hardness of the stone walls bare of stonecrop and lichen, and to the length of the winters in a climate where May can be as cold as February. I have lived in the county for nearly 40 years now and have grown to love the space and the remote places and would not change them for any other landscape.

There is infinite variety in Derbyshire. Some of the most important mines and related heavy industry in England are just a few miles from high, lonely, limestone hills, criss-crossed by light grey drystone walls making tiny enclosures of crazy shapes. There are old lead mines and a few thorn trees and ashes, windswept villages of stout stone buildings, incomparable views of a green and grey landscape inhabited by sheep and the ubiquitous Friesian cows. The scenery of the dales with their sudden clefts is made more dramatic near Buxton and Wirksworth by immense quarries, the man-made cliffs outdoing the natural ones and just as beautiful in their own way. Another kind of lonely countryside is the moorland around the Derwent Dams, those engineering marvels of lakes surrounded by heathery hills and indigenous woodland. The stone buildings of the dams have a monumental quality and look as permanent as the hills themselves. This is the home ground of the Woodland Whiteface sheep, an ancient breed which was nearly extinct a few years ago until revived interest in it and other rare breeds ensured its survival.

The start of the Pennine Way is at Edale, and so popular has this walk become that the paths have become wider and wider, and the heather and other vegetation is receding under the thousands of feet which pound it every year. Kinder Scout, 2,088 feet above sea level, is the highest point of this inhospitable but fascinating country of grouse moors and hill sheep, where shepherds and their collies rule and the high road of the Snake Pass is the first to be closed by snow every winter.

RIGHT: The crescent, Buxton, built by John Carr of York. BELOW: One of a chain of three reservoirs created by the damming of reaches of the River Derwent in 1912, 1916 and 1945. BOTTOM RIGHT: Haddon Hall, a medieval castle-cum-manor house dating back to the 12th century. CENTRE RIGHT: The viaduct at Monsal Dale.

If the hills are remarkable so are the rivers. Lord Byron asked Thomas More, "Was you ever in Dovedale? I assure you there are things in Derbyshire as noble as in Greece or Switzerland." Izaak Walton and Charles Cotton spent most of their lives in happy contemplation of the Dove . . . "The finest river that I ever saw and the fullest of fish," wrote Walton.

The Wye is another crystal-clear trout stream. It rises near Buxton and runs through Miller's Dale, Ashford in the Water and Bakewell, under Haddon Hall to join the Derwent at Rowsley. The most exciting stretch of the Wye is Monsal Dale, where the tall railway viaduct joins the hills. This is a prime example of the change in fashion in what is admired and what is denigrated. Ruskin was infuriated by its building and what he considered to be the ruination of the dale just so "every fool in Buxton can be in Bakewell in half an hour". Now it is revered as a triumph of engineering and for its own regular beauty.

The very names of the villages invite a closer look – Parsley Hay, Chapel-en-le-Frith, Alsop-en-le-Dale, Dove Holes, Peak Forest, Monyash, Foolow, Edensor, Stoney Middleton, Hope, Fenny Bentley, Stanton-in-Peak, Thorpe Cloud, Wigley, Earl Sterndale; and the dales – Chee Dale, Miller's Dale, Deep Dale, Monk's Dale, Demon's Dale, Cressbrook Dale, Lathkil Dale, Crackendale, Beresford Dale and many more.

There are caves, notably Poole's Hole near Buxton and the Great Rutland Cavern under the Heights of Abraham at Matlock Bath, a restored 17th-century lead mine in working order. The wealth produced from lead mining was of great importance to the county and the Barmote Courts, where lead mining disputes were settled, are still held at Wirksworth and other places. The miners' tools are carved on the Moot Hall, and the big brass dish used as the measure for lead ore since 1513 is preserved here.

The mineral unique to Derbyshire is blue-john, the yellow, mauve and blue fluorspar which for centuries has been made into urns, ornaments and even table tops, as well as small objects like knife handles and jewellery. Under the shadow of Peveril Castle at Castleton you can go into the blue-john mines. The Peak Cavern has the largest cave entrance in Britain. In the Speedwell Cavern you travel for half a mile in a boat on the underground canal, and Treak Cliff Cavern is remarkable for its stalactites and stalagmites. Small quantities of blue-john are still extracted.

There is silence and solitude in the uplands of the Peak District at all times of the year. The blue-john and lead mines were like cottage industries compared to the coal mining district around Chesterfield and Clay Cross and the iron and heavy industries of Staveley, Alfreton and adjacent towns, where the night is lit by the flames from the chimneys of the works which carry on their noisy trade 24 hours a day. Good arable land runs alongside opencast coal works, reminding us that industry and farming have lived together in the county since the Romans worked the lead mines. In the 18th century Sir Richard Arkwright set up one of his first cotton mills in Cromford. By 1777 there were 22 cotton mills in the county. Now there is great interest in industrial archaeology and the Arkwright Society is preserving some of the more interesting mills for visitors to see.

Derbyshire is physically and psychologically divided into north and south round about Matlock, where the midlands seem to end and the north begins. This was recognized soon after the war, when the local government offices were moved from Derby to the old spa hotel buildings in Matlock, a much more convenient centre from which to administer the county. At Matlock the accents change and the scenery turns from productive corn land into harsher, higher grass country.

You climb to a height of 1,000 feet before you reach Buxton in the north, where the 5th Duke of Devonshire and Carr of York built the glorious Crescent. Here the average mean temperature in July is 57.5°F – mean indeed. No wonder the inhabitants delighted in the warm mineral springs. Buxton and Matlock were important spas when such treatment was fashionable. Alas, the baths are no more. I have an abiding memory of a happy afternoon in a peat bath at Buxton, a "perk" of the Mayoress which I was at that time. It was the colour and consistency of a huge cow pat. I lay in it up to my neck, happily sweating, till ordered out by the attendant who then sprayed me with a jet of clean, cold water to remove the beneficial but clinging brown stuff. I never felt better, or smoother-skinned, in my life, and I rue the passing of the baths.

The denizens of Derbyshire are not as restless as those in the south. A few years ago our doctor did a survey of the village of Hartington to try to discover more about goitre, or Derbyshire Neck as it is called from the commonness of the disease in this neighbourhood. He found that 90 per cent of the people living there had been born there, a statistic unlikely to be equalled farther south. Surnames like Wildgoose and

A Derbyshire landscape of drystone walls and a wide, wind-raked sky.

The remains of a lead mine in Monsal Dale in the Wye valley.

Burdekin, which are not uncommon round here, never fail to surprise "foreigners". In Derbyshire you don't make tea, you "mash" it. If someone says he's "starved" he means he's cold, not hungry. I know several natives who say "thee" instead of "you". My daughter at a Pony Club camp on the outskirts of a remote Peakland village heard the farmer threaten his erring son, "Eh John, if thee don't shape theeself I'll belt thee one." Some swear words have never had the meanings given to them farther south. Anyway they sound different in a Derbyshire voice. When my husband stood for Parliament a friend came to Chesterfield from London to canvass. She asked the driver who met her at the station how he was getting on. "They like 'im, but they say booger 'is party," was the answer. His candidature was never successful (he was soundly beaten in 1945 and 1950), but there is no better way of getting to know a town and its inhabitants than to be a candidate and we both have a deep affection for the place and still have many friends we made 35 years ago.

An old Derbyshire custom, derived from the ancient ceremonies of blessing the water, is Well Dressing. Villagers go to immense trouble to make pictures, usually on a religious theme, on large wooden frames set up over the wells. The frames are soaked in water for some days and trays with several inches of evenly laid damp clay are set into them, and it is on this that the pictures are made. The design is pricked out with a knitting needle, the colours decided upon by the artist, and the outlines made of any natural material which is dark and definite, from sunflower or rhubarb seeds to twigs or strips of bark. Moss and lichen, leaves and petals, maize, wheat, barley and oat seeds, berries, cones, and even wool are pressed into the damp clay. It takes many people to complete the pictures as speed is vital to preserve the freshness of the living materials. The pictures stand by the wells for a week or more and remain amazingly fresh even in hot weather. They have become a major tourist attraction and Tissington, Youlgreave, Barlow, Ashford in the Water, Tideswell and the other villages well known for their petal pictures are visited by large crowds who make major contributions to the churches or the charities chosen by the Well Dressers.

Eyam is famous for its villagers' courageous behaviour. In 1665 a box of clothes contaminated by the plague arrived from London. To prevent the infection from spreading, Eyam's parson, the Reverend William Mompesson, persuaded the villagers to stay in Eyam. The deadly disease ravaged the small population but it was contained and Mompesson and the survivors are honoured at an annual outdoor service held in the field where he preached.

Much of Derbyshire is Robin Hood country. Inn signs, plantations, a group of rocks near Elton and a big stone outcrop high up in the woods above the old park at Chatsworth carry his name. The legend about Robin Hood's Stone is that he shot an arrow from it saying he would be buried where it fell. It reached Hathersage, 8 miles away as the arrow flies. There is no sign of Robin Hood's grave but Little John was buried in the churchyard there. His grave was opened in the 19th century and a thigh bone 32 inches long was found, which must have belonged to a man at least 7 feet tall.

Derbyshire has more than its fair share of beautiful country. It also has some remarkable houses which are open to the public. In the south there is Sudbury Hall, home of the Vernons, which now belongs to the National Trust. Its somewhat forbidding exterior does not prepare you for the beauty of the plaster work inside, described by Pevsner as "luxuriant and breathtakingly skilful". Near Derby is Kedleston Hall, Lord Curzon's Adam palace, and Melbourne Hall with its splendid formal garden. Not far from Bakewell is Haddon Hall, that most English and romantic of Elizabethan buildings, and east of Chesterfield is Hardwick Hall, Bess of Hardwick's surviving masterpiece which never fails to astonish the visitor by the vast scale and beauty of the presence chamber and long gallery on the second floor, and the mysterious sweep of the staircase.

I live at Chatsworth. I leave it less and less, but every time I come home after a spell away I am struck anew by its aura. To be surrounded by such beauty is something I will never take for granted, and to live and work with people who love the place and who are part of Derbyshire is my good fortune.

Chatsworth is the most palatial house in a county of great houses. The west front, which was probably designed by Thomas Archer aided by the Duke of Devonshire, bears the Cavendish family arms over the pediment.

Herefordshire

Photographs by Julian Calder

Brynmelyn, a house near Hay-on-Wye purchased by my grandfather's cousin William Booth in 1905, stands in Herefordshire but looks across Offa's Dyke into Wales and the Black Mountains. Its name is Welsh, and so is the name of the surrounding valley, Cusop Dingle. Indeed, old farmers assure me that this is really part of Wales. I cannot disagree with them. On as many Sundays as possible, I ride my horse up the deserted bridleways into the hills. There are hundreds of miles of these trackways, and hardly a mile of road suitable for cars. In an infinite number of trips I cannot remember having met a single human being in this hinterland, but a hundred years ago there were as many as three hundred people living and working there. Innumerable quarries, a lime kiln, a brick yard, a vanished cider house, derelict cottages and farmhouses – too remote to attract affluent urban dwellers – all testify to the destruction caused by modern agriculture and the supermarket.

According to Ella Mary Leather in *the Folk Lore of Herefordshire*, the last fairies in the British Isles were seen here, and I love the place with a passion for which I would abandon every town in the world. The radicalism it gave me, which means that I look West rather than East for my allies, has inspired my whole understanding of Herefordshire.

From the top of Cusop Dingle I can look across fifty miles of the county to the Malvern Hills, and I know from my own travels that Herefordshire is a kind of vast fortified bowl with hills at every extremity. The long drag up difficult hills has always contributed to its isolation. Cobbett never penetrated to the interior, and even in the age of motor transport a snowy night will immobilize lorries at Clowes Top on the Kidderminster road, or on Frome's Hill on the way in from Worcester. The natural fortification of West Herefordshire is reinforced by scores of minor castles which mark the limit of English expansion, and at my own castle in Hay the river ceases to be navigable. The glorious remoteness which this situation created was savagely removed fifteen years ago by the construction of the Severn Bridge, and Hay-on-Wye now gets as many visitors from Bristol as from Birmingham. Our opposition to this invasion is deep, but silent. If possible, we try to ignore the synthetic culture which ease of communication brings.

LEFT: Abbey Dore, founded by Cistercians in 1147, is now St Mary's Church. BELOW: Ross-on-Wye. The "medieval" tower to the left of the church is 19th-century.

A view from Merbach Hill, north-eastwards to Staunton-on-Wye.

From the choice of a few dozen castles within ten miles of Hay I prefer, for equestrian reasons, to take the course of the old railway line to Clifford. The natural history of railways is far superior, these days, to that of farmland — especially when the wild orchids are in flower. I always think of Clifford, the home of Tennyson's Fair Rosamund, as a typical castle of West Herefordshire. It is a pragmatic defender of the soil whose quality of stonemasonry attests to a craft which has steadily declined over 800 years. There is supposed to be a two-mile secret tunnel linking the castles of Clifford and Hay, but I have yet to discover anything but an abundance of local rumours. However, the full restoration of Hay Castle may yet reveal something. From Clifford I can ride my horse across the Wye at the Bronydd, which is always a thrill for a relatively inexperienced rider such as myself.

The nature of my business forces me to spend some thirty hours each week in a car, during which time I feel like the squashed interior of a crab, but an exploration of the rest of the county might demand the use of a vehicle. I approach North Herefordshire by joining the A49 at Leominster. This means that I can go through Weobley (a standard local joke is that some pee-ople go to Lee-ominster via Wee-obley), one of the most perfect black-and-white villages in England and not in any way spoiled by a few brick buildings having been painted to match. I might, perhaps, make a detour into Kington where Hergest Croft has one of the finest arboretums in the county, even though somewhat overmature. Strong memories flow at Sarnesfield for, although I have never visited Sarnesfield Court, I know it to be the home of the Marshall family whose Treatises on Regional Agriculture, written in the late 18th and early 19th Centuries, must put them in the same class as Arthur Young. The current owner is a great player of spoof (guessing how many coins are in the hands of opponents) in the pubs of Hay and, as such, I regard him as a friend. Leominster is typical of many Herefordshire towns built for horses but which has now been spoilt by cars. These towns were served by outlying villages whose pubs would stable horses, but the view of Leominster is dominated by a half-completed ring road which leads one past filling stations, Chinese restaurants and partially-restored outbuildings.

A few miles south of Leominster lies Hampton Court, until recently the home of Lord Hereford – the premier viscount in England. A few years ago, before restoration by its new owner, the house provided an extraordinary monument to the power of the regional bosses in England. The 15th Century gatehouse stood proud, but the chapel roof had collapsed and the squash court was filled with cobwebs. Even while unoccupied, a huge picture of a dog used to glare down at the inquisitive visitor. Superstition ruled that it would be too unlucky to remove it.

From Hampton Court the A49 goes south to Hereford, and must have been that city's main commercial artery in the 18th Century when it was the road to Liverpool. In the 19th Century, the dominance of Birmingham reduced the regional importance of Hereford, an influence which is now reinforced by the M5. Twenty years ago, 3000 workers were "decentralized" here and the town achieved a rise in prosperity, but it may have been at the expense of local control and local pride, which may have had greater long term value. Either way, the town had always appeared to Welshmen as a

Hereford Cathedral with its early 14th-century crossing tower.

place of unbelievable wealth – bigger than any half-dozen towns in Breconshire and Radnorshire put together. Even now, I believe at least twenty-five per cent of the people of Hay have never been to London. For them, a trip to Hereford represents a major excursion.

In the Cathedral, with its unique and priceless chained library, and its lavish tombs in alabaster and marble, the wealth of Hereford – which must have been one of the foundation stones of Britain – is clearly shown. This wealth, which was mainly agricultural, achieved its finest laurels with two products: cider and beef. The Wykham de Worde Bible of 1420, which is in the Cathedral, has the word "cider" in place of the more usual "strong drink" and until twenty years ago it was possible to go into any number of pubs where there would be a dozen glasses on the bar from which you could taste a dozen different ciders.

In 1890, the cider wealth contributed to the production of Hogg and Bull's "Hereford Pomona", whose eighty colour plates make it the finest book on cider apples ever produced (it now fetches nearly £1500), and throughout the county there were tens of thousands of rare and finely cultivated cider apple trees. Amongst the poor, cider drinking was universal. A pint of cider cost half the price of a pint of beer, and beer was half the price of Scotch. Eventually, taxation and regulation drove out most of the local cider makers. With the local production went local pride and hundreds of years of tradition. Chemical cider moved in, and now we hear the frequent and bitter complaint that a pint of cider is more expensive than a Scotch.

I like to imagine Hereford when it was a vast medieval fortress, almost as large as Windsor Castle, filled with lowing cattle which had been driven in for protection from the Welsh. I retain a particular affection for Church Street, one of the few surviving medieval streets leading to the Cathedral, which has always been the centre for secondhand booksellers in the town. In the past they were usually bow tied and blue suited, and I remember one who regularly nipped around the corner for double gins in the Conservative Club, in between disposing of 18th Century books from a Monmouthshire country house.

Across the Cathedral green and a little way along Broad Street, is the Green Dragon Hotel. Here, the carpeted interior, leather-topped furniture and immaculately laid tables seem to demand the wearing of a tie. I rarely visit it, but much respect the need of every town to have a large hotel with mahogany doors. Love and pride in the town seem to be universal, but they are epitomised for me in a slim volume of poems by Geoffrey Bright – partner in the leading firm of auctioneers, Russell, Baldwin and Bright – called "Hereford is Heaven". Leaving Hereford along the A4103 towards Worcester I pass acres of hop fields looking onto the Malvern Hills, but back on the A49 from Hereford to Ross, I am entering unfamiliar territory which leads to the Forest of Dean. Ross is ringed with hotels which are converted country houses, and its industries are among the biggest in Herefordshire. Here, I feel that the Midlands has already begun but Lea, the last village before Herefordshire becomes Gloucestershire, has a pub called the Crown which affords the opportunity to gossip about mutually-known stalwart drinkers, as the landlady is from Hay. The roads from Ross to Hay lead through some of the remotest lands in the county and it was on this route, with fog coming up from the Wye valley, that I failed to negotiate a right-hand bend and plunged through a hedge. I expect to do so again since, like a horse, I always go faster going home.

This last phase of the return journey takes me through the Golden Valley and gives me the chance to visit Abbey Dore and Kilpeck. These are the places I most frequently visit when visitors to Hay need to be entertained. The wonderful medieval church at Abbey Dore is one of the few not laid out on an East-West basis, and the 12th Century carvings at Kilpeck rank with the Chained Library as marvels of survival. The country houses of the Golden Valley I have known as neighbours. As a bookdealer, one generally sees them in decline – nevertheless, one loves them all the more.

Poston Manor is a beautiful small manor house, one of whose owners saw the Golden Valley railway built and removed in his lifetime. It was also the home of Lewis Carroll's niece, and when the present owner bought it he discovered white rabbits living happily in a derelict part of the property. Michaelchurch Court – another romantic house – was owned by a lady who departed for Portugal in a chartered Viscount with eighty Pekinese – because the whalemeat there would provide cheaper food for her dogs. Moccas Court, where Handel once played, was inhabited by an American heiress who, in poverty, wasted thousands on new Harrods blankets for her dogs. These are memories that will always be with me.

As rural life dies, so farm museums are born. Near to Hay I have a friend, John Johnson, whose museum I enormously admire. In addition to running a 175 acre arable farm, on which he fattens cattle in the winter, he has built up one of the largest collections of agricultural tools and implements in the country – not to mention an impressive number of horse-drawn vehicles from farm wagons to carriages. In collecting everything from chaff-cutters to milk floats, and cheese presses to breast ploughs, John Johnson expresses the conscience of a generation by doing homage to a non-chemical age.

Back on the border, close to Hay, I am reminded that there are more Iron Age monuments here than those of any later period. Arthur's Stone, near Dorstone, where I ride frequently to visit a friend on a neighbouring farm, is one that always attracts me. Several generations of an Iron Age family were buried here in view of the Welsh hills. No more beautiful place can be imagined and no more beautiful tomb can be made. On the Welsh border we like to imagine we are in the land of King Arthur, and it is another fantasy of mine to see every castle respecting more the tradition of the past and acknowledging that we have lost many more skills than we have gained.

JACK SIMMONS'
Leicestershire

Photographs by Caroline Penn

The modern county of Leicester is a fusion of two old ones, Leicestershire and Rutland, carried through ten years ago. There were some sound reasons in favour of that union; but anyone with a sense of the past may well reflect that it went into force in 1974 on All Fools' Day. They were two very different entities. They had this however in common: both were small units of government. At the time of the merger Leicestershire stood twenty-seventh in size among the old counties; Rutland thirty-ninth – it was only a fraction larger than the smallest of all, the Isle of Wight. The amalgamated county appears today about half-way down the list, both in area and in population.

So Leicestershire is small. It is also secret, keeping to itself. For all the efforts of the East Midlands Tourist Board – and they have not been negligible – it remains one of the least visited of English counties. You see few foreign cars on its roads. (I ignore the M1, which belongs to no county.) How many of your friends ever go there, sight-seeing or on holiday? Yet by not going they miss a good deal.

The River Soar divides the county into two unequal parts, running through Leicester itself on its northward course to the Trent. To the west of it and in Leicester lie nearly all the mechanised industries – hosiery, footwear, coal-mining, quarrying, and engineering; the country to the east of it is mainly agricultural. The few substantial industries in the old Rutland were based on the exploitation of its own resources; they were brewing and the quarrying of its splendid limestone. As late as the 1950s the Ketton cement works had a single tall chimney, and that was the only one in the entire county.

These divisions have their basis in geology. West Leicestershire includes a slice of the coal measures, an outcrop of granite at Mountsorrel, the beautiful slate of Swithland (alas, no longer worked), and the pre-Cambrian rocks of Charnwood Forest, interspersed with clay farming land, undulating very gently. Leicester itself is partly built over a main geological boundary. The county to the east of it is all jurassic, lies within the old Leicestershire, oolite within a large part of Rutland.

The landscape expresses this clearly. Leicestershire is sometimes thought to be flat: a notion quite untrue, for it denies some of the qualities that have made it what it is.

Had it been flat it could never have become the pre-eminent foxhunting county, the heart of the Shires: the rolling grass lands of East Leicestershire made it that. Nobody who has ever seen the church of Breedon-on-the-Hill from the south, teetering as it seems on the very cliff face of a large limestone quarry, could subscribe to the idea of a flat Leicestershire; nor any motorist driving along A47, especially up or down Wardley Hill in winter. The county is flat in the central Soar valley alone, and there the long dark range of Charnwood dominates it to the west, just as the Hambleton Hills dominate the broader and more level Plain of York.

How did Leicestershire and Rutland come to form units of local government? It is only to the south that they had any long continuous natural boundaries, the Warwickshire Avon and the Welland. For twenty miles however to the south-west Leicestershire has a clear man-made boundary: Watling Street (now A5), part of the Roman road running from Dover and London to Wroxeter. Here it divides Leicestershire from Warwickshire.

At High Cross on that road Watling Street intersects the Roman Fosse Way in its diagonal course from Devonshire to the Humber. Leicester itself grew up on the Fosse Way, and other Roman roads joined it there. It was the most considerable Roman town in the English Midlands, its so-called Jewry Wall still testifying to the scale of its public buildings. Though largely – perhaps for a time wholly – deserted after the

Romans' departure, its importance remained fixed by its position at the crossing of the Soar. It re-emerged as a distinct place in Saxon England, then became one of the main centres of the power of the invading Danes, and finally the capital of the unit of local government called Leicestershire in Domesday Book.

Leicester was that capital in one most particular sense. It stood right at the centre of its shire. No other county town had such a position except Shrewsbury, perhaps Winchester. Not only that. It was already the largest town in Leicestershire, and it has remained so ever since. Its market was outstandingly important, reached easily by buyers and traders from almost everywhere in the shire. When mechanised industry developed in the eighteenth and nineteenth centuries, Leicester became the chief centre of distribution for its products. In 1974 the city had a population of 280,000; neither Loughborough nor Hinckley, the next largest towns in Leicestershire, had as many as 50,000. So Leicester has always been both central and dominant.

Rutland did not become fully recognised as a shire until the thirteenth century. Oakham was its capital, and always remained so; Uppingham its only other town. In 1889 it acquired its own County Council. Fifty years later the elaborate and costly devices of modern government were clearly becoming too much for its small band of ratepayers. First the fire service, then the police were merged with those of Leicestershire. A move to amalgamate the two counties came in 1961 and was defeated by opposition from Rutland. David fought Goliath, and once again prevailed. But that spirited victory was short-lived. The Act of 1972 settled the matter, and two years later Rutland was incorporated with Leicestershire.

To a traveller moving round Leicestershire today there are very clear differences between its eastern and western parts: not only economic differences but others of landscape and building. Very few of the smaller English counties can show within their borders so great a contrast as that between the Charnwood district and Rutland. The sombre rocks of Charnwood Forest outcrop sternly, like the granite tors of Dartmoor; the range of colour round about runs through the rough purple "forest stone" to the pink Mountsorrel granite. Drive down from Mountsorrel to Leicester, and then eastwards only about thirty miles to Ketton, and you move through a whole colour spectrum, expressed in building. For two centuries and more Leicester has been a city of red brick. Though the tall and dingy concrete blocks put up in the 1960s denied that, brick is now – happily – back in favour there again. It is the prevailing material everywhere on the clay lands, but as you move eastwards you begin to find the rich tawny ironstone in the churches, here and there elegantly combined with limestone, as at Melton Mowbray.

The roads from Melton eastwards are rewarding: high over the wolds to Grantham, with a vision of Belvoir Castle – something out of a fairy story in the hazy distance, romantic like a castle on the Rhine; due east to Stapleford, with an interesting great house and a refined Georgian Gothic church concealed in a wood, then on southwards to Oakham. The great hall of Oakham Castle is one of the most perfect secular buildings remaining from the twelfth century anywhere in England. Add the impressive church, with the buildings of the large school clustered round it, and the admirable new Rutland County Museum, and Oakham becomes a place well worth seeing. Only a mile away, moreover, is the big new Rutland Water, a reservoir carefully making its own shapely landscape.

The Rutland churches preside gracefully over their villages; they include two – Tickencote and Brooke – that are of no great promise externally but remarkable inside. Further west these good things are scattered: for instance at Bottesford, Noseley, King's Norton, and Stoke Golding. At the north-western edge, very close to Derbyshire, two exceptionally interesting churches lie within one parish, Breedon-on-the-Hill. Breedon church is remarkable both for its site and for its fascinating frieze and sculptured stones of the eighth or ninth centuries. Two miles away is the chapel of Staunton Harold, begun by the Royalist Sir Robert Shirley as a piece of defiance thrown at the republican government and completed about 1665. It has kept nearly all its original fittings and is now securely in the hands of the National Trust. With the big Georgian house adjoining, it makes an unforgettable landscape composition.

The industrial development of Leicester itself makes it appear to belong almost

BELOW: Volcanic rocks in Bradgate Park, Charnwood Forest, with Old John, an 18th-century prospect tower, on the skyline. ABOVE RIGHT: Staunton Harold Hall and its chapel, Holy Trinity, built during the Commonwealth. BELOW RIGHT: Leicestershire's delicacies: the misnamed Stilton cheese.

wholly to the nineteenth and twentieth centuries. Some of the big factory buildings that remain from the Victorian age are impressive. On the ridge rising up to the south, close together, are two striking monuments of the modern world: the northernmost of Lutyens's great series of memorials of the first World War (1925) and the Engineering Building of the University (by Stirling and Gowan, 1963), generally accepted as one of the key structures in recent British architecture. That ridge is linked to the old city below by the New Walk, three-quarters of a mile long, laid out in 1785 first as a boundary and a promenade, later becoming a residential street. It has always essentially remained, in our jargon, a "pedestrian way". Wheeled traffic is strictly prohibited on it. In recent years the planners have appreciated its value. It fell into a disgraceful condition after the Second War, the lower end becoming a slum. Now it is well cared for. When a major road had to cut across it, the engineers accepted the need to take it underneath, in an expensive cutting. So the New Walk remains in the possession of the walkers.

Although the people of Leicester use it constantly, they take it very much for granted. It is however unique: something not to be found in any other English industrial town. All that is characteristic, part of the secret — almost secretive — quality of Leicestershire itself. It has never gone in for self-advertisement. In the modern world this may well have become a serious weakness. To the visitor, however, such uncommon reticence is engaging; it leaves much of what is best in the county to be come upon as a surprise. Let me end with one of the chief oddities of this kind.

Stilton cheese got its name in the eighteenth century from the Bell Inn at Stilton in Huntingdonshire, where it was offered to stage-coach travellers stopping to dine. People naturally assumed that it was made there. No such thing. It came from the pastures of east Leicestershire and the Vale of Belvoir, and still does so. The main centre of its manufacture now is Melton Mowbray. That town is also esteemed for its pork pies. (When Sir Thomas Beecham conducted in Leicester he used to be given one at the end of the concert, to his delight and wonderfully-feigned surprise. "A Melton Mowbray pie", he would exclaim. I can hear him still.) The best of these pies are succulent and distinctive. A Melton Mowbray in France would be a little gastronomic capital, so designated in the guidebooks. In Leicestershire it is just a busy country town. Its one conspicuous industry is the manufacture of pet foods. The really distinguished human foods it makes are produced quietly and efficiently, with no special attempt to announce their merits. Its cheese — the most famous in England — remains attributed to Stilton. Leicestershire has never made any attempt to claim its own.

Northamptonshire

Photographs by John Brown

Northamptonshire is a county more often encountered on the way to somewhere else than as a destination in its own right. It is the M1 between Junctions 15 and 18, the scenery whirling past the Inter-City from Euston after it has left Bletchley and before it reaches Rugby, the slow crawl to Silverstone on Grand Prix day or waiting for the lights to change at the crossroads in Towcester where, every summer weekend, east-west holidaymakers and their caravans and boats on trailers snarl up with north-south holidaymakers and their caravans and boats.

It is where the Princess of Wales comes from and where Peterborough used to be, until hived off to Cambridgeshire in the local government reorganization of 1974, thereby depriving the county of a cathedral. Northampton itself, characteristically, is where the University of Cambridge once planned to re-site itself but needless to say did not. Even those of us who have settled in Northamptonshire, and come to love it, did not always mean to.

In our case we had been house-hunting around Buckingham when someone said that property was both cheaper and easier to find if you strayed across the border, Northants lacking the social cachet of Bucks. It was only when we had found our present home and become immersed in searches and surveys and solicitor's letters that I realized I was coming back to within a couple of miles of Plumpton Wood, where in the summer of 1943, between school and army, I worked in a volunteer forestry camp. We slept under canvas, subsisted on a diet of inch-thick cheese sandwiches and lukewarm cocoa and sang dirty songs, of which a contingent from Merthyr Tydfil had an inexhaustible and learned supply.

The "forestry" proved to consist of clearing underbrush, scratchy and tedious. But when harvest time came we were released to work on a local farm, heaving straw bales hour after hour under a scorching sun until at last it dipped below the trees and the sky was shot with colour and the world was magic. Also, in the farmhouse kitchen the farmer's wife would lay on such a spread as we townies had not seen since rationing had come in nearly four years before. Thirty-five years later, when my son was working on the same farm during the school holidays, I began to feel that perhaps I belonged to this hidden, solid midriff of England.

TOP: The farmhouse at Astwell, with its battlemented tower. CENTRE: In the south, near Silverstone. LEFT: Stoke Bruerne, where there is a waterways museum.

125

ABOVE: Warkton still gives an idea of
what all Northamptonshire villages
were like 50 years ago. RIGHT: Althorp,
ancestral home of the Spencer family.

We are in the Northampton Uplands, to use the rather grand name on physical maps for what is in fact a continuation of the ironstone ridge that gives the Cotswold scenery its ups and downs and Cotswold towns their honey-coloured charm. With us the landscape is at first sight more contained. The fields make a very English patchwork of plough and pasture, separated by hedgerows and spinneys and lines of elms, now sadly depleted. Not until you peer into the distance and see how the patchwork goes on and on, crest beyond crest, the scale ever finer, do you remember that we are 500 feet above sea level.

It is good hunting country, for those who care about hunting. Northamptonshire is one of the traditionally horsey midland counties known as The Shires. The Grafton meets round our part, the Pytchley farther north, and in premechanization days the Army's great equestrian centre was at Weedon, up the A5. When we first moved here one of the things I noticed most was the number of horsemen about, together with the flocks of yellowhammers suicidally gleaning squashed insects from the metalling of the country lanes.

The building stone varies in colour from pale fawn to dark rust, depending on its exact source and whether it was newly quarried at the time or filched, as was often the case, from some lately dissolved monastery. Sometimes courses of light and dark were laid alternately to give a striped effect. One end wall of our house has this design; a full-scale and striking example is the Bede House in Higham Ferrers, of which more in a moment. The one thing you cannot often say of the masonry is that it has charm, in the Cotswold sense. Armada House, in Weston, has massive walls and embrasure-like windows that make it look like a fortress. The farmhouse at Astwell *is* a fortress, or at least embodies an ancient, battlemented tower. Even the vernacular architecture of the villages, compared with the picture book prettiness of Bibury or Burford, has a down-to-earth, used look – or in some cases abused, by the slotting in of some hideous new development in fake stone or pallid brick. But there are a couple of nicely cosseted villages called Weekley and Warkton, just north of Kettering, which retain a high proportion of thatched roofs and give not too rosy an idea of how they must all have been half a century ago.

As for the people – well, this is where it becomes quite unrealistic to generalize about a longish county, top to bottom, and geographically much demarcated. Round us they have always been farmers. The same few surnames occur in the parish records for centuries. Their heirs today are taciturn, practical, mostly prosperous on various mixes of cereals and cattle (either milking or beef), sheep and EEC subsidies. The difference nowadays is that none of the farms employs more than a couple of hired hands where once it would have been a dozen or more, so people are collected by bus to work in packing stations or the Plessey electronics factory in Towcester, while others commute to office jobs in Milton Keynes or Northampton.

To the north of the county, surrounding the fantastically romantic Rockingham Castle perched up on its spur of high ground, and also in the south, Silverstone way, huge forests covered the land until comparatively recent times. I am not sure about Rockingham but around Silverstone (literally, *sylvan town*) there were settlements so isolated and inward-turned that they were known as the Lost Villages. As late as the

1890s, according to the topographer Herbert Evans writing in 1918, children grew up in them "who could neither read nor write, but they made *excellent* domestic servants". Working in the saw-pits the menfolk developed prodigious muscles and a useful pugnacity. In the 18th and early 19th centuries quite a few became professional bare-knuckle fighters, and every village had its team of pugilists to take on teams from neighbouring villages, as they do at darts today.

In the middle and eastern parts is located the chief – or anyway, traditional – industry. "Northampton?" breathed the cobbler where we previously lived when I told him we were moving. "That's the *capital* of the footwear trade." And so it is, just about. Barratt's stately Footshape Boot Works (the name picked out in the stonework of the façade) is empty now, and no longer making boots or even shoes, but Norvic and Lotus, Church and Brevitt, and the esteemed Crockett & Jones are still in Northampton, along with a score of other makers. Barkers are in Earls Barton and John White is to Higham Ferrers and Rushden as Ford is to Dagenham.

Nondescript as these little shoe towns might seem, and indeed are when approached through a wilderness of industrial estates, mean streets and maddening roundabouts, they are where the novelist H. E. Bates was raised, and the setting of many of the early stories of his, which I devoured as a boy. The county has its share of literary associations; a splendid John Clare collection in Northampton Library; the poet Dryden's connexion through the family manor house at Canons Ashby, now owned and restored, after years of neglect, by the National Trust; at Harlestone the grounds and lake of a house, itself now demolished, which may have been the original of Jane Austen's *Mansfield Park*. But Bates is the one who made use of the terrain and the people.

There is a neglected small masterpiece of his, *The Feast of July*, whose heroine comes walking into the Bates country as she follows the river Nene on a pilgrimage to find her faithless lover. The midwinter landscape of clay heights, wide valleys crossed by viaducts, the river reflecting the sullen sky, is marvellously sketched. She arrives at last at "Nenweald" which must be Higham Ferrers, though possibly with some elements of a larger town, say Wellingborough. The period is late Victorian; behind the terraced houses are countless little family workshops where boots and shoes come from the factories to be finished. When times are good the smell of leather and glue

Typical Northamptonshire countryside.

hangs in the air, when times are bad the children are sent "running" on everlength-ening expeditions to beg work from manufacturers in all the towns around. Chapel and pub compete for whatever hours are not occupied by toil. Yet at least once a year there is always feasting and dancing.

The Elizabethan manor of Canons Ashby, seat of the poet John Dryden's family.

If the people of the county have any common characteristic, it could be the matter-of-fact endurance which Bates details so well in this and other stories. They have all had their hard times: the foresters as the forests were enclosed, the farmworkers when wages were cut, the shoemakers when the army cut back on boots after the Boer War; and now the steelmen of Corby, attracted from Scotland during the last great depression only to fall victim to this one. Dreamers are not needed, but practical men prepared to do something about it. It is surely no accident that both political and religious dissent have always been strongly rooted in Northampton-shire. Just across the fields from us is the derelict farm called Cathanger where the Baptists used to hold clandestine services before they gained acceptance.

Stuck at the crossroads of Britain, Northamptonshire also had to learn to bear the passage of armies with stoicism. The Civil War was much fought in these parts, often setting neighbour against neighbour. Our village was Church and Royalist; Weston half a mile along the road Chapel and Roundhead. It is a county that has weathered much, that keeps itself to itself and does not much care if you do whizz through. With the exception of some stately homes which I cannot be bothered to list and the cheery little waterways museum at Stoke Bruerne, it has few show places dinkied up for the coach trade. Its whole attraction lies in the way that the old and the new, the industrial and the rural, the rare and the everyday, are mixed together. In prosaic Earls Barton is the Saxon church that starred on a postage stamp a few years ago. In Higham Ferrers, I almost forgot to add, that striped Bede House (almshouse) forms a perfect little precinct with another remarkable church and what was a tiny grammar school, now chapel; and in the street beyond are the raised, railed pavements just as H. E. Bates described them.

ALAN SILLITOE'S

Nottinghamshire

Photographs by Anne Cardale

Two hours on the train from London and I am back in Nottinghamshire. There is little to keep me in Nottingham city because all those warren-like streets, once packed around the centre, no longer exist. Even Victoria Station has gone, except for the clock tower.

The only thing in the town that does not change is the accent — and a few pubs such as The Trip to Jerusalem and The Royal Children and The Salutation. The recently contrived thoroughfare of Maid Marian's Way lies like a wicked sabre slash between the castle and Slab Square and, though there are tunnels for pedestrians, to cross on the surface is a sort of "motorway roulette" played by the Nottingham Lambs on Saturday night — over the railings and take a chance.

The only area to keep me in the city is the lace market. Recently saved from the planners' devastation, it is a fine conglomeration of 19th-century lace warehouses and I like to wander between the sombre buildings of Broadway, imagining the liveliness in the heyday of the lace trade when hundreds of people worked there.

A bus gets me to Balloon Houses, the supposed hill-site of a Montgolfier-type lift-off in the early 19th century. It is the traditional western outpost of the city and, if a balloonist had in those days stationed himself a few hundred feet above ground, he would have viewed the industrial part of Nottinghamshire bordering the Erewash valley: coalmines, mills, foundries all in full glow, blast and rattle. That kind of industrialism has had its time, and a much quieter landscape is the result.

Along the bridleway there is silence except for the crunch of my own boots. Trowel Moor provides the first real peace this side of Nottingham, with only the occasional whistle and shunt of a far-off train, or the panic wing-rattle of a wood pigeon rising from the dark button of copse or spinney. A privet hedgerow, buttressed by Queen Anne's lace, borders the footpath. Nettles, dog roses and deadly nightshade thicken the base. Flowers appear without fuss or notice and go in the same manner. Thin, dark clouds litter the sky and spread a Netherlandish glow over much of the moor which, once upturned by opencast coal-rippers, now looks settled except where the motorway crosses. Even that is more vocal than visible.

Over a wall in Strelley village seven fat bullocks and a horse share the umbrella of a

130

LEFT: Almost hidden among the trees, Moorgreen Church and Farm. ABOVE LEFT: The River Poulter which flows through Clumber Park to the River Idle. ABOVE RIGHT: The pithead gear of Clipstone colliery. BELOW: Hardwick Grange, a 19th-century estate village, situated at the north-east end of the lake in Clumber Park.

chestnut tree. Wormy sandstone walls are roped and enlaced in thick ivy. Pevsner refers to the church as the most important on the western outskirts of Nottingham. As a youth I cycled or walked by it scores of times, and remember rich hedgerows in a late summer's dusk when out that way with a girlfriend.

The traffic noise of the motorway persists, like a sea-tide that never quite comes in nor goes very far out. One whole wood I knew has been erased for a service station. Church Cottage in the village of Cossall was the home of one of D. H. Lawrence's early girlfriends and became the setting of Honeymoon Cottage in his novel *The Rainbow*.

A plaque on the church wall tells that three men from Cossall fought at the Battle of Waterloo. The memorial is grand for such a village, commemorating John Shaw and Richard Waplington who died in the battle, and Thomas Wheatley who came back. Shaw, tall and mad-drunk, killed eight Frenchmen before he fell.

The sides of the disused canal approach each other, as cuts often close when left alone. The relatively sylvan way skirting the sad graveyard of the Industrial Revolution becomes a place of dead dogs, rotting car bodies and decomposing sofas. A once handsome farmhouse lies in ruins. Slates are shed from its roof and a water-butt squashed flat looks as if a strongman has hit it with a drainpipe.

In spite of dereliction there is a persistent noise of machinery, with definite signs of life reasserting itself over the ruins. Around the elegant Piranesi-like viaduct are lush meadows and ripe hedges. The new factory a mile away has as yet a discreet existence, but is renewal, nevertheless.

Tenacious vegetation proliferates, and footpaths are heavily marked. But farms, cottages and railway lines have vanished, and I get lost on land I knew well, so that I use a map and compass to get up into Eastwood. I spend the night at the Two Counties Motel, a quiet, old-world place by the banks of the Erewash.

Eastwood straddles a ridge, and I have not been here since coming on the trolley-bus from Nottingham in 1950 to have tea with Alderman Willie Hopkins and talk about D. H. Lawrence. In those days the Lawrence cult had hardly begun, but now a museum has been made out of his birthplace. For 20p I file in behind a couple of Americans and an English schoolteacher. The shop-windowed interior has been reinstated as that of a miner's house of 1885. Mrs Goodband, the curator, devotes her time to keeping the place impeccable but homely. The parlour, which you enter straight off the street, was only ever used on Sunday or for special occasions. There is a smell of piety and self-respect – and of poverty held at bay. A huge Bible on the table is topped by an aspidistra, a green-spreading crown on the book of law and wisdom.

What Mrs Goodband does not know about Lawrence and his works would not amount to much, and we discuss the Great Bert while going around the house. In the ground-floor kitchen, where the family lived, is the usual black-leaded grate with a boiler to the left for heating water. I have not seen one for 40 years, and nostalgically examine the little black box of water with its square iron lid and tongue of a handle which you held with a cloth to stop your fingers being burned while the scalding water was ladled into a bath on Saturday night.

In the backyard is a wash-house with a copper-boiler and an ancient mangle outside, together with a tub and an antique dolly-ponch to bash the dirt and daylights out of the clothes on Monday morning.

Down from the museum is a double row of buildings known as The Breach, where Lawrence lived for most of his young life. Climbing some 200 feet I look back and see the town sprawling up the hill, but in front the countryside is as fresh and peaceful as any that can be found. Just as flesh is sweetest close to the bone, so these bucolic pockets near mines and towns can have an intensity of beauty which vaster stretches can never quite match.

I walk by Willey Wood Farm on my way to Hucknall. Moorgreen reservoir is the scene of a tragic chapter in *Women in Love*. From the ruin of Felley Mill I ascend into a silent, evergreen country of loam and pasture, feeling that the grass of southern England rarely has this fresh, hay-like odour.

From this point on, the geological map shows a layer-cake of complications: the swampy wood of coal measures, then more open over Lower Mottled Sandstone and Middle Permian Marl, through Boulder Clay to Lower Permian Marl to Lower Magnesian Limestone around Hucknall and Linby. The solid-and-drift determines the clothing of the surface, which decides the density of population.

Recrossing the motorway by a mere cat-plank I notice that in order to make room for it Annesley Lodge – mentioned by Thoroton and indicated on his plan of the Park and House in 1790 – had to be demolished.

As a youth I often cycled to Misk Hill on summer evenings after a day in the factory to enjoy wonderful views of Nottingham and the countryside nearby. The route into Hucknall is increasingly urban and I call there to visit the church where Byron is buried, or those of his organs that had the good luck to get back from Missolonghi. There has always been some dispute as to what these were, but there seems no doubt that his heart, at least, was among them. On July 16, 1824, an immense procession followed the hearse from Nottingham, perhaps in recognition of the fact that Byron had been the only one to speak up for the starving weavers in the House of Lords.

Beyond the mining area of Linby the Duke of Newcastle pub in the village is closed, but undaunted I make my way through some old stone quarries to Newstead Abbey by private footpaths. The habit of looking on all countryside as my own personal jungle dies hard, no matter how many notices say otherwise

At the Abbey I make for the tea room to slake a ferocious thirst, then go on a conducted tour of Byron's private apartments, paying the same amount as to see Lawrence's place. Byron said he would never sell the Abbey, though he did so for £100,000 when creditors demanded their money. The place changed owners several times in the 19th century, but Sir Julian Cahn presented it to Nottingham in 1931.

Our guide seems to dislike Byron almost as much as Mrs Goodband had respected and liked Lawrence, perhaps because he turned the monks' mortuary into a plunge bath for himself and his dog, Boatswain. Byron's room is more or less as it was left, and has to be seen by anyone who is familiar with his early poems. It must be said, however, that during my childhood and youth Newstead was as well known for its tuberculosis sanatorium as for having been the poet's home.

Keeping to footpaths needs good maps, but the Ordnance Survey never lets you down and I continue using them over the hills to Mansfield. In Fountain Dale stands

Nottingham's lace market; a fine conglomeration of 19th-century warehouses.

the cloven rock of the Druid's Stone – a 14 foot geological freak. The gloomy glen was also the scene of Robin Hood's encounter with Friar Tuck. In fact every copse, conery and clearing has some connexion with the Sherwood Gang. The eastern part of Harlow Wood is marked on the map as Thieves' Wood, another reminder of the ubiquitous Robin.

The next day I walk up through new housing suburbs out of Mansfield to reach open country, going along a ditch called Vicar Water. Clipstone colliery was the first mine I went down, but only on a day's visit after I had become a writer. Beyond the old village of Clipstone the way leads uphill to the isolated Duke's Archway, with rooms above which were once used as a school, built by the Duke of Portland in 1842 and said to be a copy of the Priory Gateway at Worksop. On the south side of the structure are figures of Robin Hood, Little John and Maid Marian, while on the other are effigies of Friar Tuck and Alan-a-Dale. A quaint building to meet on a lonely walk, it is still thought of by the locals as "The Duke's Folly", though to me it marked a suitably impressive entrance to Sherwood Forest.

The middle of the Forest, known as Birklands, is relatively untouched. Only the Major Oak area is visited, by many children and trippers. The tree itself is enormous, though not high, but so brooding and threatening that at any sudden movement the world would have to get out of its way. It is black, gnarled, broad and stumpy, but for all its bull-like strength the geological gout has set in. Three or four great pit props support the outer branches. People formerly crowded under it for photographs, but their weight impacted the soil, making it difficult for tap roots to get sustenance, so a fence now keeps us away from the trunk.

The heathland of Budby South Forest has always been an army practice ground, used also by the Sherwood Rangers and the South Nottinghamshire Hussars for their annual territorial camp and tactical training area. A tank dug into the sandy soil indicates that much of this least populated part of the county is still War Department property.

My favourite spot was and is Hardwick Grange in Clumber Park, at the north-east end of the lake. To reach the Dukeries I used to cycle from Nottingham, a 60 mile day-trip, and wander around the 19th-century estate village with its home farm and estate workers' houses and simple war memorial.

I walk now over the ford of the River Poulter and stand in some of the most peaceful country in the world. To me, all of Nottinghamshire is beautiful, even the places where "dark satanic mills" have been, not least the area around Langar aerodrome where I worked as an air traffic control assistant. But the two places that come fundamentally to mind when I am absent from the county are the old lace market and Hardwick Grange.

I have been over the county by most forms of transport, but the best ways are still by cycle and on foot. I am fond of other parts of England, but Nottinghamshire is the only county which I feel actually belongs to me, a sensation in no way diminished when after my three-day, 50 mile footpath walk I reach the Grange Farm at Norton and put up for the night.

FAR LEFT: Church Cottage, Cossall, was the home of one of D. H. Lawrence's early girlfriends and the setting for Honeymoon Cottage in *The Rainbow*.
LEFT: The Major Oak in Sherwood Forest.

SUSAN HILL'S

Oxfordshire

Photographs by David Gallant

I can lay no claim to Oxfordshire as my native county. I was born in Yorkshire, on the north-east coast. There, I feel, my roots lie buried, there I belong in imagination and in spirit, for there my childhood was spent; all my deepest influences came from there.

Yet my claim to "belong" to Yorkshire now must be a pretence; I have lived for longer *out* of that county than I lived in it, virtually all my adult life has been spent in what can loosely be called the Midlands. Ten of those years I spent in two towns of south Warwickshire, on the fringe of Oxfordshire, and I travelled into the northern end of the county often, and drove through it from Leamington Spa and Stratford-upon-Avon on my way to the Thames Valley. I got to know the market towns of Banbury and Bicester and Thame 15 years or so ago before they began to expand; I watched field and hedgerow disappear, become covered over by the spreading stain of light industrial estates and raw new housing developments, felt the traffic increase, in volume and in size, so that the old buildings in the centres of those market towns shook and trembled, pedestrians dived for cover, the pleasant sound of shoppers' footsteps and voices was drowned by the din of lorries. The arteries of those places became furred and clogged with traffic, which flowed ever more slowly and painfully.

I came to live in Oxfordshire itself in 1978, first of all actually in the city of Oxford and, after two years, out 6 miles to an extraordinary bit of the county of which I had been completely unaware, and to a place, a village, a house, a corner of the landscape, which has entirely changed my life.

I have spent a good deal of time travelling by road and rail through Oxfordshire. I have stopped to wander and to shop, to eat and examine churches, and to gaze out across the countryside in a large number of small towns and villages to north, south, east and west of the county. I have walked footpaths and fields until I know every inch of them in the radius of my own home. I still do not feel that deep sense of belonging here – I don't know why. But I have come to love Oxfordshire, and unexpectedly, too, because its praises have been so often and so well sung in literature that I have resisted falling so easily where so many others fell first. Besides, in my heart and my imagination I respond most intensely to quite different kinds of English landscape: to the wide open marshes and flat fens of East Anglia, all sky, or the bleak, inhospitable North Yorkshire coast, and the wild, wild uplands of Hardy's Dorset. Oxfordshire is altogether lusher and more verdant, a pretty, civilized sort of county.

But it does have its more exposed, barer aspect. Travel along the high, narrow backbone of a road that runs towards the Cotswolds from Oxford in the Cheltenham direction. Below lie the charming honeyed villages of mellow stone, tucked well into their pastures beside the River Windrush. But up here, especially in the depths of winter and the gales of March, it is bleak indeed. You can see for miles around, there is nothing to stop the wind, which you feel on your face like a blade; the tough little Cotswold sheep huddle close together and the trees have all bent their backs.

If I cannot live by the sea at least I can live near the river and Oxfordshire is fretted with waterways. It is a county of river valleys and river views, from the broad sweep of the Thames running down towards Berks and Bucks to the Oxford Canal that winds north, and all the little tributary rivers in betwen.

Beside the towpath outside Oxford there are the rowing crews sculling madly through the harshest weather of early spring, as well as the glorious heat of high summer – hulking, muscular medics from the colleges, as well as gangling boys from Radley, knees to chin like hunched-up grasshoppers, yet slipping with such infinite, silent grace, sleek and speedy as arrows in the morning mist.

One of Oxfordshire's "honeyed" villages, Swinbrook, beside the River Windrush.

Through the narrow, terraced back-streets of Jericho, the Oxford suburb where Hardy's Jude the Obscure had his lodgings, you come abruptly out on to the canal among warehouses and woodyards where there are still some working barges, but more pleasure craft. Take the train to Banbury and you pass Upper Heyford and Tackley where the holiday narrow boats are moored in their bright dozens.

In many ways and for a variety of mainly social reasons I disliked living in Oxford. But oh, the glory of it, the joy of being able to walk about among those mighty buildings! The city is at its best first thing in the morning, and when my daughter was in a push chair I used to go into the city centre for shopping before nine o'clock and just walk – walk down the avenue of St Giles, and up the Broad, and down the Turl, or under the "Bridge of Sighs", or along Catte Street, and there would be no

ABOVE: A church spire rises from Burford on the edge of the Cotswolds RIGHT: Chastleton House, built on land bought from the Gunpowder Plot conspirator Robert Catesby. FAR RIGHT: The "Bridge of Sighs" in Oxford, which links the buildings of Hertford College

one about except the last people walking or bicycling briskly to work, and the first to library and lab and lecture. Then the towers and spires and domes rose into heaven above my head, then the sight of the Radcliffe Camera made me sing, then the corners of ancient quads, glimpsed through archways, were like the sight of the gardens of Paradise, visible, unattainable. And I loved the way you could so quickly put it all behind you, when so much beauty was enough for a working day, turn a corner into Market Street, or cross the Cornmarket, that short, narrow road that divides town from gown as dramatically and simply as death divides this world from the next. Then we were among the modern shopping arcades full of chain stores, and our pavement companions were the like of ordinary shoppers anywhere.

And back home to north Oxford; the glories of *that* are the trees, all those magnificent horse-chestnuts and oaks and limes and cedars, in their prime now. I have thanked the Victorians and Edwardians daily for planting so many, and later generations and an enlightened council for preserving them; and the villas and mansions sit back behind them, up gravelled drives.

And every time I have driven or ridden or walked in spring down those two great arteries, the Woodstock and the Banbury Roads into the city, I have said Betjeman's lines about bonny Bellbroughton Road, with its prunus and forsythia, gleefully in my head.

Ten years ago I often drove down through the county towards Henley. The best bits are up through the beeches of the Chiltern Hills towards Watlington, and then on again through narrow lanes, between tree-graved cornfields, winding and dipping past graceful Stonor House and Park. I love the names of those places, Pishill and Bix Bottom and Christmas Common. I love the flint-faced brick farmhouses that stand so four-square.

Two and a half years ago we came to live in the small village of Beckley high on a hill overlooking Otmoor. It is at the end of the line, we lead nowhere, we have no through traffic. Below us lie those ancient, mysterious, empty acres, haunt of rare butterflies and grasses, of legends and ghosts, crossed by dykes and ditches, dotted about with villages known as "the seven towns". A man may still be lost in the mist out there.

Our cottage was built, like the other stone dwellings in the village, in the mid

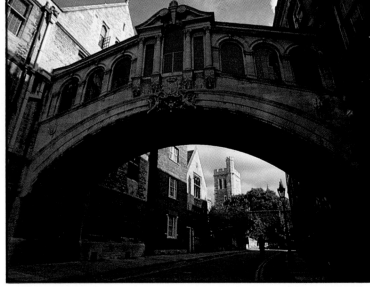

18th century. Immediately beyond it are unspoilt, undulating meadows, coursed just below the surface with hundreds of tiny streams dropping down on to Otmoor itself. On some days the mist encloses us so closely that we cannot see beyond the garden wall; but often we can see for miles, over to Brill, across to Bicester.

Every county has its famous beauty-spots, its much visited great buildings, and they are none the less beautiful for being familiar. Oxfordshire has Blenheim and Broughton Castle, it has Burford High Street and Dorchester Abbey. I like the lesser-known nooks and crannies. I love Chastleton House, on the Gloucestershire edge of the county. It is an Elizabethan manor house set formidably behind wrought-iron gates. The tiny village itself is a backwater, best approached by the single-track road across country from Charlbury; you can drive in the height of the summer season and never see another soul. But I prefer the place in winter, on any lowering, grey November day of early dark, for then it presents its real face, it is eerie and forbidding, and the ghosts lurk.

I love the village of Cropredy in the far north, as you look down upon it from the road above – a typically tucked-in Oxfordshire hamlet with good farm architecture, handsome, serviceable stone, and exactly the sort of place that is often cut off by snow – we get harsh winters here.

I love Swinbrook with its ford and its stone effigies, lying on their shelves in the light and airy church where the Mitford sisters, Nancy and Unity, lie in the austere graveyard.

I love Noke Wood, that nestles at the bottom of a sloping field 100 yards from my home. In autumn its fringes are set with berries – sloes, elder, and crab apples. Inside

RIGHT: An inhabitant of Charlton-on-Otmoor. FAR RIGHT: The Radcliffe Camera, built as a library by James Gibbs and now included in the Bodleian Library in Oxford.

Brasenose College, Oxford, founded in 1509.

it is never silent because of the small stream that trickles through. In spring, if you stand at its centre, you will be surrounded by so many bluebells, smelling so achingly of childhood past, that you will weep.

I love the sight of the spires set against the red, late afternoon sky of a frosty winter's day, as I come to the crest of Elsfield Hill. At last after seven years the scaffolding has been taken down from Magdalen Tower and it has resumed its rightful place among the others. The college has done the rest of the world a great service – the sight of the tower catches and lifts the heart.

It is all Oxfordshire.

JULIAN CRITCHLEY'S
Shropshire

Photographs by Anne Cardale

Shropshire is a castellated county, blue, green and gold, a county of long vistas in which the horizons are indented with the sharp profiles of distant hills. The north of the county is pastoral and quiet, an extension of the Cheshire plain, but south of the Severn you enter a different world. The area of the south Shropshire hills was the first in England to be designated as of outstanding natural beauty after the passing of the 1949 Act, and the crown is well deserved.

Travelling across the south of the county from east to west you are aware that the country changes perceptibly from English to Welsh. The Clee Hills dominate a landscape where the soil is Devon-red, while the view from Wenlock Edge, a wooded ridge 20 miles long, is of the bare whale-back of the Longmynd and beyond it to the wild country of the Stiperstones, with their tors and the dark Welshness of the Clun Forest.

Shropshire has always been for me "the land of lost content" and Housman its poet. Housman was a Worcestershire lad who fell in love with an unknown Shropshire. Looking westwards, the Clees were his "blue remembered hills" and when later he wrote *A Shropshire Lad* in the aftermath of an unrequited love-affair with Moses Jackson, he plucked from the gazetteer such Shropshire names as Clun, Wenlock and Ludlow as the settings for his melancholy, even morbid, poems.

My mother was born in a cottage in Wistanstow in 1898, the fifth of six children of a railwayman later killed by a shunting engine. My grandmother brought up her family on next to nothing and her eldest son, my uncle, now well into his 90s, still lives there. I was evacuated to that cottage in August, 1939, and I can remember quite clearly listening to Neville Chamberlain's sombre yet peevish broadcast on Sunday, September 3, the hot sun streaming in through the open door.

My grandparents were proud Salopians. They were poor and they were Tory. This was not so much from conviction, although they held strongly to their views, as from the fact that they were English and went to church. Shropshire is border country into which the Welsh, once driven safely beyond Offa's Dyke, have returned. They did labouring jobs, went to chapel and voted Liberal. Politics were as simple as that.

My idyll, which consisted of rabbiting, riding on the cross-bar of my uncle's bike and of running a stick along the corrugated iron sides of the outdoor lavatory inside which crouched one or other of my terrified female cousins, was brought to an end by school. I went to three Shropshire schools. To the first, the village school, I was packed off at the age of eight. I was placed for my safety in the girls' half.

I survived, although my piping West London accent seemed to anger the natives who would pursue me up the lane yelling "rotten tatters" in West Saxon. No sooner had my voice taken on a Shropshire lilt than I was moved to Brockhurst, a preparatory school up the road in Church Stretton. There I was punched for not talking sufficiently posh and my education took on that hard, middle-class gloss brought about by gym and God.

Church Stretton is a Shropshire beauty spot situated between the Longmynd and the Stretton hills, a row of neat volcanic peaks which are like a fleet of great ships in line ahead. In the van is the Wrekin, some 15 miles to the north, the hill which is the subject of the Salopian's toast "All friends round the Wrekin". Towards the end of the last century Church Stretton, then a black-and-white village with a market-hall by John Abel, Charles I's carpenter, became a fashionable holiday centre, and the Wirral rich moved south to build their Victorian villas. The market-hall disappeared. On half-holidays the school, in pink blazers and caps, would take to the hills, scrambling to the summit of Caer Caradoc in search of its cave, or following the course of Ashes Hollow as it climbed the 1,600 feet to the top of the Longmynd. There it was all wind and whinberries, with views over the Black Mountains and Plynlimmon, and the school and its formidable headmaster – a sailor who called the dormitories after admirals – happily reduced to size.

At the age of 13 I went from Brockhurst to Shrewsbury. The county town can be pronounced in one of three ways: "Shrozebury", like the school; "Shroosbury", which is the most common, or "Salop", which is not the alternative name of the county as Peter Walker believed, but the name given to Shrewsbury by the older country people. The school on its site above the Severn suffered from no such equivocation. We were not allowed to have doubts. The régime was rigorous, the food execrable (we were on almost permanent hunger strike) and the heating non-existent. I am told its living standards now match those of the public sector. In our spare time we either rowed or ran. In the winter terms the whole school would stream out of the gates on 6 mile runs, urged on by huntsmen and whippers-in. My chief memory of four undistinguished years was running for my life through the indescribable mud and filth of some Shropshire farmyard chased by savage dogs. But life at Shrewsbury had two compensations: the town, to which I went as often as I could get permission; and Sunday afternoon bike rides.

On Sunday afternoons from a quarter to two until six o'clock we were free to bicycle across the country. The whole of Shropshire to a radius of 15 miles or so was ours, and the roads in the late 40s were empty of traffic. We would pedal along Telford's A5 as far as Nesscliffe, where we would climb the rocks and finish with egg and chips at a pub. In the opposite direction we would scale the Wrekin and explore the ruins of Uriconium, the Roman city once the fourth largest in England and to this day largely unexcavated. To the south we could get as far as Stretton and to the west to Pontesbury on the fringes of the Stiperstones, a wild and desolate stretch of hill

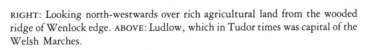

RIGHT: Looking north-westwards over rich agricultural land from the wooded ridge of Wenlock edge. ABOVE: Ludlow, which in Tudor times was capital of the Welsh Marches.

LEFT: The oldest house in Coalbrookdale, built in 1636, contains a forge. ABOVE: The cricket pavilion at Shrewsbury School, where the author spent four undistinguished years.

country pitted with lead mines and on the top of which is the Devil's Chair, a 200 foot mound of frost-fractured quartzite which, when shrouded with cloud, indicates the Devil's presence. "He's in his chair," mothers warn their children.

The Stiperstones is Mary Webb country. The novels of Mary Webb, praised by Stanley Baldwin and so popular in the 30s, were to be found on the shelves of the House library along with Henty and Rider Haggard. I read them greedily, which is more than could be said for my housemaster who was unaware of their lubricity. The heroes were petty squires with names like Gideon and Seth, who galloped across Shropshire in pursuit of virgins called Hazel who were disappointingly fleet of foot. Good was symbolized by earnest young preachers who went equally unrewarded, and rainstorms were for ever battering upon cottage windows. There was a lot of hot breath and purple prose, much of which was written in a Shropshire dialect which my experiences in Wistanstow village school allowed me to decipher.

My favourite town in Shropshire is Ludlow, confidently proclaimed by Professor Joad as the "prettiest small town in England". I agree with that cantankerous and wrong-headed old man. Ludlow is beautiful and is not yet pickled in aspic like so many other small Georgian country towns, such as Farnham where every lamp-post is protected and even the policemen talk posh. Ludlow is a workaday town packed on market days with farmers' wives in Doris Archer hats, full of seedsmen and saddlers, and butchers selling their own black puddings. Ludlow is a hill-top town with the finest castle ruin in the Marches and a parish church, St Lawrence's, on which was lavished all the piety and prosperity of the medieval wool men. The country can be glimpsed at the end of every street and the river Teme encircles half the town. The alleys and courtyards are black-and-white and the main streets Georgian, the best of which is Broad Street, which runs down from the Butter Cross where the clock still chimes "See, the conquering hero comes" as in Housman, to the town gate. In the 18th century the gentry wintered in Ludlow in houses which still sell for half the price of their equivalents in the south.

Ludlow is good for the spirit. It is overlooked by hills, to the west by Bringewood

RIGHT: Heath Chapel, an original Norman chapel, near Cold Weston.

FAR RIGHT: The butcher's shop that supplies the "quite excellent" pork pies sampled by the author.

146

where more Ludlovians have been conceived than would be readily admitted, to the north by Wenlock Edge, to the east by Titterstone Clee Hill, whose profile when seen from the Knighton road is the most elegant in England, and to the south by the rolling red and green lands of Hereford. It is unspoilt and protected from the Black Country by the Clees and 20 extra miles of bad roads. Ludlow is a secret to be kept to oneself.

I left school at the end of the summer of 1948, taking the train from Shrewsbury to Paddington. Only a year after nationalization it was still recognizably the old Great Western Railway with its green and gold engines, the reek of buttoned carriage cloth and sepia photographs of Paignton. I return to Shropshire at least once a year, staying with relatives in Ludlow, and devote a day or two to gentle exploration.

A. J. P. Taylor said that Shropshire was "remote", and that is part of its charm. To those tired of London, if not of life, a week in Clun at the Sun Hotel or the Lion at Leintwardine (now in Hereford but until 1898 a part of Shropshire) would be a marvellous restorative. Follow the road that leads from Craven Arms westwards through the villages of Clunbury, and Clunton, Clungunford and Clun as it climbs steadily between the hills of the Forest until the road peters out at the gates of Peter Walker's hill farm. No one really does go to Wales that way.

On the other hand you could go east from Craven Arms and drive slowly up Corve Dale, a valley which lies between Wenlock Edge and the two Clees, the Brown, the highest hill in the county at nearly 1,800 feet, and the Titterstone, which appears to be higher. The earth in the Dale is red and the farming the richest in Shropshire. Diddlebury ("Delbury") has a church with Saxon tiling, and high up on the slopes of Brown Clee, near the aptly named and almost deserted village of Cold Weston, is the chapel at Heath, an original Norman chapel untouched since the 12th century standing alone in an otherwise deserted field. It is unlocked. Holdgate has a church built like a castle and is completely unrestored. Not even the Gilbert Scotts, those indefatigable refurbishers of country churches, managed to lay their hands on it, so remote are the villages of the Dale.

Shropshire has had an industrial past, relics of which can be found along the Severn at Ironbridge and Coalbrookdale. The remains of 18th-century ironfounding are displayed in several open-air museums, and the scars are hidden in a steep and bosky countryside. There is a New Town called Telford on the eastern fringes of the county looking towards Wolverhampton but I have no intention of going there. It more properly belongs to the Black Country.

Shropshire is careful not to blow its own trumpet. Its county town is not a city, and in cricketing terms it rates only as a minor county. Its most famous sportsman was Captain Webb, who was the first man to swim the Channel at the turn of the century. It has no Dukes; it does have many great houses but not the sort with zoos. Shropshire is famous for its Tories, its scenery and its sheep. Painstaking detective work has placed Blandings Castle in the county.

PHIL DRABBLE'S
Staffordshire

Photographs by Charles Milligan

Strangers visualize Staffordshire as industrial sprawl from the Potteries in the north of the county to the Black Country in the south. Nothing could be further from the truth; nowhere provides a richer variety of countryside.

This variety is highlighted in the north of the county where the congestion of the five towns, where some of the most delicate china in the world is still produced, melts into moorland within a few miles, and where desolate land meets empty skies over the hills between Leek and Macclesfield.

This is stone wall country that has not changed since primitive men tended their flocks of sheep here. Curlews still sing the same wild song and life can still be as hard for the farmers who struggle to wrest a living much as their ancestors did. One man, who is part-time road-man and part-time farmer, told me that in the terrible winter of 1947 he was snowed in on January 25 – and it was still taking him two hours to get his milk, on a sledge, to the public road in April.

But for visitors in fair weather these hills are the perfect escape from the pressures and tensions of what we have come to regard as a more civilized life. Sportsmen come here to shoot the grouse and gentler folk are content to revel in the grandeur of the scenery. Many a tripper near the Roaches, a wild cascade of huge rocks, has rubbed his eyes in disbelief when he has thought he saw a wallaby. A landowner's collection of exotic animals escaped when the Army were there in the last war, and a small colony of wallabies miraculously survived; in winter, when the snow covers their food on the lower slopes, they eke a living on the most exposed hilltops, where the tempest clears the snow from the heather.

One of the drawbacks to having beautiful scenery so close to cities like Stoke-on-Trent and Sheffield and Manchester is that too many people wish to see it. The river Dove divides Staffordshire from Derbyshire, the grandest part of Dovedale being on the Staffordshire bank, and the Peak National Park suffers from erosion and congestion because so many people yearn for escape to quieter places.

To siphon off some of the pressure, the planning authority have authorized a major amusement centre at Alton Towers, a few miles to the south of Leek. It was once the home of the Earls of Shrewsbury and the gardens are still on the grand scale of generations ago, though the house itself is mostly in ruins. Not that that matters to

LEFT: The Abbots Bromley Horn Dancers and their Fool giving their annual performance at the beginning of September. BELOW: A stubble field at the edge of Blithfield Reservoir.

the trippers who congregate there, for they come for rides on big dippers and similar fairground attractions. If you disregard the opinions of the local inhabitants, this concept of creating "honeypots" to attract casual visitors and relieve pressure on sensitive beauty-spots is successful.

Part of the Staffordshire Way, one of the chain of national long-distance footpaths, passes within a mile or so of the village of Alton and Alton Towers. It uses part of the Churnet valley, which is steep-sided but richly wooded, in complete contrast to the wild moorlands just to the north. A stream meanders through a chain of pools, and the trees close in overhead to make it one of the quietest and most peaceful spots imaginable. Such sudden changes from open moorland to noble trees, peppered with showbiz razzmatazz, is typical of a county that ranges from primitive farming to sophisticated industry.

The area around Uttoxeter is among the best dairy country in England. The watermeadows of the river Dove are superb pasture and the local belief is that "in April Dove's flood is worth a King's good" because, when the rains come just at the right time, it is almost possible to see the grass grow. This central part of

BELOW: Fishing in the canal near Great Haywood. BOTTOM: A small cottage near Grindon. RIGHT: Phil Drabble and his dogs.

Staffordshire is untouched by development. From Uttoxeter in the north to Rugeley, about 15 miles to the south, and almost from Stafford to Burton-upon-Trent on the east and west the country has hardly been spoiled at all. It is an area comparable to the Dukeries in Nottinghamshire, and the reasons for the absence of development are much the same. Until relatively recently, this part of Staffordshire has consisted of a chain of great estates.

The Marquess of Anglesea could once drive across Cannock Chase to see his neighbours the Earls of Shrewsbury or Lichfield several miles away and the Marquess's Drive is still on the ordnance map to prove it; far more important, it is now a public right of way. The Lichfield lands abutted the estates of Lord Bagot who then owned the part of Needwood Forest where I am now lucky enough to live. Needwood Forest is still heavily wooded, being owned by the Duchy of Lancaster which is part of the Queen's estates. And when the aristocracy began to crumble the beer barons of Burton-upon-Trent, the *nouveaux riches* of their day, took care that the riches distilled from their beer were not despoiled.

The village of Abbots Bromley, on the edge of Needwood Forest, still maintains the ancient custom of holding an annual Horn Dance in September. Some say that the origin of the ritual is lost in long-forgotten fertility rites; others believe that it commemorates the rights of commoners to collect fuel and turf or to hunt the beasts of the forest. Nobody really knows how the dance began, but it is performed by a team of dancers with reindeer horns that hang in the parish church for the rest of the year.

The villagers pick their own dancers, who are often the sons or grandsons of men who performed the same ritual in generations past, but the vicar is in charge of the horns, which may not be taken outside the parishes of Abbots Bromley and Blithfield. Since the members of the Horn Dance team are not necessarily members of the congregation, this has given rise, in the past, to some dissent between the vicar and his parishioners. Indeed, when the dancers were invited to perform at the Albert Hall, replica horns had to be made.

Blithfield Reservoir lies on each side of the main road between Abbots Bromley and Rugeley. It is about 2½ miles long and is spanned by an exceptionally ugly concrete bridge which originally had a solid concrete parapet. There was so much public objection to this monstrosity that a few panels were taken out of the middle of the bridge to leave a reasonable view of the reservoir over a short span. The south-eastern end of the reservoir has a small section reserved for sailing, while fishing and bird-watching are allowed over the whole area.

Passes for bird-watching are sold by the river authority. It is an exceptionally good area for wintering wildfowl – a few comparative rarities, such as osprey, call in on migration. The reservoir fills from the Kitty Fisher brook and the river Blythe in the basin of the Trent, which lies about 3 miles to the west and, rising sharp above the Trent, is the escarpment of Cannock Chase. "The Chase" – and it is never known as anything else to Staffordshire folk – is about 16 square miles in area and is clad half in softwood Forestry Commission trees, half in open moorland. It is trendy, in some circles, to scorn the monoculture softwood trees of the Forestry Commission, but it was not they but our forefathers who despoiled the Chase.

It lay near enough to the heavy industries of the Black Country for it to supply the insatiable demand for fuel. Before the invention of furnaces which could smelt iron with coal, charcoal was the universal fuel and the ancient oak woods of the Chase were systematically felled to make it, though the finer specimens were occasionally diverted to the ship-building industry. Even when I was a youngster vast tracts of heather and bilberry covered the industrial deserts left by the medieval charcoal burners. Most of the waste has since been planted with fir and pine trees and the Commission has been progressive in its attempts to combine the requirements of commercial forestry with wildlife conservation.

There are large herds of wild fallow deer as well as a few red deer and tiny muntjac. The Commission has planted deer lawns of several acres apiece in the centre of the forest, in part to encourage the deer to feed where they will do no harm instead of straying on to vulnerable farm crops on the periphery.

Apart from the deer, there is a wide variety of woodland birds, as well as badgers and foxes and other animals. The open part of the Chase is administered by the County Council, which is sensible in guarding it as far as possible from overexploit-ation by declaring large areas as motorless zones: experience has shown that only a tiny minority are prepared to expand the effort to go far from their cars on foot.

Castle Ring, an ancient hill fort on the edge of the Chase, commands spectacular views. The local belief is that, though it is only about 750 feet above sea level, there is nothing higher between the Ring and Siberia. I cannot vouch for the truth of that, but I do know that on a spring day, when there is a bitter east wind, it is enough to turn strong men's vitals to water.

The Black Country lies to the west, though it is no longer visible from many vantage points because the trees have grown too high. The most spectacular time to see the Black Country is on a clear night, and the best viewpoints are Sedgley Beacon, Rowley hills or the hill where Dudley Castle stands. The M6 motorway has spoilt the view now because much of the carriageway has been lit by lamps, so that it snakes across the horizon precisely as any other motorway does anywhere else.

The prospect is best described, for me, by a man called Elihu Burritt. He was the American consulate official in the Midlands in the middle of the last century and part of his brief was to send reports back to the United States about the condition of trade in his area. He was an imaginative man. Instead of penning a report in bureaucratic language, he decided to do his reports anecdotal and he called them *Walks in The Black Country and its Green Borderland*. The picture etched most clearly into my mind – and I lent his book years ago and never recovered it – is of the Black Country seen by night from Dudley Castle.

Climbing up the circular staircase in the tower, Elihu says that the light outside was so brilliant that it shone red on the walls through the arrow slits overlooking the moat. The light was provided by no fewer than 90 blast furnaces, all blowing at once.

Nevertheless, the Black Country still has a strange beauty. It still throbs with life and there is still a rare sense of community among its people, whose ancestors no more than about three generations ago flocked in from the surrounding countryside during the Industrial Revolution.

Although such folk are urban dwellers on a census form, they still have a deep

LEFT: Pastoral scene on a farm between Stafford and Uttoxeter.
BELOW LEFT: The early 15th-century church at Tong, which contains a remarkable collection of monuments, mostly of the Vernon family.
BELOW: The main street of Alton village.

nostalgia for the country pursuits of their forebears. I know because my father was a Black Country doctor and I learned my trade as a naturalist from coal miners, descended from the same stock. They were as clever poachers as any horny-handed son of the soil. I now live a mile from the nearest road in the remnants of Needwood Forest and my neighbours' local patriotism is just as strong. I feel I almost need a passport to go over the borders of Staffordshire, and there is nowhere in the country I would rather be.

Warwickshire

Photographs by Cressida Pemberton-Pigott

I am always proud to claim Warwickshire as my home when, on my frequent visits abroad, I am asked where I live. To the foreigner, Shakespeare's England, the Heart of England and Leafy Warwickshire are all names which conjure up a romantic image, and Shakespeare and Warwickshire are inseparable to the thousands of annual overseas visitors.

There are three places which claim the title of the centre of England – the cross at Meriden, High Cross on Watling Street, and the centre of England oak which used to stand at Lillington in Leamington – and I naturally argue that my home at Coleshill is only a stone's throw from the real centre, Meriden. At least it was accepted that the Meriden cross was the appropriate stone to put in the centre of Battersea Park during the Festival of Britain in 1951, and cyclists from the world over converge on Meriden each year for a memorial service.

As a landlocked county, Warwickshire has in recent times more ominously become the motorway hub of England, and in a period of rapid change it has been trying to cope with 20th-century industrial installations, particularly in the north of the county.

I was born in 1925 at Park Farm, Ansley, rented by my father from the Ansley Hall Coal and Iron Company. This is in the centre of the north Warwickshire coal fields and, while the Ansley mine is now closed, the district still shows the effects of mining operations, although a number of spoil tips have been removed. I have vivid and happy memories of my childhood, when Joe Phillips, grandfather of Captain Mark Phillips, was the owner of the mine, and reliable part-time labour by miners was always available for seasonal farm work. Miners were also expert poachers and I probably learnt more about country life and country pursuits from them than from farm workers, particularly catching rabbits with ferret and lurcher. The old Chinese temple and hermitage in Ansley Park no longer exist, but a visit to the ruins of the hermitage in my youth was a ghostly experience and the stories were legion.

Ansley lies west of Nuneaton and is surrounded by villages which once formed part of the Forest of Arden. The forest has been replaced by rows of miners' cottages and, although they do not make the most picturesque landscape, there has been little change in their architecture in my lifetime. I still feel the warmth and friendliness of the sons and grandsons of the mining families when I motor through the villages.

A number of villages in north Warwickshire are continually threatened by an expansion of modern Coventry or Birmingham, but I am encouraged by the action of many people who, through civic societies and local authorities, are determined to protect the fabric of the villages and maintain village life. This is something we can learn from other European countries and particularly areas like the Black Forest in Germany or Bavaria, where small industries and private enterprise have kept local communities together.

Warwickshire is, however, divided into two types of countryside and, living and farming where we do in the industrial north of the county, people often assume that no farming land survives. A walk along the bank of the River Blythe on a summer evening corrects this impression.

I joined my father in a farming partnership and started married life with a girl from Bentley in 1947. Our farm at Coleshill is sandwiched between the two great conurbations, Birmingham and Coventry, but the town is still one of great antiquity with a mixture of timber-framed, Georgian and Victorian buildings, which lead to the crest of the hill and the parish church. On Church Hill is an old market-house,

Farming country near the village of Over Whitacre in north Warwickshire.

155

outside which can still be seen the combined whipping post, pillory and stocks that contrasts with the new construction beside the church, erected on the site of a row of fine old buildings which were demolished. Views obviously differ over this development, but I believe it completely destroyed the grace and character of the area.

Standing on the hill you can see the vast industrial complex and housing estates that separate Coleshill from the narrowest of green belts. The view beyond is closed by the electric power station and cooling towers of Hams Hall and the redundant Lurgi gas-producing plant, now millions of pounds' worth of industrial scrap. Over your shoulder lies the sprawl of housing estates at Kingshurst and Chelmsley Wood, and many of the older residents of Coleshill would claim that the character of their home town's surroundings has vanished during their lifetime. It is difficult to believe that the postal address was Birmingham near Coleshill at the turn of this century.

From Coleshill the A47 crosses the River Blythe, a tributary of the Tame. Across the fields is seen Blyth Hall, the present home of Sir William Dugdale. He is descended from the famous antiquary, Sir William Dugdale whose *Antiquities of Warwickshire* was published in 1656. Continuing through the villages of north Warwickshire and passing the great Whitacre reservoir, it is difficult to appreciate the change and improvement in soil structure from the Blythe valley, dark and stony, to red sandstone. Many of the small farms have disappeared, giving way to large arable fields with fewer hedgerows. Between Coleshill and Atherstone there are now only about four dairy herds on farms, compared with 44 some 20 years ago, but the total number of cows is about the same. Modern technology has brought with it a revolutionary change in methods of farming and taken much of the drudgery out of the work.

My grandparents moved to Hall Farm, Over Whitacre, in the early part of this century when so many farms were vacant and Cheshire families were moving south. What a performance it must have been moving stock, machinery and furniture on horse wagons. The villages of Over and Nether Whitacre lie either side of Furnace End, which took its name in 1700 from the furnaces of the Jennens family in the Bourne valley. As children we were always being reminded by Squire Weston, who lived and owned a farming estate in Over Whitacre, that "Over" means superior and "Nether" inferior – a statement accepted only if you lived in the right village. At Nether Whitacre, however, little remains of the old village except the 16th-century church of St Giles, and at Over Whitacre on a prominent hill-top is the isolated church of St Leonard, built in the Baroque style of 1766. From the churchyard, where my grandparents are buried, the cooling towers of Hams Hall dominate the skyline.

North and west of Coleshill there are numerous similar villages among the Warwickshire coal-fields and large granite quarries around Nuneaton, rarely seen by strangers. A sad fate has befallen some, many of which are recorded in the Domesday survey. They no longer have separate identities, even if you can find them among the urban sprawl. Kingshurst, Marston Green and Kitts Green are all now part of the vast Chelmsley Wood estate, built since 1950 by the City of Birmingham on part of the green belt. Also surrounded by local authority housing developments is Castle Bromwich, its historic centre struggling to survive.

South of Coleshill, running alongside the M6, is a group of villages of great

The 17th-century Blyth Hall is overshadowed by Hams Hall cooling towers in the industrial area of Coleshill.

antiquity, some with their manor and great estate. To the west lies Maxstoke, a delightful village of timber-framed or brick houses and cottages, on land of red loam which is some of the most fertile in Warwickshire. The ruins of the Augustinian priory, which was dissolved in 1536, remain, but Maxstoke Castle, surrounded by its moat, has been carefully restored by Captain Fetherston-Dilke, the descendant of Sir Thomas Dilke who acquired the property in 1589. This castle, resembling a fortified manor house, is one of the finest examples of its type in the Midlands, its impressive red sandstone walls forming a square-on plan with towers at the angles, its moat crossed by an 18th-century bridge replacing the original drawbridge.

You cannot leave the villages of north Warwickshire without mentioning the parish of Great Packington, east of the River Blythe. Much of the area is occupied by Packington Park with its fine woods and pools, most of them landscaped after the extraction of sand and gravel. They are now stocked with fish, and fishermen come from miles around to enjoy a few hours' relaxation. There is no village and the church stands about mid way between the Old Hall and Packington Hall, the seat of the Earl of Aylesford. The church is unique in this country, built in 1789 and based on the

ABOVE LEFT: The whipping post, pillory and stocks outside the old market house on Church Hill, Coleshill. ABOVE: Ruins of the Augustinian priory at Maxstoke, founded in 1336. LEFT: The brick Church of St James at Great Packington, designed in 1789 by Joseph Bonomi on the Byzantine inscribed-cross plan with domed corner towers.

Maxstoke Castle, built in the 14th century from local sandstone.

style of a church near Rome. The small organ was bought from Charles Jennens, Handel's friend, and Handel is thought to have used the instrument to compose parts of the Messiah.

The hall has an impressive interior, and among its showpieces is the Pompeian room designed by Joseph Bonomi, employed by the fourth Earl from 1782 to redecorate the house. Tragically there was a serious fire two years ago and the present Earl and Lady Aylesford were forced to move to the Old Hall. The fine landscaped grounds were first laid out by Capability Brown.

Having mentioned a few of the surrounding villages and the countryside from my home town of Coleshill, and neglected some of the better (and admittedly more attractive) parts of Warwickshire, I return to where I started, Meriden. This village is the headquarters of the oldest archery society in England, the Woodmen of Arden, formed in 1785 and limited to 80 members. Meetings are held at the Forest Hall on the lawn said to have been undisturbed since the time of Robin Hood, whose Loon is supposed to be the one hanging in the entrance hall of the building, used when the outlaw competed in archery matches in the old Forest of Arden. Not far away is the village pond where traditionally water flows out of one side into the Humber and from the other into the Bristol Channel.

Worcestershire

Photographs by John Frye

Sir John Betjeman once called Worcestershire "a gloriously dim county". It is certainly one of the smallest, far from the sea and tucked away in the Midlands. Betjeman described its shape as that of a fruit tart burnt black at the northernmost edge where it encounters the industrial towns. Indeed Dudley was so burnt that the borough became detached from the rest of the tart, an island of Worcestershire lost in Staffordshire. Similarly bits of the unburnt tart at the southern extremity floated off centuries ago, so that places like Northwick and Daylesford proudly maintained that they had nothing whatever to do with Gloucestershire where they had landed up. But these delicious irrelevancies have been neatly ironed out by a series of preposterous local government reforms, the last of which lumps Herefordshire and Worcestershire together in one county!

Unspectacular Worcestershire may be – a flat plain framed by the Clee, Clent and Lickey hills on the north, the Long Ridge Way and the Cotswolds on the east, Dumbleton and Bredon hills on the south, and the Malvern and Abberley ranges on the west. Through the centre of the plain flows the Severn, to be joined by the Avon at Tewkesbury.

It is impossible for me not to picture Worcestershire in the past, and a distant past too, for my earliest and sharpest memories of it go back beyond 1914. I was brought up there during the First World War, shuttled between my parents' house in the south of the county near Evesham, and my grandmother's in the north, close to Bewdley. I do not think there is a town or village in the whole county that I have not visited, certainly not a single church, and probably no country house when it was still privately inhabited.

This sounds boastful. It is simply explained by the fact that architecture has always been my chief interest and, for the greater part of my working life, my job. When other boys played cricket or football, my brother and I would in the 1920s bicycle to churches within reasonable distance of our parents' and grandmother's houses. Solemnly and seriously, with our box Brownies propped on piles of hassocks and prayer-books, we would take execrable time-exposures of squints and rood-screens, to the disgust and contempt of our sporting father who considered these expeditions

ABOVE LEFT: Worcester, with its cathedral begun in the 11th century, lies on the River Severn. ABOVE RIGHT: The rococo interior of Great Witley Church. BELOW: The Malvern hills formed the western boundary of the old county of Worcestershire.

RIGHT: Part of the Worcester and Birmingham Canal. CENTRE RIGHT: The untypical but best-known Worcestershire village of Broadway. BOTTOM RIGHT: The more representative Dormston Moat Farm. BELOW: The ruins of Witley Court.

unhealthy and unnatural. Unhealthy they surely were not, considering the miles of pedalling we covered. Unnatural they may have been because I frankly confess to a preference for stones, bricks and mortar to human flesh and blood, and on the whole a preference for the historic past to the unhistoric present.

Actually the historic dead with Worcestershire associations are not so numerous. For the most part Worcestershire men are humble and diffident ("dim" perhaps!), as Wordsworth discovered when he came upon a gravestone in the cloisters of Worcester Cathedral with the single word "Miserrimus" upon it.

I was never much interested in Layamon, rector of Areley Kings around AD 1200, who is described on a tablet in the parish church as "the earliest writer in the English language". I feel sure the author of *Brut*, a mythical rhymed history of the Britons, is unreadable. Not so the monk William Langland, however, who flourished a century later. The soporific alliteration of *The Vision concerning Piers Plowman* epitomizes for me the spirit of the lush and earthy country Langland saw from the Malvern beacons.

I like to think of that later and hardly less visionary clergyman, Lewis Carroll, staying in his brother's Georgian dolls' house rectory at Alfrick. And while talking of poets I have a weakness for the irascible, blustering Walter Savage Landor who was born in Ipsley Court which, when a sick old man in far-away Florence, he recalled in melancholy: "I hope in vain to see again Ipsley's peninsular domain." Which he never did. Landor I could not have known but the author of *A Shropshire Lad*, who was born at Fockbury in 1859, I remember as an old maidish, fragile and droopy don. A. E. Housman, Edward Elgar and Stanley Baldwin are surely the three greatest Worcestershire men of this century. I am proud to have met and known, however slightly, the two last. They were positively steeped in love of Worcestershire. Elgar's music expresses the same dream-like pastoral quality as Langland's verse. It, too, conjures up visions of heaven across chequered hedgerows, orchards and hop-fields. My memory of Elgar, with his Poona colonel moustache, spats and trilby hat, the would-be squire, is in complete variance with what one expected a famous maestro to look like. Baldwin on the other hand looked exactly what he was, the produce of Worcestershire clay with a dash of Redstone Rock. I must be one of the last people to remember him when he was a mere backbench MP who attended croquet parties on summer evenings, and was considered rather unimportant.

Nothing indicates to me so strikingly the change of the times as the fact that, while Prime Minister, Baldwin would spend two or three days walking, pack on back and a Mary Webb novel in hand, down the lanes, stopping at pubs for a tankard of cider, or even a bed, alone and unaccompanied by a single detective. Francis Brett-Young was another favourite novelist of Baldwin's. He lived in elegant Craycombe House near Pershore. The measure of his inferiority to Mary Webb may be gauged by the seriousness with which he took himself. I recall his wife warning me to pass his study door on tiptoe, while she put a finger to her lips, murmuring, "Let us not disturb the master's inspiration." This made me decide at the time that were I ever to become a writer, I would endeavour not to appear a fool.

Of all the fine villages of Worcestershire, Broadway is the best known. It is also the least typical, belonging as it does to the Cotswolds. It ought to be in Gloucestershire: the typical Worcestershire villages are not built of limestone, but of timber, lath and plaster, or red plum brick. One thinks of Abbots Morton, Great Comberton and Cropthorne, with their black-and-white, thatched cottages, which look as though they are growing out of the wooded soil. The small manor houses are mostly of this construction too – Dormston Moat Farm, Middle Beanhall Farm, Dowles Manor House (a miniature manor with Elizabethan stencilled designs spread over timber studs and plaster fillings alike), recusant Huddington Court with its hiding-holes and hauntings, and Mere Hall, where the Bearcrofts have lived since the 14th century. These have to be sought far off the beaten track. Of the brick villages, Feckenham, where needles and fish-hooks were once manufactured, contains a number of splendid Georgian houses of the sort the ladies of *Cranford* inhabited. As for small towns, Bewdley and Pershore among the plums and meads are unsurpassed. Long may they be preserved from the fate that has overtaken Worcester, which until the end of the last war was a medieval and Georgian city, almost intact. Whereas now – words fail me to describe the havoc that has been made of it. It retains no more quality or tradition than Slough or Stoke-on-Trent.

The grander country gentlemen's seats are not more typical of Worcestershire than of any other county, although Madresfield Court, where the Lygons have lived since 1321, is still moated. It was much aggrandized by the fifth Earl Beauchamp in the 1860s. Ombersley Court, ancient home of the Sandys family, was respectably refaced with drab stucco in the early 19th century, Croome Court (Lord Coventry's) and Hagley Hall (Lord Cobham's) are splendid Palladian edifices which would look just as appropriate in Norfolk. Of the foreign-looking Victorian seats, Château Impney can have few rivals in all England for pretentious French mansard roofs, turrets, dormers, prickly spires and spikes (it was built for a Droitwich tycoon in 1869). And Woodnorton, near Evesham, once the retreat of the exiled Duke of Orléans, in red brick and half-timber, is sprinkled with crowns and fleurs-de-lis. Its famous "golden gates" on the road impressed me greatly as a child. It took me years to acknowledge that they were of a commonplace design, and not wrought in gold at all.

One of the houses I dearly loved as a child was Hanley Court, a fine George II house demolished in the 1930s. It belonged to a very eccentric, elderly friend of my grandmother's who fancied she was the Virgin Mary. The friendship ended on a sad note. She was to have lunched with my grandmother a day or two before Christmas but telephoned to say that her condition made it unwise for her to leave home. Moreover she terrified my grandmother's butler by insinuating that he was St Joseph. As it turned out she was removed to a "home" of another sort which we children considered mysterious and rather romantic. Another loved house was Tickenhill, Bewdley, once a palace of Arthur, Prince of Wales, but in my time lived in by that enchanting collector of bygones, J. F. Parker. I spent many an evening with him listening to music-hall songs played on a phonograph cylinder of the 1890s while being plied with heady cowslip wine.

But my two favourite country houses in architectural terms are Hanbury Hall, of rose-red brick, the epitome of what is called Queen Anne, and Witley Court, a palatial monster in ruins. Witley was burnt down in 1937 during a drunken spree, so we were informed; the remains are sheer romance. The church of Great Witley, attached to them, was spared. It is one of the most rococo buildings north of Bavaria.

The nave is an orgy of stucco grotesques, the ceiling paintings are by the famous Laguerre and the organ case once held the instrument which Handel played upon at Canons.

Exotic Witley Church is no more true Worcestershire than the Catholic church at Droitwich, lavishly encrusted with Byzantine mosaics. But on the whole Worcestershire's parish churches are unpretentious. Few have spires. Most have rather squat, square towers. Many are built on little hills, or mounds. Hanbury and Croome d'Abitot churches (both Georgian) contain the finest collections of monuments in the county. And monuments are the first things I look for on entering a church. They are the best recorders of parochial history and often works of art.

To find Bowater Vernon's effigy to be by Roubiliac and Lord Coventry's tomb by Grinling Gibbons is exciting. To learn from Thomas Woolner's effigy of William Prescott in Bockleton Church that the estimable youth of 21 contracted fever while tending his dying gamekeeper is edifying. To learn from a memorial at Childswickham that Mary Lane died in 1741 aged 133 is curious, and at Cleeve Prior that Sarah Charlett reached the age of 309 is more curious still. Then there is the carving on pillars, pulpits and fonts. In Bretforton Church St Margaret is represented on a capital being swallowed and evacuated by a dragon, her petticoat and feet protruding from its mouth, her decorous head from its other end. The genuine Norman font of Chaddesley Corbett displays carved creatures with bared teeth and plaited tails. The bogus Norman font in Holt Church displays sacred images of a questionable character sculptured by Mrs Sales, wife of a Victorian rector. As the *Building News* of 1858 said, "We refuse to criticize them as they are the work of a lady."

County loyalty may be sentimental. But it is harmless. The truth is that people love most the places where they were reared as children, unless they come from unhappy homes. Even so I have known friends whose parents were cruel to them, but who shed tears of nostalgia when speaking of the homes where they spent years of thraldom. I am aware that my deep-seated love of Ribbesford on the west bank of the Severn is irrational, and probably meaningless to others. But to me it remains such a sacred place that I cannot bring myself to return to it. I know it has been spoilt. But my memory of it, as once it was, a large nondescript house in a small park – a paradise of seclusion, tranquillity and trees – is indestructible.

And when I wish to tap that memory all I have to do is to evoke smells. Smells of the muddy river after rain, of hops and cider apples, of walnuts, blackberries, Michaelmas daisies and rotting sycamore leaves; smells of hot bread, silver polish, croquet balls, even the acrid stink of acetylene gas. Now I come to enumerate them, they are not vernal but autumn smells. Worcestershire is, on account of its fruit and harvests, pre-eminently an autumnal county. And that is how I think of it.

EAST ANGLIA

JACQUETTA HAWKES'
Cambridgeshire

Photographs by John Farnham

The west front of Ely Cathedral, founded in the 7th century, which dominates the surrounding countryside.

Few people, I think, would name Cambridgeshire as their favourite county. I remember when, as a child, I first saw mountains with their swift rivers and dashing streams I was tremendously excited and felt this was how the country ought to be. I had a perverse sense of homecoming: that this was where I belonged.

And yet . . . and yet everyone must keep a particular love for the place where he was born, for the surroundings of childhood. One knows them with an intimacy of detail never to be equalled in later life. This feeling I have for Cambridgeshire, memories spreading in widening rings from our house in Grange Road on the outermost limits of Cambridge. There were the meadows clumped with moon-daisies over our garden fence, then the glories of the college "Backs", cowslips at Madingley, bluebells at Hardwick, and finally, with the mastery of the bicycle, all those villages within a dozen miles of the town. (This must be the point to declare that for me Cambridgeshire remains the narrow county I knew of old: I am aghast when in up-to-date guides I see Huntingdon and Peterborough listed as Cambridgeshire towns. What blasphemous absurdity!)

I showed sense and sensibility in developing at a tender age a fondness for Gothic architecture in a village setting, for my county, outside its university rather poor in great houses or fine urban buildings, keeps much of its charm and interest in modest villages with their dominating but equally unpretentious churches. Although there are regional differences, the characteristic old cottages do not make a show of their timber framing but are faced with daub, nearly always painted white and snug below deep thatching.

Good stone for the churches might have been brought from the Jurassic rocks in neighbouring Northamptonshire, while where chalk was near the surface its flints were taken for building of all kinds, though seldom for the ornamental knapped work so much to be admired in East Anglia. Another building stuff used for cottages and for the interior of churches and colleges is that hard and ancient variety of chalk known as clunch. I was proud of our Cambridgeshire clunch: it sounded solid – and so it is when sheltered from wet weather.

It was, I suppose, the quality of the names that made me associate clunch with the even older, more brutal-sounding gault, a stiff, bluish clay plentiful beside the Cam. For me the chief product of the gault has always been unpleasing – though many would disagree with me. From late medieval times, and most freely from the 18th century, this pure clay was made into the pallid bricks of which so much of the city of Cambridge is built. Inevitably it penetrated the villages as well, and I regard any buildings in this harsh, unyielding material as unwelcome intruders on the native village scene.

Beginning my exploration of the countryside as a young bicycle rider made me very conscious of its structure, so much do contours affect pedalling. Like Britain for Julius Caesar, Cambridgeshire for the geologist can be divided into three parts: the chalk uplands, once known as Whitelands, to the south-east; the low, rolling clay and greensand country to the south-west; and to the north that unique part of Cambridgeshire, the Fenlands, stretching their vast flats as far as Lincoln.

Cambridge was formerly on the very edge of the fens, and the townscape itself is all but flat, save for the mild slope up from the river to the pudding-shaped motte of Castle Hill and the adjoining still milder slopes of Mount Pleasant. No wonder that we all had bicycles and that few university people were burdened with motor cars. Indeed motor traffic was thin enough then for the rural roads I frequented to be almost free of it. Instinctively I loathed cars as a threat to much that I loved and made a practice of scowling at any that passed me by.

Our Cambridgeshire hills would hardly be noticed by Britons from the highland zone such as Welshmen or Yorkshiremen. Yet to us they were considerable. Of the two nearest Cambridge one, on what is now the A45, though imperceptible to the motorist, was an important test of nerve: no one was an approved cyclist who had not flown down it with hands off the handlebars. The other hill is of far greater note, indeed one of the best-known features of the county – that spur of the chalk called the Gog Magog Hills that rises to the dizzying height of some 200 feet a few miles to the south-east of the town.

It seemed quite a stiff pull up to "the Gogs" but when you reached the top, threw your mount into the hedge and set off along the Roman road, you were in delightfully different country. There were chalk-loving flowers such as harebells, and the fields were pale and scattered with flints, offering nesting places for the peewits which tumbled above them with their ecstatic cries. Even the light seemed paler, more rarefied, than in the familiar valley of the Cam.

There was history as well as natural history to be enjoyed up there. The high point of the Gogs is crowned by the ramparts of Wandlebury, one of the few prehistoric earthworks in the county. Yet the chief attraction must always be the green track itself, the continuation of the Roman road known as the Via Devana that cuts through Cambridgeshire from the Huntingdon road. Here, on climbing the chalk, it breaks free to display a well-preserved agger which can be followed for many miles. Not far from Horseheath it crosses the more ancient thoroughfare of the Icknield Way and heads on towards Colchester.

Some miles beyond this significant crossroads the Icknield Way, traversing southern Cambridgeshire between Royston and Newmarket, leads you first to the Fleam Dyke and then the Devil's Dyke. These two massive embankments seem to have been raised by the Saxons in the sixth century as barriers against the briefly triumphant Britons. The Fleam Dyke was a blissful place for walking, noted for butterflies and flowers and above all as one of the rare haunts of the downy, purple Pasque flower. Having walked the crest thinking of Britons and Saxons, I loved to lie in the deep fold of the ditch where the silence and solitude were profound.

These uplands were the part of the county I liked best. Balsham, where the Fleam Dyke ends, has a fine church and the neighbouring hamlets of Great and Little Abington and Hildersham always delighted me. The appeal of Balsham increased when I began to take an interest in monumental brasses. There are two beauties there, while those up at Westley Waterless of Sir John de Creke and his wife are as elegant examples from the 14th century as any in the whole country. A friend and I used to set out with rolls of lining paper across the handlebars and blocks of cobbler's heel ball in our pockets intent on brass rubbing. In those days you merely went to the

The market square in Cambridge.

vicarage to ask permission — and we soon began to classify vicars into the disagreeable, the interested and those who invited small girls in to tea.

We did not dream of a future when swarms of rubbers would have to be denied access to original brasses, yet there was already a hint of it. As far as I know the famous early brass at Trumpington was unique in being protected by a sheet of glass and a charge of 10 shillings to make a rubbing. It was an outrage, yet added to the pride of possession when the money had been saved and the rubbing made.

The valley of the Cam above Cambridge and the mild country to the south-west were easy bicycling, but familiar and unexciting. The many villages, starting with Trumpington and Grantchester and widening out to the Shelfords, Harston, Haslingfield, Barton and Coton, were already beginning to be colonized by university people even while motor cars were rare.

All these are names celebrated or denigrated in Rupert Brooke's "Grantchester",

BELOW: Gibbs building, King's College, Cambridge, and the west front of King's College Chapel. BOTTOM: The Roman road at Wandlebury.

and to this poet and his verses is partly due the special renown and affection that that village possesses in Cambridge hearts and minds. But only partly, for it is a delectable place in itself attended by spirits – Chaucer, Byron, Tennyson, as well as Brooke. It was good to walk there by the footpath through Grantchester meadows, sharing it with dons deep in talk or meditation; but better to go by punt, tie up at the Orchard Tea Garden and stuff cakes which, despite discomfort and wasps, tasted better under the apple trees. Then there was the bathing in Byron's Pool where, a highly selective memory would have me believe, I always splashed and swam in the green shade of a canopy of young leaves.

The greater and most distinctive part of Cambridgeshire is the Fenland. The area falling within Cambridgeshire has, of course, been much enlarged by the inclusion of Huntingdonshire, but the truth is that in my bicycling days these vast, lonely stretches of flat ground, the black soil of the wide, treeless fields cut by drainage ditches and straight artificial waterways, were too much for me.

Special expeditions were made to admire the marvellous angel roof in St Wendreda's Church in the little railway town of March, and to Wisbech, farther down the Nene, where the charming houses of the North and South Brinks show the influence of the Dutchmen who came to drain the fens. Outstanding among them was Cornelius Vermuyden who had the backing of Charles I for his great work of cutting the Old and New Bedford Rivers, diverting the Ouse and running it direct to the Denver sluice. This was the first fully successful drainage since the efficient Romans had driven Car Dyke from near Cambridge round the western edge of the fens to Lincoln. It was vainly resisted by the wild marshmen, the "stilt-walkers", who knew it would rob them of their fishing and fowling. Wisbech is still a port in a small way, and now has another link with Holland in the bulb-growing that has brought sheets of colour to a once sombre countryside.

This northern extremity of the county always seemed strange and infinitely far away, but Ely was one of the wonders of my world, while I had some favourite haunts among the villages fringing the Fenland on its Cambridge front. A strenuous round could be begun by pounding along the Via Devana and turning off just before the then Huntingdon boundary for Fen Drayton, where there were not only Dutch gables to be seen but an inscription in that language on a cottage dating from 1713. Then on to Over, a real fen village on the banks of the Ouse with boating and fishing to be had. At Over I once saw the villagers carrying their Sunday dinners to be cooked in the baker's oven, a big domed one equipped with those long-handled wooden shovels for lifting the loaves. Eastward again to Cottenham, long associated with the Pepys family, but for me rather with the family of my nanny who grew fruit for the Chivers jam factory at Histon on the way back to Cambridge. I recall gorging strawberries there, but even more vividly remember the myriads of summer butterflies which rose and fell in clouds along the hedgerows.

Yet the villages I liked best of all were those bordering the Fenland to the east: Bottisham, the two Swaffhams, then on to Burwell. To reach them you set out along the Newmarket road, passing first the site of the famous Stourbridge Fair and next the perfect little Norman church known as the Lepers' Chapel. While all these villages and their churches are well worth seeing, I was always most enchanted by

Swaffham Prior for the preposterous spectacle of two substantial churches, St Mary's and St Cyriac's, side by side in one churchyard. The lofty Perpendicular church at Burwell does not fall far short of those built by East Anglian woolmen. Burwell is one of the largest villages in the county with good domestic building and appropriately fenny industries such as barge-building and turf cutting.

I liked Burwell and rubbed both sides of its palimpsest brass, but for me its greatest virtue was that it was on the approaches to Wicken Fen, which lies between it and Soham. Soham once adjoined a wide mere which has now vanished, but in the 700 and more acres of Wicken generations of scientist-conservationists have fought to maintain a remnant of true fen with all its abounding natural life – and succeeded. Indeed, I believe its wildlife is now even more various than it was in the days when I found it a world apart, a watery world of enchantment. My special desire always was to see a swallowtail butterfly flash past, but it was rarely satisfied. The once derelict windmill has been recommissioned and now helps to maintain the water in lodes and pools. Though its old function is thus reversed, it still represents many hundreds of mills that faced the Fenland winds before steam pumps.

Wicken is not far from Ely, but it was not by this route that you went to the noblest building in the county, but directly by Akeman Street running almost due north from Cambridge. The presence of the Romans hereabouts is further commemorated by the name of Chesterton and a stretch of the Car Dyke, while at Wilburton are Dutch gables and the Bridge Inn, at 8 feet above sea level claimed to be the lowest-sited pub in England.

We used to say that the road did not rise 1 foot between Cambridge and Ely, and it was true that all the way the attention was held by the great cathedral on its low hill as it grew from what might have been a white sail on the horizon into a glorious harmony of Norman, Early English and Decorated architecture. Before their drainage the marshy fens were broken here and there by little islands of glacial clays and on many of them monks were to settle. They seemed safe from the world, but most of their holy refuges were destroyed by the Danes – some for ever. Among those restored to flourish through the Middle Ages Ely, founded in the 7th century by the Lady Etheldreda, was always supreme. From the days when Hereward and Abbot Thurston (himself a fenman) strove to defend the abbey and the Anglo-Saxon cause against King William, gifted builders added to their church. Perhaps the greatest of them was Alan of Walsingham, Sacrist in 1322 when the central Norman tower crashed down. Showing "the most complete and wonderful mental skill" he filled the gaping hole with a stone octagon, crowning it with the lovely bell tower, or lantern, built of timbers so huge "that they had to be sought for far and wide". Many judges would, I believe, put the lantern as second only to King's College Chapel as the most beautiful and original of the medieval buildings of Cambridgeshire.

My rides around Cambridge created for me a personal realm, every feature of which was known, named and significant and where 10 miles was a very long way. I hope to return some day and explore it again, if not on a bicycle then at least in the leisurely style it still merits and will repay.

MICHAEL WATKINS'

Essex

Photographs by Phil Rudge

It is a melancholy fact that whenever I find myself in Chelmsford I long to be in Kathmandu. I cannot put hand on heart, swearing that the county town of Essex fills me with a sense of beatitude. The Romans were of another mind, naming the place Caesaromagus, elevating it as the only British town with imperial prefix; and, in so doing, confirming my opinion that they were barbarians. Brave Queen Boudicca would have had my support in her campaigns to send them packing.

You should not expect passivity of a lover; and I do love Essex quite fiercely, and will defend her if I can. They say, who know no better, that she is wedded to London, inhaling fumes from the great metropolis, her arteries clogged by urban traffic. It is partly true and useless to deny. As, over the centuries, London has over-indulged, gorging on industrialization, shipping and mercantile prosperity, so it has put on weight, spreading its contours into Romford, Purfleet, Grays, Tilbury, Stanford-le-Hope, Canvey. There is even an argument for considering Southend-on-Sea a London suburb. Yet I can lead you into an Essex wilderness which is one of the last remote corners of England, a bare 50 miles from Piccadilly Circus.

Consider these: Brightlingsea, Mersea Island, Heybridge Basin, Northey Island, Osea Island. Belonging to the Blackwater estuary, these are manacled to the past, home of a superstitious people, God-fearing — but fearing also the dark one of their bad dreams. Some have turned their backs on the world; others merely shrug, accepting that times have advanced while they stand still, stranded on the isthmus of their own independence. A few cling to this past, reassured by the village they once inhabited. They have obliterated the present, remembering 50 years ago better and more clearly than last week.

You could say perhaps that they are an uncritical breed, that they have little and do not need much more. Historically, they were vulnerable, exposed to invaders, some who came to pillage, others who settled. A 10th-century epic poem, *The Battle of Maldon*, records the heroic stand in AD 991 by Byrhtnoth's Anglo-Danish defenders against Viking warriors camped on Northey Island. This same terrain is scoured by winds unbroken by any land mass all the way from Siberia. It is the wind that makes the countrymen mutter; they talk with their mouths shut because they do not want to let the east wind in. But they work a steady stroke, unconcerned with metaphysics and by clever modern men. Occasionally newcomers who settle among them say: "They could kill you with silence."

There are other aspects to their several natures. They are not innovators, nor do they question the order of things. Spanish peasants of Old Castile have a legend: "We are born, we fight and we die." It is a philosophy well suited to men of the Essex marshes. When called to arms, they went: to Agincourt, as archers and pikemen, to Waterloo to hold the thin red line, to Passchendaele, Alamein, the Injim. They have shed their youth and their blood in foreign fields. And no doubt they swore as they went down, disbelieving at the last gasp that anyone could better a man from Brightlingsea.

These marshes are forgotten, secret — sinister, too, some say. The sea ebbs and flows into creeks, gouging out inlets where in summer the common tern flies upriver on fishing trips. At high tide water courses on to the flats where avocets feed. If you are patient you will hear skylarks and spot a hovering kestrel. You will hear the cronk and gabble of wild geese. Over the seasons sea water has smothered the land, poisoning trees with its taste of salt; at low tide old gate posts rise like dismembered limbs from pools of mud. They have a skeletal look. The land is drowned, derelict, to the benefit of wildlife, waders and wildfowl, curlews, duck, sea-swallows and herons. There is loneliness, a fractious wind, a calloused touch to everything under the massive sky. The colours are of marsh reed tarnished gold, mute greens and misty blues; no magentas or vermilions scream into the solitudes.

Men live with one foot on the land, the other in tidal saltings; they live by the plough and by the tiller. "Native" oysters have always been partial to estuaries and creeks flowing over cold London clay. In Colchester oyster feasts and ceremonies for mayor and corporation go back at least to 1667; but the Romans were gobbling oysters at Colchester long before. It was their main reason for making Colchester "Britain's Oldest Recorded Town" — such is the claim of Colin Brookes, oyster-man and historian of Heybridge Basin. It was only after Roman discomfiture in Colchester during Boudicca's revolt of AD 61 that they decided London would make a safer administrative capital; although it is still tempting to think of the A12 dual-carriageway as leading out of Colchester to London rather than vice-versa. Neither lose sight of the truth that when Essex was a Saxon kingdom, London was its capital. Partisans still consider London a minor satellite of Essex.

Aboard his dredger, *Karenda*, Colin Brookes is fearful of the oyster's future: "It's a dying industry," is his lament. "Once there were nine pubs, now we're down to two, the Old Ship and the Jolly Sailor . . . but there's still about seven gun punts between here and Maldon," he announces proudly. The village may be changing hands — from pirate, smuggler, Elizabethan seaman, Napoleonic privateer, poacher and deckhand, to people with thinner, etiolated blood from city bank and insurance house — but ancient sports survive.

There is plenty of hard work getting a punt across the tide, especially if you have had to sprint half-way down the other shore before crossing over to an island hide. Some guns have 2-inch bore and fire 1½lb of shot as big as pills. The gunner waits, face down, camouflaged in a reed-bank, until he has a target, then he pulls the lanyard. The thing goes off like a howitzer, there is smoke like Guy Fawkes night, the punt shoots back in the water, and birds are laid out all about.

On Christmas Eve, 1920, Dr John Henry Salter of Tolleshunt D'Arcy went down to these marshes at 4 am, up to his knees in water "with", according to his diary, "an east wind blowing strong and rain in torrents". He then fell into deep water "shooting under the worst circumstances of weather from 5 to 10 am, a walk of the beastliest description for 8 miles and then 50 miles of patient-seeing afterwards . . . a good wholesome day for a young man of 80". During his lifetime he owned 2,692 dogs; between 1865 and 1925 he shot 62,504 head of game and wildfowl. He won 1,400 prizes for fruit, flowers and vegetables. He brought more than 10,000 Essex babies into the world.

They never really die, these marshmen; if you are sick in Tolleshunt D'Arcy today, the GP gives you a prescription which you take to Mrs Bore at the village shop. The prescription is handled at Tollesbury and returned to Mrs Bore in a "Salter bag".

There is a certain Essex quality which is imperishable, too: stubbornness is that quality, downright cussedness that refuses to be brought into line. But there is no common purpose, no uniformity in this obstinacy; it is simply a series of unconnected statements of implacable self-confidence. One is aware of it in patrician Frinton and equally aware in proletarian Southend-on-Sea.

Frinton is an anachronism. It is a seaside resort preserved in aspic, petrified since the early 1900s when nannies wore starched white aprons and gallants paraded in striped blazers. Sartorial habits have changed; so, too — though only marginally — the mock-baronial architecture; otherwise Frinton remains inviolate. Mafeking may have been relieved, but the news has not quite got through to Frinton. Once you have filtered through passport control at the town's periphery you enter the Immaculate Zone where certain commandments ordain one's lifestyle. To isolate its inhabitants from the Sodom and Gomorrah temptations of the outside world, pubs, fish and chip shops, cinemas and buses have no place in Frinton. Nor is there any overt advertising. I rather doubt whether dying is permitted; senior citizens transfer from Frinton-on-Sea to a kindred Valhalla on a slightly more celestial plane.

Southend-on-Sea would give a good belly-laugh at such refinement, for Southend has never made any pretence to ladylike behaviour. She is loud, she is obvious, she hasn't an aitch to her name, and she has a heart of gold. She has the longest pier in the world, wears kiss-me-quick paper hats, eats candy floss, jellied eels, stewed eels, pie and mash. She plays bingo and rides the Big Dipper; she sings "Knees Up Mother Brown" and gets tiddly on Guinness. She would live for a cuddle in the back of a charabanc, and die for a friend.

Parts of Southend have the look of downtown Miami in this year of grace. There are areas where she has been given a lick of paint and the kiss of death. Basically, she remains unscathed: her jewellery is a thousand flashing neon lights, her corsage a bouquet of palm trees, each a trifle stunted, like desiccated shaving brushes. Frinton and Southend have nothing in common except an invincible zest for survival.

Essex can be downright contrary, but not in the least neurotic; there are few schizoid bumps, few depressions in her topographical makeup. There are no

RIGHT: Low tide at Heybridge Basin, popular yachting and caravaning centre on the north side of the Blackwater river.
BELOW: Southend-on-Sea, the county good-time-girl, shows off some of her many seaside wares.

ABOVE: Fishing the Thames at Tilbury, London's major port for container ships, situated across the estuary from Gravesend. LEFT: Some 16 miles inland in Dunmow, Joe Smith perpetuates a skill that has been in his family for three generations.

mountains or ravines, the countryside undulates undramatically, unfussily. The marshes and estuaries are full of surprises, packed with guile, blasphemous and gritty; dark deeds and heroism are part of the emotional tenor. The marshlands are not favoured for neutrality. For peace and gentle hearts you must travel to those final frontiers of urbanization, to where London stops being London, sensibly becoming Shellow Bowells instead. Which leads to Chignall Smealy, Good Easter (rhymes with Chester), the Rodings (rhyming with "soothings"), and eventually to Saffron Walden, the prettiest dwelling-place in Essex. Just a small town, you should understand, whose inhabitants go about their business, breathing in and breathing out, walking past some of the best preserved pargeting in England – on the walls of the Old Sun Inn, nowadays an antique shop.

Nearby stands Audley End, the vast Jacobean palace that supplanted Walden Abbey as a dominant influence on the life of the town. It is a handsome house, made handsomer by its mill-race and riparian setting, which Capability Brown and Adam had a hand at landscaping. Vanbrugh, too, left his signature on Audley End. With three such illustrious names, who could deny this masterpiece of classical elegance?

Thaxted, too, is a joy. Thaxted, originally "a place where thatch comes from", is high among the most popular British symbols of not only thatching, but the whole picturesque mood of vernacular building. Stand at the foot of cobbled Stony Lane, looking up towards the church: fine oversailing houses of wattle-and-daub and exposed timbering. It was here that Conrad Noel was appointed to the living by Lady Warwick in 1910, thus beginning one of the most turbulent and controversial incumbencies of the century.

The phrase "Dedham Vale" has become synonymous with "Constable's country", itself already used in John Constable's hearing as he boarded the London-bound coach in 1832. Dedham itself, clustered in the broad Stour valley, clings to the episcopal skirts of another great church, famed for its flower festivals. As in the Suffolk clothing towns, Dedham's climax of prosperity came in Henry VII's reign; and this prosperity was never really eclipsed. Spearing, the village grocer, is the rural answer to Fortnum & Mason; each house in the high street is a little grander than its neighbour. I am sure the people of Dedham observe the rules of truth and beauty, and never have unkind thoughts or cheat at cards. It is just that it all seems a bit self-conscious, a fraction too good to be true. If Dedham expelled a collective swear-word, I would feel happier. Perfection is an uncomfortable bed-fellow.

It reminds me of the Dunmow Flitch Trial not many miles away: a flitch of bacon is awarded to the couple who, under cross-examination, best convince the judge and jury that not for one split second in 12 months have they regretted their marriage vows. They would never convince me.

Any more than I am convinced that East Anglia's outstanding visual attribute is the sky. You can see the *whole* sky, it is said. To be honest, I am not at all sure I want to see the whole sky. I like hills, towering forests, sprawling valleys. What strikes me about this landscape is the mud. There is such a lot of mud. It has different colours and hues, a variety of texture; it is heavy, adhesive, clinging to your boots, binding you to the soil. That is what I like when I go walking over Essex mud — the very feeling that I am bound to the soil.

Essex's majestic, cloud-banked sky photographed near Frinton.

NICHOLAS HERBERT'S
Huntingdonshire

Photographs by David Gallant

In the early years of this century – I think it was 1903 – my grandmother watched a statue of Oliver Cromwell being unveiled in the market square of St Ives. She had to observe the ceremony from behind the lace curtains at an upper window of the Golden Lion because her companion was her mother-in-law, who was married to the rector of a royalist village. The statue had been offered to Huntingdon, Cromwell's birthplace 5 miles away along the Great Ouse, but Huntingdon was a Cavalier town and rejected the monument.

Fifty years later, when plans were being made to celebrate the Queen's Coronation in the twin villages of Hemingford Abbots and Hemingford Grey, my father observed a reluctance on the part of the representatives from one village to attend meetings in the other. Abbots, nearer to Huntingdon, was royalist; Grey, now almost contiguous with St Ives, was Roundhead.

Too much can be made of this; the county is no longer rent by civil strife. I retell the stories because they epitomize one of the country's most enduring traits – a deep-rooted sense of history. The county is aware that it produced something of crucial significance to our democracy three centuries ago and a man who has been called "the most typical Englishman of all time". It is a matter of subconscious pride and if there is tension, most of the time it is creative.

There is plenty of history to go on. At Hemingford Grey, Lucy Boston, whose children's books are so popular, lives in what is believed to be the oldest inhabited private house in the land. It is an extraordinary experience to sit under the stone Norman arches in the sitting room upstairs and sense the presence of so many previous generations. Hemingford Abbots celebrated its millennium 10 years ago. Characteristically the high spot was a pageant in which villagers re-enacted events of the past 1,000 years.

Equally, back in 1953, the Coronation was marked by a pageant. Episodes from the country's history were enacted in the grounds of Hinchingbrooke House, home successively of the Cromwells, one of whom had the King beheaded, and the Earls of Sandwich, one of whom brought the next King back in his flagship from Holland. It is typical of Huntingdonshire that the house should be rescued from decay and made

RIGHT: The author's house, the old rectory of St Margaret's Church, Hemingford Abbots. ABOVE: Sunset over water meadows of the Ouse river near Hemingford Abbots.

the focal point of a comprehensive school which is the successor to the school where both Cromwell and Samuel Pepys were educated.

Horace Walpole once described Hinchingbrooke as "old, spacious, irregular, yet not vast or forlorn". It has been much altered, rebuilt and demolished but now presents a mellow stone front to the world. Standing on a rise just west of Huntingdon, it overlooks both Pepys's cottage and the county's greatest asset, the Great Ouse, meandering on its way from Buckinghamshire and Bedfordshire to The Wash.

For me the river is crucial. Strong, slow, relaxed and mellow, it offers a feeling of peace and continuity which I have not experienced anywhere else. Yet it can also be troublesome and burst its banks. In 1947 the rector had to deliver coal down the High Street of Hemingford Abbots in a punt. The river authority has imposed its will now and domestic flooding is not the menace it was, but the water meadows across to Houghton flood every winter and, if the skaters are lucky, freeze as well.

When the sun is setting behind the mist on a winter's afternoon, there is a mystical quality about these meadows which more than makes up for the lack of dramatic scenery. And in the summer, when the Queen Anne's Lace is as high as an elephant's eye and a limpid heat haze floats on the fields, the river bank can still be peace personified. The motor cruiser is a threat but there are still places where it does not obtrude, and the punt, though an endangered species, still survives. The Hemingfords still combine to run the only village regatta in the country on the stretch below Battock's Island. When the Vicar's Sculls are won, church bells ring out, a sound which seems in perfect harmony with the scenery.

Daniel Defoe recognized it long ago. "Here are the most beautiful meadows on the banks of the River Ouse, that I think are to be seen in any part of England," he wrote. "And to see them in the summer season, cover'd with such innumerable stocks of cattle and sheep, is one of the most agreeable sights of its kind in the world." The stocks may not be as numerous as they were in his day, but there are still sheep on the meadow opposite my garden. Elm disease has wrought some havoc, but the river remains embellished by willows and chestnuts and all the noble trees which contribute so much to a typical English scene.

I cannot fully agree with A. C. Benson, who wrote of Hemingford Grey that "it seems an enchanted place, where there can be no care or sorrow, nothing hard, or unlovely, or unclean, but a sort of fairyland, where men seem to be living the true and beautiful life of the soul", but with allowances for poetic hyperbole I know what he meant.

Benson also noticed that, as he put it, "the place was alive with the calling of old voices". Some of these, as I have already mentioned, were eminent; other less so. In the Coronation pageant my mother produced the episode celebrating the "Beautiful Miss Gunnings", notables of a sort because they married two Dukes and an Earl between the two of them, but hardly on the lips of every schoolchild. They grew up in Hemingford Grey in the manor house where Mrs Boston now lives. Near by the Victorian artist W. Dendy Sadler lived, behind the boathouse which used to figure in one of those prints that decorated railway carriages in the 1940s but has now disappeared.

Bust of Potto Brown, wealthy miller and philanthropist, in Houghton village.

Sadler was a pen-and-ink man who worked best indoors, but this is watercolour territory *par excellence*, which reminds one of the seven Fraser brothers. They were an eccentric lot, who paid their debts with paintings that are now quite well thought of, and who used to hold meetings of the White Cockade Jacobite Club in the local pubs at the end of the last century. The best of them, artistically, was Garden Fraser, who signed his pictures W. F. Garden to distinguish himself from his siblings, and there are a good many of his works in the villages where he worked because, to the end of his life in 1921, he was always hard up.

Charles James Fox was married at Houghton, but our family walks across the water meadows had as their destination the statue of Potto Brown which stands in the centre of that most attractive village. He is hardly in Fox's class, and I do not think he would have approved of the Misses Gunning, because he was a strict Nonconformist. His statue is only a bust, but there he sits looking benignly out over the community where, according to the legend on his plinth, he "spent his life devoting himself to the best interests of those around him". Not a bad epitaph.

Potto was also the tenant at one time of Houghton Mill, a spectacular 17th-century water mill where as many as nine stones ground flour, raising so much dust that a sophisticated air-conditioning system had to be installed. The Mill was a Youth Hostel, but the National Trust have now opened it to the public and ambitious plans are afoot to get the machinery going again. The great water wheels, which old photographs show to have clung to each side of the Mill giving the impression of a lumbering paddle steamer, have gone, but inside most of the machinery survives.

If Potto Brown was obscure, his existence is at least certain. The same cannot be said for St Ivo, who gave his name to St Ives. He was apparently a Persian bishop who travelled through from Cornwall in about the year 600 converting and baptizing the heathen. He is said to have died at St Ives but the circumstances in which his alleged bones were dug up and taken to Ramsey Abbey give little grounds for confidence. The town was then known as Slepe, a name which in my youth was still perpetuated by the telephone exchange.

The town's most notable feature, however, is dedicated to St Leger, who underwent unspeakable tortures in France in the seventh century. He was thus less obscure than St Ivo, but why the little chapel on St Ives' handsome bridge should be dedicated to him is not clear. The chapel, though similar to others at Rotherham and Wakefield – the only three bridge chapels in England – appears to be unique in that it has living quarters built in. It is now empty, there being no need to collect tolls, but it can be visited on application. It used to have an upper storey of wood, but this has now been demolished, and the bridge itself has been much relieved in recent years by the construction of a bypass.

It is necessary to state emphatically, because there is much misunderstanding on the point, that St Ives, Huntingdonshire, is the scene of the famous trick riddle about the man with seven wives. Do not ask me to prove it, but we in Huntingdonshire know that it is so – not that polygamy is, or so far as I know ever was, rife.

St Ives, once a centre for the production of woad, was the site of one of the great medieval fairs because of its accessibility, via King's Lynn and the river, to the Continent. That is a reminder of the importance of waterways in this low-lying land on the edge of the Fens. The story of how the Fens were drained, resulting in the land subsiding at the rate of "the height of a man in the life of a man", belongs elsewhere. But at Earith in the north-eastern tip of Huntingdonshire is the start of the Hundred Foot River, cut by the Dutchman Cornelius Vermuyden in 1630 to carry the water of the Great Ouse more directly to the sea.

The northern part of the county, embracing the ancient settlement of Ramsey, with its ruined abbey, and up to Whittlesey on the edge of Peterborough, is genuine Fen country with a character quite different from the mellower reaches between St

RIGHT: The church of St John Evangelist, Little Gidding, where Nicholas Ferrar's religious community worshipped in the 17th century. FAR RIGHT: The church's unusual "college" seating facing across the nave.

184

Ives and St Neots. There they talk of Fen tigers, descendants of those who originally tried to fight off Vermuyden, and of Fen blows, winds which, passing allegedly without impediment from the Ural Mountains, whisk away the topsoil. But the soil remains among the finest in the world, though it has sunk below the level of the roads which wind their way drunkenly across the landscape. Dorothy Sayers lived in the fruit-growing area north of St Ives, where the orchards and strawberry fields flourish.

In the early 1950s when we had no car these were remote places almost as foreign as Bedford or Northampton, but later, playing cricket round the county, I came to know them as communities which, though enclosed and perhaps even narrow, housed people with the same basic stability and independence of mind that I admire here.

If the waterways had much to do with the early nature of Huntingdonshire, the motorways are with us now. I use the term not in its technical sense because the M11 turns into the A604 (the Roman Via Devana) before it enters Huntingdonshire and the A1, though superior to the M1, is not a recognized motorway.

The A1, passing up west to St Neots and Huntingdon, picks up the line of Ermine Street towards Sawtry, where highwaymen used to be especially active. The road divides off the third sector of the county, the western area, where rolling hills set the little churches up on the skyline and provide the natural basin in which man created Grafham Water. On these gentle hills in pre-Roman times the British tribes made their fortifications against the pirates coming up through the Fens. So the area has always been somewhat separate.

Here is Kimbolton, an attractive little town of lath and plaster and peg tiles and a broad high street. The Castle, now a flourishing public school, was conveniently empty when Henry VIII was looking for a safer house than Buckden Palace for Catherine of Aragon to live in. Not surprisingly she did not take to the place ("dark and damp Kimbolton" she called it) and she died there in 1536.

The present castle was remodelled on the site by Sir John Vanbrugh. It is a fine four-square building set in stately parkland. Defoe said of it "no pains or cost has been spar'd to make the most beautiful situation still more beautiful, and to help nature with art". Inside are some splendid murals by Pellegrini.

Also in this western part of the county is Little Gidding, where Nicholas Ferrar established a unique religious community in the 17th century. Charles I used to visit, but the little church has now been remodelled in 18th-century style with the seats set facing each other across a narrow aisle. Once again a religious community is flourishing there.

Leighton Bromswold near by provided an ancestor of mine, the poet George Herbert, with his first living, but the association is dimmed somewhat by the suggestion that not only did he never live there but probably never even went there! Still he did have Ferrar rebuild and refurnish the church.

Considering that only Rutland is smaller, Huntingdonshire is thus remarkably varied. The motorists may pass through almost without noticing it and the jet pilots from Alconbury and Wyton flash across from east to west in minutes. Huntingdonshire takes them all in its stride, but only those who are prepared to linger longer will know this little county's real merits.

STEVE RACE'S

Lincolnshire

Photographs by Janine Wiedel

The radio interview with Sir John Betjeman was over and I could not resist bringing out my copy of *Summoned by Bells* for the poet's signature. "Where are you from?" inquired Sir John. When I told him, he wrote on the title page "Ah, Lincs! The glorious home county of Steve Race." Then to my further delight, he added an ink drawing. It showed a long line of electricity pylons striding across a stark fenland landscape.

"Glorious" is not perhaps the first word that comes to mind in describing the county of my birth. One might rather say that it was remote, stern, beautiful, rich in history – certainly large. It is, in fact, the second largest county in England – or was, until Lord Redcliffe-Maud's preposterous committee snipped off a chunk of north Lincolnshire in order to create the bogus county of Humberside, an administrative unit to which no one owes the slightest allegiance. I join with every other proud son of Lincolnshire in utterly ignoring the Local Government Act of 1972 and consigning His Lordship's report to a dustbin, preferably in Cleveland or some other equally implausible region.

Large my county certainly is, the distance from Stamford to Barton upon Humber being equal to that from London to Stamford. Only the most determined walker can claim to have tramped the whole splendid Viking Way, which stretches from Oakham (in Rutland, as I still call it) to the Humber Bridge which links, but never unites the arrogant folk of Yorkshire with the proud natives of Lincolnshire.

Proud they are, even standoffish. The plain fact is that isolation is in the very blood and bones of Lincolnshire men and women, bred to the view that the best way to greet a "foreigner" is to heave a stone at him first and ask him his business afterwards. "A proud, conceited, ignorant people," as one 18th-century poet summarized us. Henry VIII was even blunter: "One of the most brute and beastly of the whole realm", said he, referring to my county, admittedly while under the strain of a little difficulty regarding monasteries.

In earlier centuries to penetrate Lincolnshire at all required physical persistence, even a kind of mad courage. Enter from north or south, and if the Humber or the Wash did not get you the bogs would. An approach from the west was not much

The contrasting landscapes possible in a county the size of Lincolnshire.
OPPOSITE ABOVE: The fens north of Boston. OPPOSITE BELOW: The wolds south of Louth.

ABOVE LEFT: Some of the attractions of Skegness. ABOVE RIGHT: A tenant farmer at Friskney. RIGHT: The Maud Foster windmill in Boston, built in 1809.

RIGHT: The ruins of Crowland Abbey, founded in 716. FAR RIGHT: The statue of Herbert Ingram, founder of the *Illustrated London News*, in Boston, with the Church of St Botolph and its "stump" behind.

easier: the river Trent remained unbridged below Newark until 1790. But the rewards for the determined traveller were considerable. They still are.

Who, for example, could resist our rattling, galumphing place names? One could make them into a poem of sorts: Snitterby, Scrivelsby, Scamblesby, Stow, Worlaby, Pyewipe, Cowbit, Scartho, Sloothby-with-Willoughby, Swallowbeck, Torksey, Ashby Puerorum, Slash Hollow and Keal.

Who would not walk with jaunty step from Haxey Tubaries to Burton Coggles? From Wrangle to Aslackby? Do Lincoln boys still cycle, as I so often did, between New York, Waterloo and Jerusalem, all of them hamlets within a bat's flight of Lincoln Castle?

For Aslackby the visitor might inquire in vain. Call it Aizelby, though, and you may conceivably be directed there. Similarly Margaret Thatcher's birthplace of Grantham was a *ham* not an *am*: one should therefore call it "Grant'um" when conversing with a local purist. Skegness is more likely to be referred to as Skeg, Skeggy or even Skegsnest, while your true Yellowbelly still manages to turn Louth into two syllables (Lou-ath).

Yellowbellies – an unlovely nickname. How did we Lincolnshire folk acquire it? Some say that our ancestors had a yellow tinge to the skin caused by eating a bilious local seaweed. Military scholars, more plausibly, point out that the old Lincolnshire Regiment tunic was yellow. For all I know some early resident of Spalding clasped to his chest an armful of yellow tulips. Any derivation is acceptable, except that we were "yellow" in the cowardly sense.

No cowards we. Awkward, perhaps; stubborn, yes. And incomprehensible to outsiders, though Lincolnshire speech is not so much a matter of dialect or accent as of intonation. There are special words, of course: onomatopoeic gems like *slape* (meaning slippery underfoot) and *melch* (humid). Someone petulant and ill-tempered is *mardy*. There are special speech forms, too, as in *while* as a substitute for *until* ("not while Tuesday"). But the Lincolnshire sound is, I maintain, an inflection, a cracking tone of voice, rather high in pitch, such as one surely needs in order to call the cattle home from Drinsey Nook or shout down a furnace at Stamp End. Tennyson understood it, perhaps even spoke it.

Tennyson – one of our sons, of course. Our sparsely populated county encourages introspection, which is why Lincolnshire's sons and daughters contribute notably to the nation's heritage in the sphere of arts and sciences. Archbishop Langton, Lord Burghley, Sir Isaac Newton, Sir John Franklin, John and Charles Wesley, William Byrd, Alfred Lord Tennyson, John Foxe, Jean Ingelow, Matthew Flinders – it is a proud roll call, to which can be added the more recent Dame Sybil Thorndike, Tony Jacklin, Neville Marriner and that lady occupant of 10 Downing Street.

Nor should one forget the Lincolnshire-born Pilgrim Fathers who reached the New World. Some of them, led by John Winthrop, set out from Boston in the south of the county, where they are remembered with understandable pride. Present-day Boston is a typically busy market town, but with a tang of the sea in its air. Ancient tidal waterways snake almost into the centre of town, their chunky vessels tilted on banks of dark mud. That most feminine and elegant of church towers, known so inappropriately as "The Stump", casts a morning shadow across the town's main statue, which is of one Herbert Ingram. He looks worthy and somewhat pleased with himself, as well he might, having been the founder of *The Illustrated London News*.

The visitor who explores Lincolnshire from the south finds himself first in Stamford, once a major staging post on the Great North Road. Sir Walter Scott described High Street and St Martin's Church as "the finest scene between London and Edinburgh". "Much finer than Cambridge!" sang Celia Fiennes in 1697. For most of my lifetime the scene was less than fine. "This is Stamford – stay a while amid its ancient charm" pleaded a sign by the roadside, as traffic clogged the winding streets and yet another multi-ton juggernaut shaved the corner off yet another elegant Georgian building. Now, thanks to the by-pass, one can linger there, and the ancient charm has returned to those honey-coloured streets.

On to Crowland along the county's southern rim, where the streets were once waterways, so that at an intersection the villagers had to fashion a triple stone bridge shaped like the Manx symbol. It is still there, dry as a beached whale, not far from the brooding Crowland Abbey, where a superb Norman sawtooth arch pierces the sky.

I find it impossible to describe the appeal of the Fens, especially to anyone brought up in the soft luxury of the south country. Imagine endless miles of flat, reclaimed seabed, yielding magnificent crops from the dark rich earth. A lapwing wheels away across a frozen dyke towards a grey stone church tower. A forlorn windmill leans against the penetrating North Sea gales, long ago stripped of its sails. A single tree 10 miles away is an "event" in the sky-laden landscape. Does that sound appealing, I wonder? I promise you that it is. Visit the rest of Britain in high summer if you will, but experience our Lincolnshire fens in some crisp winter, when the hoar frost is on the reeds and the fieldfares quiver with their backs to the wind.

As you move north into the county subdivision of Lindsey the farmland notably softens, giving place to the delectable Wolds, those neat, gently folding hills where the great Tennyson mused. No longer is this "the drowned country" in which Daniel Defoe heard "a sigh like the sound of a gun at a great distance". (It turned out to be the boom of the bittern.) This is a kinder landscape, though still earth-gripped. Not far away, in their season, are Brent geese, snow bunting and redshank, while trout, pike, bream and roach police the dykes in cool silence. There are over 60 nature reserves in present-day Lincolnshire. Some of them, like Gibraltar Point near Skegness, can be visited without causing any discomfort to their proper residents, who perch unconcerned on the sea buckthorn or paddle on the meres with no more thought for the tourist than for the seals basking offshore at Outer Knock.

"Skegness", the posters tell us, "is so bracing". And there to prove it is John Hassall's famous painting of a jolly fisherman frisking along the shore. Admittedly, some of our other beach resorts seem to me to have less to recommend them, like Cleethorpes, which is too near to Grimsby, just as Grimsby is altogether too near to Grimsby for my taste. A skilful football team and a lively MP cannot compensate for overdevelopment, any more than Gainsborough's fame as the setting for *The Mill on the Floss* can make up for an industrial preoccupation with linseed oil, flour and malt.

In Lincolnshire there is no urban substitute for the city of my birth, Lincoln itself. "The cathedral looks nobly on approach" wrote the 18th-century compulsive traveller John Byng. Indeed it does, and from every direction, too. Lincoln is – am I prejudiced? – a work of art. Up there on the brow of the escarpment stands the finest Gothic cathedral in Christendom. Inside it are proportion, line, majesty. Outside is the most exquisitely light-responsive stone ever dedicated by a craftsman to his Creator. "How superior to lumbering Grecian St Paul's!" exclaimed Byng to his diary.

When you have been brought up in Lincoln you know the cathedral from every angle. It watches you while you are shopping; it peers at you through the trees; it leans on you as you grind up that last almost vertical stretch of Steep Hill between the medieval antique shops. Big Tom booms each hour at you in deep-throated admonition.

Go inside the cathedral. Find, if you must, the famous Lincoln Imp who squats in stony malevolence high on a column in the Angel Choir. Then explore the Roman remains of the city, the superb art collection in the Usher Art Gallery; visit the shopping area around the 15th-century Stonebow, so wisely turned into a pedestrian precinct. Wander into immemorial churches that were already dozing with age when Parliament met in Lincoln in 1301. I love Lincoln. I admit it. Maybe there *is* piped music in the library and a Chinese takeaway where the Band of Hope used to meet. That's progress, against which Lincoln is no more proof than any other living city.

But my civic pride has squeezed out other notable county sights which deserve mention: the fine Lincoln Red cattle and the vast sugar beet prairies; the 10,000 acres of blazing tulip fields in spring around Spalding. I ought to have mentioned the motor racing at Cadwell Park; the Royal Air Force Lancaster which stands at the entrance gate to Scampton airfield, in commemoration of the Moehne Dam raid in 1943. The pilots of today's Red Arrows see it as they take off from the same runways. A word might have been spared for the treasures of the National Trust's Belton Park, the incomparable church spire at Louth, or Grantham's old coaching inns.

All these are my joy when I return to the county of my birth. But down south in my expatriate home, at night, when thoughts wander amiably just before sleep across remembered scenes, it is the snug villages huddled round their churches that I see in my mind's eye; the long sentinel rows of poplars, the lapwings in the cart ruts, the seagulls mobbing the plough, the well cared-for barns, and – John Betjeman's symbol for Lincolnshire will do very well – that line of electricity pylons striding across the splendid, fertile fens towards an endless sky.

LORD BLAKE'S
Norfolk

Photographs by Trevor Wood

The perpendicular Church of St Peter Mancroft, which stands at one end of Norwich market square.

"Very flat – Norfolk," says a character in Noël Coward's immortal comedy, *Private Lives*. It is perhaps the most famous comment made on this county and it has the advantage of being true. No part of Norfolk rises to more than 350 feet above sea level, most of it is under 150 feet, and it shares with Cambridgeshire the feature of having a few areas that are actually below sea level. Statisticians will note that Norfolk, like the rest of East Anglia, is one of the driest parts of England, with an average rainfall of less than 30 inches. They may also note that as it covers some 2,000 square miles it is also one of the largest of the old counties, surpassed only by Yorkshire, Lincolnshire and Devon. Although Norfolk yields little joy to those who hanker after rocky gorges, mountain peaks, dashing torrents or even rolling downs, its landscape nevertheless has a charm of its own. For though it is flat, it is not so flat as Holland or the Fenland, except insofar as a part of the Fenland is enclosed by its western boundary.

There are gentle undulations which it would be an exaggeration to call valleys, so gradual are the slopes, but they have a great charm for those with eyes to see. There are long perspectives and notable views. From my own house, only a few feet above the Yare, I have a view of a horseshoe bend of the river, one of the southernmost Broads and finally cornfields on the horizon. You have a feeling of space in Norfolk and an awareness of great skies. The dry air not only makes for a general sense of well-being – I always feel more alert there than in the torpid damp of the Thames Valley – but it also lends a peculiar clarity to the scene. The fact that so many English landscape painters came from East Anglia is not accidental. As for Norfolk it has its own particular coterie, the famous "Norwich School" whose leading exponents were John Crome and John Sell Cotman, supported by much other talent. But the Norfolk landscape has no obvious appeal. It is anything but "picturesque" or "pretty". You have to live with it to appreciate its subtleties.

For this and other reasons Norfolk does not greatly attract foreign visitors. The tourists in this quintessentially English county are usually themselves English. American and Continental visitors on a short holiday often confine themselves naturally enough to the usual London, Oxford, Stratford circuit; they do not even go

to Cambridge – which is nice for Cambridge. Those with time for a foray from the heartlands will "do" Devon and Cornwall, or perhaps Wales, or even Scotland via the Lake District. Norfolk is not on the way to anywhere and it has an exaggerated reputation for cold. In fact being two-thirds surrounded by sea it does not in a hard winter get the severe frosts of the Midlands. A fine summer can be as pleasant there as anywhere in England. But it is true that especially in March and April there are times when a grey sky prevails and an east wind blows unobstructed, save by the Ural Mountains, from Siberia. The spring can be later and the winter longer than in most parts of England.

The visitor who is deterred misses much. Norfolk contains the finest assemblage of medieval churches in any county. It contains magnificent country houses, some of them, like Houghton and Holkham, virtual palaces. Its smaller market towns – Wymondham, Aylsham, North Walsham, Swaffham – are gems of their kind. Norwich is a genuine local capital with a cathedral which can rival any in the country, a museum which is arguably the best provincial museum in England, and a church, St Peter Mancroft, which in style and situation is truly magnificent. Norwich can boast much else besides. Not for nothing was it for many centuries the second city in

the realm. It suffered from bombing in the war, probably more than most cities, but less than most from the vandalism of post-war architecture. Not that it went unscathed. What major city did?

The Norfolk landscape is by no means all of a piece. On its western boundary is Wisbech, sometimes described as the capital of the Fens. The land in this corner of the county is very like the rest of the Fens and was indeed drained at the same time. Here the ground really is flat, and there are no architectural features to soften the bleak scene. The black soil is the richest in England, pure peat many yards deep. The land was reclaimed from swamp in the 17th century, and except on a few pieces of higher ground – "islands" – there are no old buildings, only square red-brick

farm-houses "standing like ships out at sea in the miles and miles of dead flat black Fenland", as John Seymour puts it in his *Guide to East Anglia*. Slightly nearer the sea you move from the Fens to the Marshland. This looks very much the same and is equally flat, but the soil is loam and it has been dry since very early times. The flatness here is relieved by some of the finest churches in England standing like fortresses silhouetted against the sky. West Walton, Terrington St Clement and Walpole St Peter are three of the best; there are many others.

If you move from Wisbech across Norfolk to the east coast there are three main routes: south-east through the Brecklands to Thetford and the Waveney valley which divides Suffolk from Norfolk; due east through the centre of the county to Norwich; north-east to King's Lynn, Hunstanton and round the coast to Sheringham and Cromer.

The Brecklands ("breck" means a very large field) are in their way as idiosyncratic to Norfolk as the Fenland, the Marshland and the Broadland. They are not quite like anywhere else. The land is light and sandy and full of flints, but for agriculturalists from earliest times to the Anglo-Saxon period it was easy to cultivate. Thetford was an important town and centre of a prosperous farming community. Norfolk became part of the Danelaw and King Canute made it his capital. What ruined agriculture in the Brecklands was the great medieval sheep boom: over-grazing reduced the land to a desert. John Evelyn compared it to Libya. By the early 1920s those landlords and farmers who had survived were happy to sell to the Forestry Commission which has planted thousands of acres of pine – Thetford Forest is now the second largest forest in England. It is monotonous scenically but it has brought life to a dead land. Little of the primeval Brecklands survives. One small area is the 30 or 40 acres surrounding "Grimes Graves" – an extraordinary congerie of flint mines dating from neolithic times.

The traveller who goes north-east from Wisbech encounters a very different scene. King's Lynn itself is a town well worth visiting. Anyone proceeding north from there ought to find time to see three notable houses – Sandringham, built by Edward VII and remarkably hideous; Houghton Hall, a vast Palladian mansion, seat of the Marquis of Cholmondeley, a descendant of Sir Robert Walpole who built it in the

LEFT: Cley-next-the-Sea on the Glaven estuary was a busy port before the 17th-century land reclamation.
BELOW LEFT: "Grimes Graves" neolithic flint mines in the Brecklands. BELOW RIGHT: The Jacobean Blickling Hall belongs to the National Trust.

The beach and pier at Cromer.

1730s; and Holkham Hall, seat of the Coke family and another Palladian palace. The Cokes, who became Earls of Leicester, descend from the great 17th-century lawyer Edward Coke. The first Earl of Leicester built Holkham and his great-nephew was the famous "Coke of Norfolk" to whom the older history books attribute an exaggerated degree of agricultural innovation. Another Norfolk grandee, "Turnip Townshend" whose forebears built Raynham, a magnificent 17th-century house near Swaffham, probably has a better claim.

Coke, Townshend, Walpole – we have still not mentioned the greatest Norfolk "worthy" of all: Horatio Nelson, born at Burnham Thorpe on the north Norfolk coast and son of the rector. The rectory, alas, has been pulled down. Relatively few objects survive in Norfolk to commemorate its greatest man, although the Norwich Guildhall has a splendid sword belonging to a captured Spanish admiral which Nelson presented to the city. But he survives in folk memory, and not only in Norfolk – one of the most extraordinary and fascinating naval commanders in the whole of history.

The coast of the Wash from Lynn to Hunstanton is rather desolate. It becomes far more attractive when one turns the corner eastwards. From there to beyond Cley the great features are the harbours and the salt marshes which divide land from sea, miles and miles of them. It is, as Mr Seymour puts it, "the very paradise of bird lovers, of fishermen, of small boat lovers and lovers of wild places. Nowhere else in England is there a piece of coast remotely like it, and it has a broken, sandy windswept beauty quite unsurpassed." Scolt Head and Blakeney Point are two notable nature reserves owned by the National Trust on this section of the coast. After Cley you come to a more orthodox coast of cliffs and beaches. I have never much liked Sheringham and

Cromer, though the latter has a superb church. I associate them with childhood Easter holidays when the Siberian blast was at its worst. This corner of Norfolk is higher than the rest, heavily wooded and rather untypical. Cromer crabs are delicious, especially with samphire, a sort of primitive asparagus which grows on the salt marshes.

Some of the churches south of Cromer are magnificent, Worstead perhaps the greatest of them all; and there are two splendid country houses, Felbrigg, bequeathed to the National Trust by the late Wyndham Ketton-Cremer, that most percipient of Norfolk historians, and Blickling, a red-brick Jacobean masterpiece also left to the National Trust by Philip Kerr, 11th Marquis of Lothian.

We are now in east Norfolk. The other possible route from Wisbech is via Swaffham and East Dereham across the centre. It is the least exciting. There is much of architectural interest but the countryside might be anywhere – prosperous farming land, as most of Norfolk is and usually has been, but otherwise rather dull. As I was born in a village on the Yare, educated at Norwich School and am married to someone from the same area, I must declare an interest. West Norfolk may be more fashionable. North Norfolk with its contingent of holiday cottage occupants from Cambridge may be more intellectual. But east Norfolk with its Broads – that unique Norfolk feature – is my favourite region.

For the Broads lying between the three rivers – Bure, Yare and Waveney – which converge on Yarmouth have no equivalent anywhere else in England or Europe. They are shallow, artificial inland lakes, some of remarkable beauty which, experts now believe, were dug out for peat in Saxon and early Norman times. They are nearly all connected with each other and with the rivers. Norfolk contains some 200 miles of inner waterways. To appreciate the curious magic of these marshy meres one has to go there by sailing or motor boat. There are far too many of the latter, and an embargo will be needed if this most touristy part of Norfolk is not to be killed by the tourists themselves.

I can remember in less mechanized days the Norfolk wherries which conveyed cargo between Norwich and Yarmouth or Lowestoft. They had a shallow draft and a high mast carrying a huge black sail without a boom. They could sail incredibly close to the wind and could "shoot" a bridge by collapsing and then re-erecting mast and sail with scarcely a pause. It was a wonderful spectacle. Today only one survives, owned by a special trust. For commercial use the Norfolk wherry is as dead as the tea clipper.

I must end with a word about Norwich. It is only 100 miles from London, but it has a curiously remote feel about it. For centuries people in Norwich and indeed throughout east Norfolk could travel more easily to Antwerp than to their own capital. Norwich was difficult of access from the south. This may account for a self-sufficiency, some might say a certain arrogance, which is to be found in the inhabitants of Norwich, indeed of Norfolk generally. I would prefer to regard it as pride – pride in a long historical tradition, pride in the beauty of a strange landscape which "foreigners" (or non-Norfolk people) do not appreciate, and pride in a sense of being different from others – which indeed those born and bred in Norfolk certainly are.

The town sign Swaffham.

SIR KENNETH LEWIS'
Rutland

Photographs by Fritz von der Schulenburg

When they took away administrative county status from Rutland in 1974 they threatened to divide it up. They (the Ministry men in London) did not get away with it: Rutland was kept on the map as a district. National sentiment, local pride, history that went back almost 1,000 years and the Rutland motto, *Multum in parvo* (Much in little), could not be ignored.

For 24 years, as Rutland's Member of Parliament, I was involved in its battles with the Whitehall bureaucracy. Despite the attempt of the Big Battalions to demolish it, it remains its own small, independent but unique and lovely district, set in the heart of England.

Rutland survives and thrives. It is an oasis between the conurbations of the East Midlands – Leicester and Nottingham, Northampton and Corby – and the growing city of Peterborough, towards the Fens. In the limestone uplands of the north Rutland is peppered with little hills and sparkles with grey stone villages. And in the south, even on the greyest of winter days, it is golden with attractive ironstone buildings. Rutland is unspoilt and those who come into it from the big cities do not harm it. They, too, want to keep it as it is: a place where hardly a single village or one of its 50 churches is not worth a visit.

The traveller should come into Rutland from Stamford on the old Great North Road. Stamford is a gem of a town, worthy to be the eastern gateway to Rutland, and it was linked with Rutland as a parliamentary constituency until the redistribution of seats just before the 1983 election. The road from Stamford to Rutland's capital, Oakham, is one on which to drive slowly. The scenery is a mixture of old and new which should not be missed: the landscape is centuries old; Rutland Water, set in the landscape, has been there for only a decade. The Water stretches for half of the way between Stamford and Oakham, as large as Lake Windermere. It fits beautifully into the landscape, has one of Europe's largest trout fisheries, a nature and wildfowl reserve, and an internationally known sailing centre. From Rutland's uplands on either side you can look at this great expanse of water in sunlight or moonlight and rejoice that God and man made it together. Right into the middle of Rutland Water juts the lovely village of Hambleton. On the other side of the lake the water laps round three sides of Normanton Church. Rutland refused to have the church submerged and raised the money to keep it. It is a copy of St John's Church, Smith Square, Westminster, but is now deconsecrated and used as an information centre.

Along the Stamford road, towards Rutland's first town of Oakham, is Barnsdale Wood, made more striking because of the fields surrounding it, rural with sheep and cattle grazing – not to mention horses. But not to mention horses in Rutland is impossible. Rutland is Cottesmore Hunt Country, so there are bound to be horses. The Prince of Wales often rides with this famous hunt which was started by Tom Noel, whose descendant the Earl of Gainsborough still lives in Rutland and who has always played a leading part in the life of the district. In the 1930s another earl, the Earl of Lonsdale who had boxed and beat John L. Sullivan, founded the Lonsdale belts, and drove to hunt from his house at Barley Thorpe in a yellow car.

The capital town of Oakham has more horseshoes than horses. You find them in what is left of the 12th-century castle, now a Court House. Here are dozens of

Normanton Church, almost surrounded by Rutland Water.

horseshoes on the walls — some small, some large, some royal, many crowned, all given by peers of the realm as a forfeit when they officially visit Rutland. Elizabeth I and Elizabeth II, with many dukes and earls and viscounts and barons, have donated horseshoes made especially for the occasion. The de Fessers family, who came over with William the Conqueror, and who were farriers, are said to have started the custom. Doubtless it helped keep them in business. Titus Oates, trouble-maker and rogue, was also born in Oakham in 1649.

Oakham, with its museum, its famous school, its stocks in the old attractive square, is no ancient monument. It is a lively town with a good mixture of small industry, a market, good hotels, excellent shopping and a railway station.

Rutland has only two towns, each with its public school. Oakham and Uppingham were both founded in 1584 by Robert Johnson. The year 1984 is therefore a special one for both of these schools which celebrate 400 years of a continuously high level of education. Edward Thring was the most famous head-master in England when he transformed a small school of 30 boys at Uppingham into an establishment of magnificent buildings with a strong educational influence.

Both Oakham and Uppingham Schools are now among the most up-to-date in the country. The ancient buildings have acquired the most modern of additions and girls and boys enjoy the best of the past, together with all that the latest technology can provide. They have the best in sporting facilities, too — cricket especially, as one might expect since it was George Finch, the ninth Earl of Winchilsea at Burley-on-the-Hill, who founded the MCC. Rutland may be ancient but, in education as in other things, it keeps up with the times.

Uppingham is the second town of Rutland. Its market place has hardly changed in several hundred years. The church is off the market place but were it not for the high tower you would have trouble in finding it: shops, a bank, the Post Office and an old inn stand in front of it. The money-changers are kept outside but only just.

Near to Uppingham is Stoke Dry which has Rutland's second lake — small and pretty to walk or drive round. Here the Dambusters practised in the Second World War. Stoke Dry is said to have been the place where the Gunpowder Plot was hatched. Sir Everard Digby, who lived there, was executed in 1606 for his part in it. One can well imagine the conspirators, gathered at the ancient inn outside the church in Uppingham, laying their infamous plans. Later a famous preacher, Jeremy Taylor, Vicar of Uppingham, preached an equally famous sermon on the Gunpowder Plot at Oxford.

In its long history Rutland has had repeated trouble with Parliament. It is appropriate that a field at Ayston, near Uppingham, is called Parliament Field. Near by Cromwell gathered an army and it is said the headquarters was at the Manor House in Preston, just up the road from Ayston. Preston is easy to pass on the main Uppingham-Oakham road but is worth a diversion particularly in the summer. On a Sunday afternoon you can get good English tea in the Village Hall, provided by the ladies of Preston.

Cromwell may have mustered the last great army to be raised in Rutland but the RAF took over, 50 years ago. Cottesmore RAF Station was famous in the Second World War. It is now multinational: Germans and Italians, working with the

British, fly the new Nato Tornado aircraft. So Rutland is in the van with military aviation progress. Cottesmore village's story dates back 4,000 years: all the ages — Bronze, Roman, Saxon, Norman — left their mark, each making its own military contribution as Cottesmore is doing today.

Rutland is also famous for Ruddle's Beer, its special brand of County Ale made at Langham which now sells far afield in supermarkets and pubs — even in Whitehall itself. There civil servants doubtless toast each other and recall what they nearly persuaded Parliament to do to Rutland without quite succeeding. They know, for example, that Rutland still has its own Queen's Lieutenant, with special responsibility for Rutland. Colonel Thomas Haywood, who was Lord Lieutenant when Rutland was still a county and was foremost among those who battled to keep the identity of the area, still represents Her Majesty in Rutland.

In Whitehall not only the pubs have Rutland connexions. So has the Palace of Westminster itself. The new House of Commons is made of Clipsham stone whose quarries are in Rutland. Sir David Davenport-Handley who owns these quarries was one of those, with Colonel Tom Haywood, the late Sir Kenneth Ruddle of the brewery, Alan Bond, the then Clerk of the County, and myself with many others who fought and won the battle to keep Rutland a county in 1962; which it remained for another 10 years, when it became the present District Council. Sir David Davenport-Handley used to say, "If you people in the House of Commons do not keep us free from total take-over I will claim back all my Clipsham stone."

In this little area in the heart of England once upon a time a little man jumped out of a pie in front of a King. It happened at the great house of Burley-on-the-Hill, owned by Jos Hanbury who is also Lord of the Manor at Oakham. Burley-on-the-Hill is magnificent to look at from the Oakham-Stamford road and is rich in history. The Romans were there, so were the Norman and Saxon Lords. It was a holiday centre for kings and queens. The renowned and profligate Duke of Buckingham owned it. Part of *Upstairs Downstairs* was shot there. But the pie story associated with it is special.

Jeffrey Hudson, born in 1619, was a very small man, only 39 inches in height. His equally small thatched house still stands off Oakham High Street. When Charles Stuart came to Burley-on-the-Hill with Henrietta Maria in 1628 a large pie was

LEFT: The maze in the village of Wing. It is 40 feet in diameter and laid out exactly like the pavement labyrinths in some French cathedrals. BELOW: The church at Hambleton.

placed on the table in front of them at a great banquet and out jumped Jeffrey, then only 18 inches tall. He became famous: his portrait was painted by Van Dyck; he went to Paris with the queen at the time of the Civil War. Sadly he was captured by some Turkish pirates and sold as a slave. Eventually he was ransomed, returned to Oakham and granted a pension. But disaster followed: he was suspected of complicity in the Popish plot and imprisoned in the Westminster Gatehouse, opposite the Parliament Building.

The association with Westminster has not always been just political. In Langham in the 14th century was born Simon de Langham who became Lord Chancellor of England and then Archbishop of Canterbury, thus serving both God and Mammon, in reverse order. It could hardly happen today. But it had a good result then: Simon de Langham persuaded Edward III to give mighty gifts to the Abbey to advance its building.

Modern Rutland has over 300 miles of good but quiet roads. You can travel from village to village alongside farms and pastures which could form subjects for watercolour landscapes. The villages make Rutland. Lyddington has its Bede House, a creation of Elizabeth I's Lord Burleigh. Bede House is Gothic perfection. Market Overton has a distinctive Saxon arch tower and a sundial given by Sir Isaac Newton whose mother came from Market Overton. At Great Casterton there is a Stone Age settlement. Near North Luffenham is the site of a siege of the Royalists in the Old Hall where they held out against 1,200 Parliament troops. Today, keeping the military connexion, there is RAF Station North Luffenham to twin with RAF Cottesmore. Back on the ground at Wing there is an ancient maze. At Preston yew trees from the Garden of Gethsemane. And if you want to come right up to date recently the tiny village of Whitwell was twinned with Paris. All of it, or just Montmartre?

The villages are rural jewels; everybody knows everybody and people get to know those who live in the other villages while shopping in Oakham or Uppingham. Rutland has had difficulty with the Post Office. The Post Office did not want people

Uppingham School.

to use Rutland in the postal address. But everybody did, of course. At Belton they went one better and added "In Rutland" to the village name, just to make sure that letters would not be lost to the other Belton in Leicestershire. The village area of Edith Weston has the most distinguished name because Edward the Confessor, who owned Rutland, gave this particular part of Rutland to his Queen Edith. On the church at Edith Weston there is a 500-year-old inscription which reads: "Crown of all the neighbouring lands. High and lifted up it stands." And when you come into Rutland from the flat Fenlands of Lincolnshire and Cambridgeshire so it is.

If you go into Rutland via Stamford you had best come out of it on the Kettering Road through Uppingham and via the village of Caldecott where there was once a Roman temple. Then you will see before you the beautiful village of Rockingham with its magnificent castle set high and, when floodlit at night, like a fairy-tale palace above the village. It is a gem of Northamptonshire but the best view of it is from Rutland.

Rutland is like that: inside looking out, or outside looking in, it is small but special.

The huge expanse of Rutland Water, though man-made, is at one with the landscape.

PAUL JENNINGS'
Suffolk

Photographs by Anne Cardale

John Constable told his engraver, David Lucas, a story which wonderfully illustrates the tremendous sense of place, of identity, of strong life-in-itself of Suffolk. A farm labourer, crossing the river Stour to the Essex bank in search of work, looked back and said, "Goodbye, old England, perhaps I may never see you more."

It is an open question whether Anne Hathaway's or Willy Lott's is the best known cottage in the world, but I count myself lucky to have been born and to have grown up in Warwickshire, the county of the former, and to have lived 24 years (and I hope for whatever remain) in the county of the latter. It is probably true to say that while Constable is not in Shakespeare's league (who could be?) he does have that same quality of proceeding from deep roots in an intense local and particular culture to an art of universal validity. It does not matter if *The Hay Wain*, that poignant glimpse of a perfect moment in the transient English summer, has been on a million chocolate boxes and playing cards; it *is* England. There is another famous Constable painting, *The Cottage in a Cornfield* (in the V & A), but "The Small Manor in a Cornfield" would be an equally typical Suffolk view. The reasons for this go back a long way historically. Norman Scarfe, *the* historian of Suffolk (*Shell Guide*, *The Suffolk Landscape* and others), points out that in Domesday Book Suffolk was not only the most thickly populated county in England, but with 7,460 freemen Suffolk had well over half the total recorded for the rest of England. Owing to a local custom of "partible inheritance" (equal division between children) "an active market in small pieces of land, of a fairly modern kind, was well developed by the end of the 13th century".

Suffolk, therefore, has had not only a great deal of historical time to develop its unique character but has also been favoured geographically by the fact that it is not on the way to anywhere except Norfolk and the pale waters of the Wash.

The isolated manor-farmhouse or the snug village, often with the beautiful timber-framed architecture recalling medieval cloth-trade prosperity, are particularly observable in the central clay belt of High Suffok, and some of them are over-exposed classics. It has now got through even to the advertising agencies that Lavenham with its famous Guildhall and film-set Tudor streets is a classic English village.

But there are two other areas of Suffolk totally different visually: the shingle-beached coastal strip, mostly wild, sandy, pine-dotted heathland with gorse and heather, especially when you get up to Aldeburgh, that pure Suffolk town of flint and brick and white woodwork gleaming in the clear sea light, so natural a setting for Britten's clear music, and Southwold, a Victorian sea town with its spacious greens, and Adnams' brewery, where the best beer in England is delivered locally from drays drawn by, curiously, not Suffolk Punch but Percheron horses, not for sentimental reasons but because they save £1,000 a year on each lorry replaced. And there is the little corner north-west of Bury St Edmunds where you get not only Suffolk's share – in fact their northern end – of chalk uplands (Newmarket Heath) that go via the Gog Magog hills of Cambridge, the Hertfordshire hills and the Thames Valley right down to Wessex, but also sandy Breckland, going on into Norfolk, where stage-coaches could get buried in sand dunes in the 18th century, where there is the Neolithic flint-mine, Grimes Graves, and there are also Forestry Commission conifer woods.

BELOW LEFT: Willy Lott's cottage at Flatford. BELOW: The timber-framed Guildhall at Lavenham, built in 1529. BOTTOM: Blythburgh village, which was until the 16th century a prosperous fishing town but which, like the town of Southwold, declined when the Reformation reduced the demand for fish.

Right up in that top left-hand corner is Suffolk's bit of pure fen country, with its local capital of Mildenhall – as good a place as any to start looking at the inexhaustible treasure of Suffolk's churches. St Mary and St Andrew has many glories, including a superb east window of *c* 1300, but what you notice first, as in so many Suffolk churches, is the marvellous roof, here a tie-beam full of angels – riddled with buckshot and even arrow-heads fired by what Scarfe calls "maniac Puritans".

In Suffolk you may find an unmatchable variety of every kind of roof: the single-hammerbeam of which St Michael, Framlingham, is a noble example (not to mention the town's castle and its unspoilt architecture, rivalled or even bettered in central Suffolk only by Eye); and you can find the ultimate fantastication of the double-hammerbeam all over the place. St Mary, Woolpit, with another incredible flurry of angels' wings, is my favourite – and what a porch! There is always some other glory as well. As for St John the Baptist, Needham Market – a rather barn-like exterior in one of Suffolk's less picturesque towns – just go in there and you will see a roof which H. Munro Cautley, whose famous *Suffolk Churches and their Treasures* is the outcome of a lifetime spent exploring these miracles, called "the culminating achievement of the medieval carpenter . . . unique and remarkable".

Nearly all these marvels are built of flint, the local material that seems to change from grey to silver to ochre to beige in the changing light of the wide skies. There are huge churches rising out of fields or marshland where you wonder how any population, at any time, could have afforded such things.

Take Holy Trinity at Blythburgh, "the Cathedral of the Marshes", full of amazing light and space, where we saw the Aldeburgh Festival's *Idomeneo* two days after the Snape Maltings, the most beautiful concert hall in the world, had burnt down, later of course to be restored better than ever. It has about 20 houses huddled round it, but otherwise there are only fields and the wind in the huge reed-beds of the river Blyth marshes which debouch into the sea at Walberswick, just below Southwold.

No wonder it was called "Silly Suffolk", the adjective being a corruption of *selig*, German for "blessed". Certainly it was a church that made the biggest impression on me the first time I ever set foot in East Anglia. In 1952 certain key troops, of whom I was one, were called up for a fortnight in something called the Z Reserve (I have forgotten what that particular crisis was – could have been the Berlin airlift). Anyway, all I had to do was sit about with my signals section knocking out idiotic messages about Redland and Blueland forces, and watch bright September clouds sailing over the noble church of Long Melford at the top of the vast green that comes after the beautiful wide (and eponymously long) village street. It is one of a chain of magical villages passed through as you go up the Stour: Stoke-by-Nayland with its majestic, ridge-dominating tower beloved of Constable, Bures, Gainsborough's Sudbury, Cavendish, Clare . . . and I thought, I wouldn't mind living round here.

We newcomers tend to be more Catholic than the Pope when it comes to loving the place. It seems to be full of writers and artists, viewed with a tolerant eye by the real locals with their deadpan humour ("Jim, there's a drop a-hangin' from yore nose," said a man in a pub to his crony with a rather large nose. "Dew yew woipe it then, boy. It's nearer to yew"), their rich dialect and their unfussy, deliberate, courteous conversation. There is a marvellous picture of them in *Suffolk Scene* by

ABOVE: Marshes near Walberswick.
RIGHT: Looking across the green at Long Melford towards the Victorian Grammar School and the 15th-century Holy Trinity Church.

ABOVE: Frost lying in the hollows of the Stour valley. ABOVE RIGHT: The church at Needham Market with its fine 15th-century hammerbeam roof. RIGHT: The wind-swept sea-front at Southwold in winter.

Julian Tennyson, a young man's labour of love (he was killed in Burma) about the county of his boyhood holidays.

Among other splendid things it contains the story of St Edmund's martyrdom by the Danes in 800 as told to him by a Suffolk ploughman. When finally captured by "them Deens, they must ha bin whully a savidge lot o' davils", he shows his true mettle. " 'Oho, me little King-o,' they say, 'yew're ketched now an yew're a goin to be kilt an no mistake. But ere's one thing,' they say, 'will yew give up yer Chrisheranity afore yew're kilt, y'know kind o' change yer relijun like, cause thass the wrong un yew got there, boy.' But young Edmund he was a werry kerajus chap, he whully stuck by what he thot was roight, dew they moight ha let im orf. 'I ain't a goin to give up nuthen fer yew,' he say, 'yew're a rotten lot o' barstids the whull bloody bag of ye . . .' "

St Edmund – here we are at the end of the article and only just arrived at Bury, the elegant, now predominantly 18th-century town where his shrine was once in the greatest abbey in England. And then there is the nearby great house of Ickworth with its park and gardens and rotunda. There are the innumerable creeks and sailing harbours, from Lowestoft to Aldeburgh to Orford to Pin Mill and the sailing capital of Woodbridge, haunted by that adorable Edward FitzGerald of Boulge Hall, who when he was not translating Omar Khayyàm or dining with Tennyson or sailing was in London pining for Suffolk.

On May 23, 1845, he wrote, " . . . there is an old hunting picture in Regent St. which I want him [his friend Thomas Churchyard, the painter and one of the "Woodbridge Wits" together with George Crabbe, son of the poet, and the Quaker Bernard Barton whose daughter FitzGerald, one of nature's bachelors, unwillingly married; he saw a pink blancmange at the reception and said "Ugh! Congealed bridesmaid!"] to look at. I think it is Morland; whom I don't care twopence for; the horses ill-drawn; some good colour; the people English; good old England! I was at a party of modern wits last night that made me creep into myself, and wish myself talking away to any old Suffolk woman in her cottage . . . "

THE NORTH

Cheshire

Photographs by Sarah King

The nice ladies who ran the Altrincham infant school during the Second World War taught that my native county, Cheshire, was shaped like a tea-pot. Its lid resists Manchester and industrial Lancashire, its base nudges the commercial pottery towns of Staffordshire (but rests more happily, I fancy, on rural Shropshire), while on either side are hills — east are the Derbyshire Pennines, and west are the Welsh mountains — with the spout (the Wirral peninsula) poking between Wales and Liverpool. It is a warm tea-pot of a county, round, snug and motherly.

Near where I was born in Middlewich there is a village stump that marked, so I was told, the centre of England. Whether this is literally true or not is beside the point. In local folklore it was believed to be so, and I was brought up with the comforting idea that I had been born in the central womb of my country, which then was the centre of the world — on the school's map in Mercator's projection it was shown to be so — and the village cross-roads was the cross-roads of the empire on which the sun never sets.

The lovely district around me was famous for its milk and cheese, for its walled parks with noble trees, for its villages and mansion houses of black-and-white timbers, for its small, delicious lakes called "meres", for its fields (which thankfully are still hedged and small) and for some rich people known as "The Cheshire Set".

Cheshire is also a plain, with red sandstone poking out of it in places (not many, for generally it is too lush and well covered), cupped in austere grey hills. It is hedged in by counties gaining their character and vitality from industrial transformations. I wonder whether Cheshire's own apparent lack of chaotic social unheaval is the reason why it has produced few eminent artists and creative people? Mind you, it suffered early rural transformations. To judge by the wealth and size of its parks, the land-clearances must have been savage — perhaps too vicious to speak of. But the county has smoothed out its history, rubbed out the palimpsest, so that it is difficult not to be lulled by a sense of unrippled "ageless" peace.

Yet my name reminds me that I am descended from invaders. There are 15 pages of "Hugheses" in the Chester telephone directory. The Celts presumably first came warring; then, I would guess, as schoolmasters and domestic servants — the two great Welsh occupations exported over the border.

My childhood and youth were spent in the north of the county, in Altrincham, which holds an ambiguous attitude towards immigrants from Manchester and Lancashire. Ambiguous because the whole character of north Cheshire — and increasingly the rest of it — is created by the wealthiest Manchester people. (Cheshire is sometimes called "a little bit of Surrey in the north".)

In the bowl of Cheshire southwards from Altrincham are the great parks, Dunham and Tatton, where the Earls of Egerton once were able to travel for 20 miles entirely over their own land from Knutsford to Manchester. The wealth of Tatton Park was made out of the industrial exploitation of Trafford Park and the docks in Manchester. Next came the cotton merchants, who built a colony of exotic mansions at Bowdon, a wooded hill overlooking the plain, sold or leased by the Lords Stamford of Dunham. (Under preservative conditions, even in those early days, they specified the types of stone and brick.) In the 19th century Lord Stamford opened his park to visitors from Manchester — many of them working people for, as readers of Mrs Gaskell will know, cotton operatives used to explore the Cheshire countryside on foot; and many of them naturalists and scientists, braving gamekeepers to trespass for their specimens. Yet philanthropy was one thing, permanent residence another. Their lordships kept "development" within bounds.

Every area has its notable places that shout out to the visitor. In Cheshire there is Little Moreton Hall — an amazing rickety pile of oak-timbered architecture. There

Sunset over Pickmere. Cheshire's natural lakes are one of its great attractions.

ABOVE: Deer graze in Tatton Park near Knutsford. TOP RIGHT: Chester's galleried streets, The Rows, date from the Middle Ages. CENTRE: Rostherne church has a beautiful situation overlooking Rostherne mere. RIGHT: 16th-century Little Moreton Hall.

are a great many such small, half-timbered manor houses, set among orchards and walled gardens. At the other extreme is the grandeur of Tatton Hall, in which one of the most striking things is the great room filled with the heads of African animals shot by an Earl of Egerton. (Though I myself would revisit to see one of the most interesting, because "uncompleted", Caravaggios – a violent, expressionist still-life painting, hanging modestly in the kitchen passageway.) There is May Day in Knutsford, when interest might stray to the bizarre row of villas in Legh Road erected by R. H. Watt, a Manchester glove manufacturer. There is Beeston Castle, a crumbling lonely fortification in the plain near Chester, and Chester itself. And for those interested in industrial history, old silk mills in Macclesfield and the salt industry set in the pastoral heart of the county at Winsford, Middlewich, Sandbach and Northwich – places where a bus can, and is, driven about the mines and where towns collapse awry into the subsidence. At Sandbach, too, are the famous Saxon market-crosses.

But all this is guide-book stuff. Smaller, more deeply felt things can better convey the place's real personality. The geography of childhood surroundings becomes the map of one's soul, and I doubt if I can write of Cheshire without the passion that comes from inner revelation. My early days were spent on a 1930s council-house estate, the land on which it was built being also an allowance of a Lord Stamford. It was a ghetto on the edge of Bowdon and, I have always suspected, a shrewd plan to provide a servant population for the nearby rich: Cheshire is soaked in paternalism, and it is to this that we owe the preservation of so much. Village paternalism was the commonest subject of my father's talk. You didn't get work, he said, if you were unwilling to raise your cap or curtsey in the street; the pawnbroker-cum-magistrate was also chairman of the Means Test Committee, growing fat on his interest in forcing the out-of-work to pawn their belongings. I knew that my father earned his right to radical anger, if only for one act of which I am immensely proud: during the Depression he was a baker's boy in Sandbach, and at the risk of his precious job he nightly left free loaves of bread on the doorsteps of the hungry.

But my mother split my soul, for she was in love with all that Cheshire offered through its apparently secure gentility. She cleaned in Bowdon's houses. And my childhood trips with her out of our utilitarian, treeless ghetto into the secret interiors of those thickly shrubberied fantasies of Victorian architecture – mixtures of Gothic cathedral, Spanish Alhambra and Indian Taj Mahal – made another split that has its equivalent in the geography of my mind. The split was expressed, too, in where we lived, which was at the end of a tentacle of houses, so that our front faced the desolate factory landscape of Lancashire, while the back looked into the fields and park of the Earl of Stamford. Thus I straddled both worlds. And no matter how much I enjoy the maternal seductions of Cheshire, the other half of my soul belongs to those more chaotic, more openly brutal, uglier but creative facts found over the Lancashire border, and also in small industrial pockets within my own county.

From earliest childhood I went south, delving into the heart of the county. First on foot, with other boys to bathe or fish in one of the tiny brown rivers – the River Bollin; or to build "dens" in the game-copses which in Cheshire entice adventure, islanded amid the fields. Something about those places made me return later and alone. Next I had a bicycle to take me farther south, visiting aunts and uncles in Middlewich and Sandbach; then on to the border to discover the rich environment of the Dee valley. Yet I was never satisfied by roads, not even footpaths, because from the beginning I saw that the land was cut off in huge tracts beyond hedges and behind old brick walls that rambled for miles. It was more than private – it was sacred, its spirit accessible only to subtle trespass, over the walls and across the parks. Sometimes I brought home the cast antlers of red or fallow deer, and one autumn dusk I listened in awe to the clashing and roaring of those "tame" beasts rutting.

Cheshire's true spirit lies beneath its genteel surface. To discover it when we were children we braved a mythical gamekeeper, whom we called Grassy – a king of the woods, supposedly having green hair and a snake-like body, who was likely to pounce upon us out of the trees, and whom I now recognize as a Cheshire descendant of the Green Man and of that priest-king who guarded the oak tree at Nemi, about whom Frazer wrote *The Golden Bough*. I do not know how he became transformed into a Cheshire gamekeeper. But though, of course, I never met him through my 15 years of trespassing, I believed in his existence as certainly as I believed in that of my own father. When I was with others I was not so scared. But I could not resist returning to Grassy's haunts alone and it was then, through watching and listening out for him that, petrified into silence and motionless, I became intensely aware of all nature around me.

Fear and trepidation, and being alone, were incitements to the reception of natural beauty. The whole countryside seemed then to be unified against the stranger, particularly if he was a roaming boy, and especially if he had the look of one from a housing estate. Thirty years ago those cottages – patchings-up of rich old brick among the black-and-white of half-timbering – were inhabited not by Manchester commuter-purchasers but by estate servants. They were united in keeping me out. No one in sight could be trusted. I crept into the lusciousness gratefully; it was like being embraced by a woman, by the great green goddess herself. No fields I have come across since have the intimacy and safety of those little hedged diamonds, growing the grass that fed Cheshire cows.

Beyond the little fields would come a fringe of woods. And at the heart of any typical stretch of mid-Cheshire country, after penetrating the wood, there would be a little winking lake, or at least a pond, surrounded with reeds and alders, with moorhens and tufted-duck scooting over the water. Though small, few lakes anywhere can have such beauty as Rostherne, Arley or Budworth, a small village grown up through centuries a field's distance away. My image of Paradise is something like Rostherne – gently rising and falling country, folding down into a mere; small scattered copses with pigeons; an old wall around it; an ancient church and village.

My soul seems buried there already. I took my mother's ashes to Rostherne, and when the vicar would not allow me to scatter them in the churchyard overlooking the mere, I spread them in the wood and planted snowdrops.

And yet also a more awake part of myself tells me that I would not like to spend all eternity in a place so sweet as Heaven.

MELVYN BRAGG'S
Cumbria

Photographs by Ian Howes

For most people Cumbria is the "Lake District" and, indeed, for more than 200 years travellers, poets, visitors and residents have glowingly reviewed this spectacular landscape soaring peacefully above the sea of troubles in the north-west plain. For this is also border country, centuries of pillage and vengeance; and, along the coastal strip, a cicatrice of the once exuberant and brutal entrepreneurial Victorian heavy industry is proof to yet another place. Beauty, war and mining – three massive pillars dominate the history and present face of Cumbria, and yet in my opinion nothing so characterizes the area as the work-a-day farms, particularly the hill farms, which bind together the heartland of the place with an extraordinary tenacity.

In a sense, to call it the Lake District is to do an injustice to its finest feature – the hills, or fells as they are called locally. These hump-backed, bare uplands are among the oldest mountain ranges in the world. For over 500 million years the geological fantasia which included vast volcanic eras, times of desert and ice, Olympian land shifts and furies of resettlement formed and reformed this involuted landscape. The lakes came later. They could go comparatively soon; silt builds up ceaselessly. But the hills, you feel – and this is the essential element in the allure of Cumbria – will stretch into the future as far as they reach back into the past.

It is the complication and the varying proportions of the place within the human scale which make it so singular. Coleridge was the first to point this out, and since then all of us who have walked there have consciously and unconsciously subscribed to the same insight. For it seems such a little spot, in a way. Runners run through it in a day and a night: Josh Naylor, the king of the fell runners, manages to pound up 20 or 30 peaks in a few hours.

Whizz along the valleys in a car and you can take in most of the big lakes between sun-up and opening time. You would miss a lot. For the only way to see it as it deserves to be seen is to amble – to follow the sheep tracks or the way drawn out by Wainwright whose hand-written guides are both folklore and functional – and as you amble, to pause, frequently. For the hills are so close packed, the lakes so different, the valleys so particular, that if you are at all sensitive to variety, the richness of it will seep into and then saturate your senses.

The weather, too, will rarely hold still for more than a few minutes and, indeed, as Turner and the other lesser artists show dramatically, it has the quality of being in several conditions at the same time: you can have sun direct on Derwentwater, cloud to the west on Catbells, a fuming storm beyond the tip of the lake in Borrowdale, and over Watendlath in the east silvery strokes of light as clear as the lines on a sun dial. The ambling itself can be easy – up Skiddaw or Gable, around Rydal or by Ullswater – but, once again, the variety can be sudden. For inside those quiet humps are steeps and screes which continue to claim victims every year. It is both docile and dramatic.

Just as the other side to the embossed intricacy of the apparently small place is the limitless grandeur you can feel high-mounted on a fell looking over a sea of peaks, so the dark side of those easy walks is only a few feet from your safe path. Rock-climbing began in this district almost 150 years ago, and still the valleys ring to the peals of ironmongery as hard-muscled young men from the northern cities batten to the rock face and seek to pick out a saving hold.

It is a fortress, this central massif, and inside its natural barriers are scattered the remains of conquerors and conquered. Although much smaller than Stonehenge, the stones at Castlerigg near Keswick have a much more lonely mystery about them. The circle stands in full view of dozens of hill-tops, as plain as an arena built to serve the seven hills of Rome – but why?

The even earlier Bronze Age circles – of which, again, there are several, mostly down in the Ulverston area – also stand bare of explanation, mockingly secure, telling no stories of those who laboured to construct them. Up in the Langdales, though, at Pike o' Stickle, you can touch the first real entry point of man in this area; you can even, still, find the instrument with which he hacked his way into the history of the place – the slate axe, quarried here, refined with the sand on the coast, so sharp it can still fell a forest and so useful that it was used by Cumbrians at the Battle of Hastings, approximately 6,000 years after it had been perfected on these volcanic hills.

The Romans came, of course, and their most lasting impression on the Lake District natural fortress was a fortress of their own – at the top of Hardknott Pass, poised there on the heights like the imperial eagle itself ready to swoop down on the constantly discontented inhabitants. The Romans left no trace in language or place-name; the Britons who had been there before re-emerged after centuries of centurions to merge with the Norsemen in what seems a reasonably amicable marriage – one which bred the dialect and character of the district so resolutely that the paternity is still everywhere apparent.

Once again Cumbria was lucky: the Bewcastle Cross and the Gosforth Cross are quite superb examples of the arts of the Anglian and Norse periods, and to decipher them is to decode a cultural portrait of those warrior-farmers. Castles from the Normans, who never, legend claims, overran the independent centre of Cumbria, begun and rebuilt at Kendal, Cockermouth, Penrith, Egremont are all about the entrances to the place. And there are the churches, above all the Cistercian monasteries, most richly remaining at Barrow in the blood sandstone which softens so much of the building, and which in its gaunt ruins still emits feelings of that godly and profitable life which captured the soul of the Cumbrian and brought cultivation to many an isolated valley.

It has been in effect, though, a place on its own since the Norsemen came with their language which became and remains our dialect. Go to the Horse Fair at Wigton, the Shepherd's Meet in Wasdale, the Hound Trails all over the countryside and you will hear words more easily understood by Norwegians. Most Cumbrian names, mine included, are Norse; the names of all the natural features from fell to stayn (stone) are Norse; and the hill farmers work the same dour land with the same independence so admired by Wordsworth of the old Norse statesmen at Hawkshead.

Wordsworth is everywhere. The particularities of his poetry graph out so many spots – the Yew Trees in Lorton Vale, Glaramara's caves, Ullswater's daffodils, Michael's sheepfold – that you can take a journey through the countryside which is also a journey through his poetry. But his magnificence in insisting, in his work, on the symbiotic relationship between mankind and nature gave nature itself a new

BELOW: The Roman fort at the top of Hardknott Pass. BOTTOM: A sheep sale at Lazonby.

dimension for thoughtful observers, and since then both literature and life have been enhanced. Around Dove Cottage in Grasmere, in Cockermouth where he was born, or in the enchanting village of Hawkshead where he gained an education in sense and sensibility, you can be present still at what was the first spinning of that revolutionary weave of poetry and philosophy.

At school I received three collections of Wordsworth's poems as prizes over the years. We know our loyalties in Cumbria. I was born a few miles to the north of the lakes and at first the rim line of northern fells seemed like a vision, some secret Xanadu, rather intimidating. School trips and choir trips in plush, musty buses were the first infiltrations and there were crowded voyages up Ullswater and down Windermere trying not to be seasick, group rambles with the Anglican Young People's Association, and later longer explorations with the youth hostels always

Ullswater.

open at 5 pm. I left when I was 20 and returned about a decade later – to the northern fells where the plain villages and the lack of lakes provide no encouragement for the general visitor and much selfish but most agreeable relief for those of us who live there. It is there, now, that I learn about a place I had taken so much for granted, read poets other than Wordsworth, go to see the hundreds of prints and paintings done of the place, make a date with the sports meetings and shows famously at Ambleside and Grasmere, but even more entertainingly in the smaller villages where Cumberland and Westmorland wrestlers in long-johns and embroidered bathing trunks engage in ancient grappling, where fell runners rip to the top of crags and cascade down like a slither of scree, and where the men with the hound dogs wait for the scentlayers to come in from their 10 mile circuit which the hounds will follow as the bookies shout the odds.

Nearer to me, though, in the early days, were the two other parts of Cumbria, one by birth – the industrial coast – the other by geography – Carlisle. The town in which I was born, Wigton, is in the magnetic field of Carlisle, a border city and capital of a rich and richly fought-over plain; to the west the mining towns of Maryport, Workington and Whitehaven were where my father's family worked in the pits.

The castle has been cut off from Carlisle now by a road which is probably efficient but leaves that splendid pile as gasping for its element as a pike on a river bank. When the road from the gates led directly into the old city, soon to reach the medieval cathedral and the equally old town hall, the place had a real feeling of its past. Here Bonnie Prince Charlie got on his white horse and entered the English city with his 100 pipers before him. In that castle kings of England and Scotland were crowned and parliaments convened. Men were hanged there for war and forgery; the heads of its defenders were stuck on the spikes on its walls; and ballads came along the high and low roads leading north to the old enemy. North past the wall, called after Hadrian, begun by Agricola, a stupendous barrier of stone and ditch and castle thrown across the waist of Britain: even now, walking along the reconstructed monument, the power of that imperial gesture can be felt.

The mining towns have taken a beating and they show the signs of it. There was a time, towards the end of the 19th century, when Whitehaven was one of the leading ports in the land, when Humphry Davy came to west Cumberland to continue his work, when discoveries in steel-making were made promising eternal riches for this remote, mineral-riddled area. Coal shafts went out under the Solway, men from Cornwall's closing tin mines came to work the iron ore, the Irish came over as they have done for 6,000 years to work on the mainland they had split away from; the place was revved up and ready to go. It went down. But still in the grid-precision squares of Whitehaven and the attractively solid streets of Maryport, which hump over to the harbour which Lowry drew so lovingly, you know that there was a time . . . Hard times now though, with the irony of atomic energy replacing the closed coal mines, the disused ore shafts, the perilous steel works.

The people in those coastal towns were largely drawn from the fells and still the same interests and sports hinge them together. Still the whippets and ferrets, the poachers and fishermen, the men with dogs and the men with guns step out of their back doors into the powerful seduction of the hills and the lakes. And the area now sees itself clearly, wants to keep what is good: volunteer wardens clean up the popular

walks; the professionals mend the paths; we amateurs make our children stuff their crisp bags in their pockets.

The Lakes today are as lovely as when Wordsworth drew his inspiration from them.

There is a fairy-tale aspect – not for nothing did Beatrix Potter invent her characters up here – and at the right time of year the lakeland towns and villages have an unperturbed serenity which taunts progress. Yet the visitors themselves have represented progress since the early 18th century when the English upper-middle classes took to their own backyard and the new turnpikes took their new coaches up into Defoe's "dreadful and horrid" wilderness of the north-west. Genteel terror was the first inducement to these parts and the printmakers and reporters laid on the horrors with all the greasepaint of circus clowns. That, too, was a fairy tale, even Wordsworth's pantheism has its fairy aspect, and the sites in Cumbria which any dutiful visitor must see – Sawrey, Dove Cottage, the Abbot Hall Museum at Kendal, the Brockhole centre on Windermere – have, too, their rather unreal dimension. Like the over-grand 19th-century mansions on the southern lakes, like the sometimes over-twee folksiness of the shops, there is something about the place which makes the unreal gesture seem appropriate: and so fantasy and folly seem set in.

Those who keep the place on the ground are the hill farmers. Around me in the hamlet in which I live are men and women whose constant and ever absorbing occupation is with the land, what it gives and what feeds off it. They know that the primal wilderness still exists: they plough it down every year. They know the basic fact of existence: the lambs freeze solid in the snow. They know the strength and weakness of their own lives: the markets and the weather test their knowledge and endurance every week. It is there in the hill farms that the truest life of Cumbria goes on, among men whose daily work takes them to the tops where they see around them the shape 500 million years have made and know how hard it is to hold what they have.

DAVID BELLAMY'S
Durham

Photographs by Trevor Wood

Of all the Counties of England, Durham has the richest legacy of history, both natural and man made. I don't say that just because I live there and work out from its Great Little University but because it is true.

The Fells of Upper Teesdale hold a unique record of the last Ice Age. Its rivers, Tyne, Wear and Tees, bore the brunt of the Industrial Revolution, if it did not cradle its actual beginnings. The towns of Chester-le-Street, Jarrow and the City of Durham are the heart of an ecclesiastic heritage which, for 600 years after the Roman occupation, was the only light in an otherwise uncivilised world. Above, below and subtending all, it has the rare beauty of a well worked landscape.

Scarred by mining and industry, the contours of its pit heaps which once smouldered buxom against the skies have been given less brazen contours, their flanks put out to grass or even shrouded with trees. Those mines which fuelled an Empire are now all gone and the manufactories which led so much industrial innovation are as silent as the graves of the millions who made them their ways of life and livelihood.

Children used to slave their youth away within the bowels of the earth and wives, sweethearts and mothers worked naked in the wet slime of the deepest pits to line the pockets and pave the streets about the stock exchange with gold. That was until the Dean and Chapter decided that such nakedness was a serpent of lust within the grass roots of its male workforce and clothed their nakedness on that account alone.

It was here among these inhumanities that trade unions found their fighting roots which are still paraded on the third Saturday in each July. Then the Big Meeting fills the City Palatine with banners, boots, beer and the real zeal of politics. Come and see it for yourself before the greed of the 21st century sweeps it all away.

History is reconstructed in the great museum at Beamish. You can sense its once massive presence, its hopes and hopelessness in the ghost of Consett and in the two up two down nettie out the back, way of life which still wreathes real smoke down wind. You can sense it in the pubs and clubs where the best beers in the world soak up chips and crisps, where talk, not conversation, has taken over from that of "bait" time at the coal face.

Your best route is to ride the heritage line from Darlington Station where passenger rail transport had its real beginnings, out and up through even greener countryside into the welcome of the dales – dales carved out by an Ice Age and three rivers. Two, the Tyne and Tees, are shared borders with the might of Yorkshire and the rural beauty of Northumberland. The third, the Wear, is the county's own for it rises with the high fells and discharges to sea at Sunderland.

All three drain off the lifeblood of the landscape as they have channelled its natural resources out to richer realms. Three estuaries have launched and berthed a million ships, sent on their way with champagne and besmirched with sewage and a fricassee of chemicals, the like of which were never found in nature.

Now as the ships and tides of commerce ebb, the Wear flows clean enough to allow the salmon to run up to the clear waters of their birth. They, like so many true Durnelmians, know the free beauty of the dalescape to which they so desperately wish to return. *En route* they run up through still murky waters which each year support Britain's oldest regatta past the great grey towers of Durham.

TOP LEFT: A view from Hamsterley forest. TOP RIGHT: The ticket office, which dates from 1867, is the centrepiece of the section on the North Eastern Railway in the Beamish Open-Air Museum. BOTTOM LEFT: The attractive Baptist chapel is one of the oldest in the country. BOTTOM RIGHT: Hamsterley parish church, mostly 13th-century, stands in a field half a mile from the village.

This is a place neither to begin nor end your pilgrimage. It is the place in which to spend time, sense history and find meaning in the ethics of a working life.

The pillars of this great Cathedral Church of God, rough hewn to perfection, spring from blessed roots at which the bones of St Cuthbert lay. They were carried here to rest in the sanctuary of a natural fortress guarded by a meander of the River Wear.

The upper dale must be visited for many reasons. Wolsingham, once the centre of wealth made malleable by lead, still makes steel in the most rural of surroundings. Close by, the first steel in the world was smelted with the strength of oaken charcoal from the forests. Today, the products of those same broad acres about Hamsterley have been commissioned for a myriad other uses and still produce oak, pine, spruce, and larch for a wood-hungry economy. Those same acres give welcome each year to the spawning fish and to tens of thousands of visitors who come to see the wildlife and understand the problems of managing such a landscape and raising such a gigantic crop. A very special part of all our heritages in the able hands of the Forestry Commission.

You can walk, drive or just sit surrounded by growing wood and listen to the strong pulse of a stream which once drove no less than 16 water wheels on its way to meet the Wear.

The Baptist Church in the centre of Hamsterley, one of our oldest, speaks loud of the time when the Ranters challenged the formal dogma of the Anglican community. Its parish church stands aloof a little outside the village, looking down over Wilton-le-Wear sitting on the edge of a thriving wetland nature reserve which, not that long ago, was still worked for gravel.

Old scars fade to become mellow memories as new ones take their place. Open-cast and quarrying on a scale undreamt of a few years ago rip black through measured coal or mark warm gold-yellow faces along the scarp of the limestone which forms the backbone of the lowland plain.

The coal still fires homely hearths, and the magnesian limestone mixed with seawater forms "magnesia" bricks to line and protect the bellies of belching furnaces which still give employment hope for some.

Such new scars reveal the wonders of our natural past: rich beds of fossil fish, the unique cannon ball limestone found nowhere else on earth, and neat knolls which were once a living part of a tropical reef – all may be seen within the sound of the famous roar of Rokers football crowd. The purple black strength of Whin Sill, which provides the strong foundations to much of the most dramatic scenery of the north east, now paves our motorways. Frosterley marble, which still veneers the beauty of living rock into many buildings, is now a tourist spectacle reminding all of their fiery volcanic origins.

Despite new scars the bounty of nature is always there, as it was at the end of the last ice age. Old quarries are a haven of wildlife and rare plants have spread from the cliffs and coastal denes – Ryhope, Crimdon, Castle Eden – to clothe their nakedness. Castle Eden dene brings a karst landscape to the edge of Peterlee and boasts of being the first nature reserve in Britain to be set up by a local authority. The thin soil of such places is home to a multitude of plants. Some, like the Fly and Burnt Tip Orchids,

LEFT: Colliery buildings at Beamish Open-Air Museum, where visitors can tour a drift mine. BELOW: The River Tees meanders through the magnificent scenery of Teesdale.

find their northern limit, while others like Blue Moor Grass and Birds Eye Primrose tell of high mountain pastures. Here too industry in the guise of Steetley Magnesite works with conservation to safeguard both jobs and 19 acres of unique limestone grassland. They are moving the whole, turf by turf, to a new safer site. Each turf is a living link with past glacial times and with the real treasure house of Teesdale. The River Tees flows down over the mighty waterfalls, Caldron Snout and High Force, the highest waterfall in the north of England.

There among the magnificence of the rolling fells and the spoil heaps of Roman and Quaker lead is a community of rare plants second to none in England, if not in Europe. Plants from the remnants of the last Ice Age crowd the fells, such as False Sedge and Northern Asphodel, Horseshoe Vetch from the warmer south, Shrubby Cinquefoil of North American and Russian stock, Mountain Avens and the fabled Gentians – all these are to be found here.

Black faced sheep do their best to remove the flowers before eager cameras can record them (please be careful of your feet). They also play their part keeping the fields free from ranker growing plants which would soon take over and choke out their diverse beauty.

Red Grouse brood over their rich clutches and rear their young on the best grouse moors in the world. Here generations of gamekeepers have used their skill, burning

BELOW: The heart of Durham, dominated by the castle and cathedral seen from the River Wear.

the heather to provide a patchwork of managed habitat which keeps both grouse and keeper well fed and safe until the birds' day of reckoning.

ABOVE: Orchids and other rare plants flourish on Castle Eden nature reserve.

Take away the "Glorious" Twelfth and all it stands for and the dale would be a poorer place. There would be less work to be done on these working fells. Take away the sheep and lambs and the same would be true; rank growth would crowd out the rare flora and fewer tourists would come to see the sights. Take away the concern of those people who decry hunting and who eat neither grouse nor spring lamb and Britain would not be the same caring place.

Durham, the County Palatine, is happy to share its hard worked roots with any who will tread its ways with care and reverence. Stand at Cow Green, walk its nature trails, look up at the high fells and down at the reservoir, iron grey white elephant of a recent past when society thought more of itself and less of its heritage. If you are brave and hardy enough, make the final pilgrimage to High Cup Knick, one of the true wonders of the world, where ice and time have carved a fluted valley out of the Great Whin Sill and left it high and dry and almost forgotten except by the wind and the stalwarts of the Pennine Way. This, we believe, was one route by which man came to develop the County of the County Palatine.

From this high vantage point, look back across the chequered beauty of these landscapes where nature and people together have managed to keep a sense of purpose.

GEOFFREY MOORHOUSE'S
Lancashire

Photographs by Sarah King

I write as a guilty man. Here I am, reviewing the shire of my origins, from "the wrong side of the hill"; and there can be no greater treachery than that from anyone born and brainwashed in either the county of Lancaster or of York (but at least I still get the order right). I look through the window and see my Pennines rolling straight up from the end of our lane, but I hear a puritan voice telling me that this isn't quite good enough now I call Wensleydale home. I take comfort from the fact that Eddie Paynter, who fought many a Roses battle on "the right side", also made his peace with the enemy and ended up over the hill. That I should be haunted still by the old imperatives in such a mobile world marks me as an alien in more senses than one. There are moments when I am not sure whether anyone else cares about these topographical loyalties any more. Our governors do not, for a start.

The last time I wrote about my native county Lancashire's boundaries were still more or less as Christopher Saxton mapped them in 1577. We shared the Pennines with Yorkshire, the sea separated us from the Manxmen and the Irish, and while the Mersey marked our limit to the south, the Lune did a similar service to the north; to which was added the outrider of Furness, extending into the Lakes. Apart from that eccentric adjunct, the boundaries were wholly natural ones, and a tremendous weight of history, stretching back to the Brigantes and including local peculiarities of culture as well as politics and economics, had been impacted within them.

For as much as a decade after the Second World War anyone living there knew, as well as he knew anything, that to be a Lancastrian was to be distinctively different from anyone else in the British Isles. In speech, most obviously; in other areas also, palpably if he took stock of his environment, paid attention to its present, informed himself of the past and compared himself with everybody else. It was to be tied up with cotton, not wool. It was to be more accustomed to tripe than Yorkshire pudding. It was to spend Wakes Weeks in Blackpool or Morecambe more naturally than elsewhere. It was to stroll behind brass bands through the centre of town ("T'top o't' street", we used to call it) for the annual Whit Walks. It was to have a communal affinity with an endless stream of names that rang; from John of Gaunt to Tommy Handley, from Robert Peel to Kathleen Ferrier, from John Bright to Gracie Fields,

230

from Francis Thompson to C. P. Scott, from Richard Arkwright to Thomas Beecham. It was to have a proprietorial interest in the Hallé Orchestra, in the incunabula that John Rylands collected, in the Pre-Raphaelites Andrew Walker bequeathed. It was to rejoice with the rest of the tribe that we boasted some of the loveliest country in Britain, even if most of us had to make the best of industrial towns which could be applauded only for their character. Haslam Mills, who was one of Scott's henchmen at the *Manchester Guardian*, once remarked that Lancashire gave itself the airs of a continent. If you kept your eyes open and traversed the county from Hawkshead to Irlam, from Blackstone Edge to Blundellsands, you could see very well why this should be so.

Post-war economics have altered much of Lancashire's substance, television (*pace Coronation Street*) has played havoc with the cultural pride, but nothing has done more to damage the old order and the old awareness than the manipulations of government. In 1974, for the convenience of public servants and no one else, the county was dismembered and has not been the same place since. There was a painful logic in the surrender of Furness and Lakeland Lancs to Cumbria (though I would have had another bone to pick there if I had originated in Westmorland) but how can any man with his faculties intact defend what else was imposed in that year?

Several million people who were Lancashire born and Lancashire bred have since found themselves bundled into an apparition known as Greater Manchester. These include the good folk of Saddleworth, who live as high up in the hills as I do myself; and the burghers of Ramsbottom, which is half-way up Rossendale; and the Wiganers, whose reputation as a sub-species of the tribe was evidently resented by government, which has no time for individualism, especially on a collective scale (no wonder Joe Gormley fled to Surrey, where he might feel that he was recognizably his own man still). I am told that a similar infliction has been visited on south-west Lancashire, in the name of Merseyside. If so I don't want to know about it, because Greater Manchester is already more than I can stomach, and I refuse to address letters to my parents thus, when they live in a village on what had ever been a Lancashire Pennine spur. Greater Manchester is a product of the same crassness that expunged the Saxon Ridings, though Yorkshire continues to be divided administratively into three. It's a peculiar world we inhabit now, and one I do not like. It has Bolton Wanderers in the Third Division and Watford in the First, and the natural order of things cannot be reversed more sickeningly than that.

BELOW LEFT: Accrington, with its viaduct built in 1847, was a thriving cotton-mill town during the Industrial Revolution but has since declined.
BELOW RIGHT: Modern development has changed the "gritty" character of Bury.

Rawtenstall in the Rossendale valley grew out of Lancashire's textile trade.

When Arthur Mee wrote a directory to Lancashire in 1936, he subtitled it "Cradle of our Prosperity", which must have made the horses at Haydock laugh and would have them positively convulsed today. As usual, when British times are bad, Lancashire has again copped it in the neck as severely as anyone and more wickedly than most. Greater Manchester, in fact, was invented at a moment when the comparative in that title was about to become more grotesquely inappropriate than at any time in local history, except when Mee was launching his fantasy. "If you want to see life," someone advised Disraeli's Coningsby, "go to Stalybridge or Bolton. There's high pressure." But that was in 1844, and the high pressure has all gone, evaporated in the loss of Empire, to be replaced by the wind and whatnot of political and industrial rhetoric. What Greater Manchester thinks today Yokohama did the day before yesterday, and already has a new trick up its sleeve to stay two jumps ahead. It hurts to say this, but it happens to be true.

There is little joy left in a contemplation of what used to be south Lancashire's industrial towns. For all their ugliness, that character I mentioned contained some precious things built of local idiosyncrasy. At Bury, where I was schooled and sang Stanford in C, our parish church (at "T'top o't' street") was the landmark round which the entire community – religiously inclined or not – swung throughout the year. It was a dignified building, but it was as black as pitch outside and pretty gloomy within. It was remarkable, apart from its commanding situation, for the flags of the Lancashire Fusiliers, which hung in two long rows from the clerestory down both sides of the nave and represented regimental history from the time of Wolfe. This was their garrison church, which they invaded every year to celebrate and lament the anniversary of their landing at Gallipoli in 1915; when, as I was constantly reminded by Grandad (who was there), they had won six VCs before breakfast and were proud of this feat.

The church was also in the path of the Whit Walks, which began in Union Square, again a shabby place but containing some notable Victorian architecture and two marvellous shops. One was the home, the birthplace, of black puddings; the other housed coltsfoot rock, liquorice root, camomile, and every other herbal remedy that Culpeper ever took note of, in a bewildering assortment of tiny drawers, each labelled with its contents in gold lettering. When you walked into those shops, they made you glad to belong to the same place as them. That was their point, as it was the point of those flags, and many other things I could recall about the Bury of only 30 years ago.

The point has been lost. The church has been stonewashed clean, which is a gain. But the flags have been removed from the clerestory and half-hidden under the aisles: had the floors been carpeted, I suspect there would have been a call to make a proper job of it (the Fusiliers, after all, have been concealed in some military amalgamation, so why not their banners as well?). Union Square has been eradicated, as if by some form of pest control, and with it those two shops. In its place Bury has been granted a parking lot and a shopping precinct, an anonymous sprawl which is already beginning to fade and could just as easily be in Harlow or anywhere else that has spawned one of Britain's gimcrack urban developments. Bury is no longer a gritty little town with a lot of character. It has been reduced to a nonentity which is not even allowed to consider itself part of Lancashire any more. They call this progress at Westminster.

I pick on Bury because I happen to know it better than most places that have gone the same way. Bolton and Rochdale, Oldham and Leigh are all in similar plight. Even the towns to the north of them, which have been permitted to escape the seepage of Greater Manchester, have been marked by the same deadening hand of the developers, who think little of style and less of durability, both of which take their toll of the profit margin. There were distinctive things about Blackburn and Burnley and the nearby communities that are the cricketing backbone of the Lancashire League, and they have been whittled away in this past generation, like the cotton industry on which they once thrived. Preston used to have much more than Tom Finney to be Proud Preston about; but it, too, is now just another Third Division place.

I am not being flippant here. The transformations of English football in my lifetime tell a great deal about the changes that have taken place in society at large; and what, in many ways, has gone wrong with us. In the same way, what has happened to Blackpool says much about our not so brave new world. The tawdry glamour of the Costa del Sludge and its like has been such a counter-attraction to the breezy familiarities of the Fylde coast that the unique spectacle of the illuminations is dimmed, because its audience has ebbed. Not so long ago it would take a couple of hours or more to drive from one end of "the Lights" to the other, so thickly congested were the crowds. When last I tried it, we drove unhampered through the lot in a quarter of that time – and there were far fewer lights to see.

The one thing that has not been mauled too badly is the Lancashire countryside. The redeeming feature of many a mill town was that you could literally walk out of it into uplands that were wildly desolate or benignly rugged according to the season of the year. It is still, thank goodness, possible to climb straight out of Littleborough and make for Jacob's Well and the traces of the Roman road, where the curlew and the peewit haunt the peat hags and the long Pennine slopes with their cries. Get yourself onto Holcombe Hill above Rossendale and you are in what some would call a wilderness, which means something not yet spoiled by man. And this is only one aspect of rural Lancs. Below the Pennines in the north of the county, the landscape near Hornby is as softly tamed as Leicestershire. The damson orchards still flourish in Bowland, and in the farmlands around Preston they still make cheeses the old-fashioned way – white wheels and cylinders that crumble under the knife and bite the tongue. Lancashire may not be able to afford the airs of a continent any more. But in its topographical variety, and what that humanly includes, it still represents – as few other counties do – everything that England has to offer now.

Nor is the spirit of Lancashire yet gone the way of Greater Manchester, in spite of all that government and the goggle box can do. I have half a shelf full of books and pamphlets, all published in the past few years, extolling old Lancastrian virtues and expressing a deep affection for the traditional peculiarities. *Old Lancashire Recipes* is one (and if you have never made potato cakes out of leftover spuds, you have not discovered that "waste not, want not" can be a pleasure as well as an ethic). *Clattering Clogs* is another, revealing that there are still 18 cloggers at work in the county. *Lancashire Evergreens* contains 100 dialect poems, mostly written in the 19th century but still recited today by people desperately trying to keep a flame alive against considerable odds. And there are a lot of such Lancastrians around, far more than some of our governors appear to think. Fred Dibnah, messing about with his steamroller after a day up a mill chimney, is not the only man who has resisted the awful tide of modernist conformity. To see him is to be reassured about many things, and to be reminded yet again of who I really am.

In spite of my settling for the other side of the hill, the old allegiance still exerts its pull. No other county cricket club shall have my member's sub, and I start few journeys as eagerly as when I set off for Old Trafford on a summer's day. I instinctively head for Lancaster and its market hall, bulging with all the produce of the Fylde, if there is "a big shop" to be done, unlike our neighbours, who loyally patronize Northallerton or even Harrogate. And when I descend the flanks of Ingleborough, get through Cantsfield and come to the tranquil valley of the Lune, I realize I am back where they have an ancient claim on me. For all that I have embraced Wensleydale, and would not now have it otherwise, I remain a Lancashire man. I know it, every time the name is called.

HUGH TREVOR-ROPER'S
Northumberland

Photographs by Richard Dudley-Smith

Northumberland is one of the most beautiful counties in England. Its beauty is multiple: it has something of everything: five rivers and dozens of islands; a long coastline, here of tidal beach or blown sand-dunes, there of rocks or the steep dolerite cliffs of the Great Whin Sill, with a string of coastal castles and picturesque fishing villages; rich pasture land behind it; then the rounded, friendly Cheviot Hills and the waste moors that separate us from Cumberland – as remote it seems to any Northumbrian, as the far side of the moon. And of course there is also Tyneside: we shall come to that.

The beauty of Northumberland is obvious at once, but it is given depth and meaning by history. Every stage of English history has left its mark, and successive ages have re-defined both the frontiers of the county and the society within them.

We begin with the Romans. What a monument they have left us! Of course, by now, the wall is a mere shadow of its former self. It was a magnificent work still in 1600 when our first great historian William Camden marvelled to see it, rising and falling with the contours of the hills. The Jacobite revolt of 1745 was, literally, its undoing, for General Wade then pillaged it to build his military road from Newcastle to Carlisle. But even its diminished remains are impressive as they follow the defensive line of the crags, looking north over that waste land. Our ancestors called it not the Roman but "the Picts' Wall". Northumberland was then "Pictish", hostile or, at best, debatable land. But the Roman roads ran forward into it: the line of the Dere Street can still be seen, running dead straight through the Western hills.

To the Romans Northumberland was beyond, if only just beyond, the pale. To the Saxons it was the heart of an independent kingdom stretching from above the Cheviots to below York. They too left their monuments: there is a fine Saxon church tower at Bywell, nestling in a romantic sylvan curve of the Tyne; and they too used pillaged Roman stones: witness the inscription of the Emperor Caracalla, upside-down in the crypt of Hexham abbey, one of the first of Saxon bishoprics.

Christianity came to Northumberland in Saxon times, from two competing sources: from Rome, via Canterbury and York, and from Ireland via Iona and the Tweed valley. Hexham was the Roman bishopric; the Celtic was Lindisfarne, the

LEFT: Dunstanburgh Castle, built by Thomas, Earl of Lancaster in the early 14th century. It was badly damaged during the Wars of the Roses and by 1538 it was in ruins. BELOW: Bamburgh Castle, founded by King Ida in 547, which stands on a 150 foot precipice by the sea. It was re-built in Norman times and restored in the 18th and 19th centuries.

ABOVE LEFT: The ruins of the Norman priory founded by Benedictine monks from Durham on Holy Island (Lindisfarne) on the site of England's first Christian monastery, destroyed by the Danes in 875, Lindisfarne Castle stands in the distance. ABOVE RIGHT: Wallington Hall, built in 1688 by a Newcastle merchant.

romantic tidal peninsula of Holy Island. There St Aidan, who could not speak Anglo-Saxon, preached in Irish, and the Saxon king of Northumbria, who had learnt Irish in exile, acted as his interpreter. Thither he was followed by St Cuthbert, the patron saint of that coast: he too came from the Tweed valley to be bishop of Lindisfarne, and would end as a hermit among the seals and sea-birds of the Farne Islands.

The frontier of Northumberland is always changing. The Romans drew it in the south, against the Picts. The Saxon defences faced east, against the terrible Viking sea-raiders, who swept down on that open coast, destroying monasteries and villages, and Lindisfarne itself. So the Saxon fortresses lined the coast – the vestigial beginnings of those medieval castles which still dominate it, whether gaunt and ruined, like Edward II's Dunstanburgh, or recently restored, like little Lindisfarne and giant Bamburgh – two rock-borne sentinels acknowledging each other across the intervening bay. Then, with the Normans, the frontier switched again, this time to the North. It was in the reign of William Rufus that the Border was fixed on its present line. Thereafter the enemy became not the Roman nor the Viking but the Scot.

Not all at once. At first it was an open frontier. The Normans settled the country: what an air of peace surrounds the little Norman church of Old Bewick, in its wooded dell, near Chillingham! In the 12th century, English monks from Northumberland planted monasteries across the Tweed, just as Celtic monks from Scotland had planted Lindisfarne. It was not till the Anglo-Scottish wars of the 14th century that the Border became a reality, as divisive, though invisible, as ever Hadrian's Wall had been. Today it remains a frontier still. Having lived on both sides of it, I am always astonished at its reality. "No, we don't know them at all", I have heard it said, of neighbours only a few miles away; "they are over the Border". Against that decisive reason there can be no argument.

It was in the age of the Scottish wars that Northumberland acquired its feudal character, then that the castles and pele-towers sprang up – not along the Border only, but in depth, from Tweed to Tyne. The whole Border area, on both sides, was then organised in "Marches". The Wardens of the Marches, and the Keepers of castles under them, were charged with keeping the peace – when there was peace. When there was war, the royal armies came up through the great castles of the coastal plain. One Sir Thomas Malory came up thus with the army of Edward IV; he looked on Bamburgh and decided that this could have been King Arthur's Joyous Gard.

There were three Marches on the English (as on the Scottish) side. The Eastern March was the old Saxon shore. Its headquarters was the town of Berwick-on-Tweed, when it was in English hands (for it changed often). The Middle March was the rest of the county. The Western March was Cumberland. Berwick finally became English under Richard III. The Scots never digested the loss, and after the savage wars of the mid-16th century, Queen Elizabeth had it solidly re-fortified by two *émigré* Italian engineers. The fine Italian fortifications are still there and, being never damaged by use, make a delightful esplanade round the old, unspoiled town. For by the time they

TOP LEFT: Country near Allenheads on the southern border. BELOW LEFT: Berwick-on-Tweed, built along an estuary crossed by three bridges. BELOW RIGHT: Part of the 73 mile Hadrian's Wall.

were completed, the wars were over, for good. In 1603, when James I became king of England, the Border lost its function; the Marches were dismantled; the castles and pele-towers on both sides fell into ruin or were converted into private houses; and Berwick, from a fortress, became a picturesque harbour-town on the road to Scotland. However, the Scots never dropped their claim to it, and so, to humour them, it has a special status in formal treaties. It is said that, having been included in the declaration of the Crimean war, it was inadvertently omitted from the peace treaty which ended it, and so is still formally at war with Russia. I do not know if this is true.

The capital of the Middle March was Alnwick. It too was a walled town, and is dominated by the greatest castle of all. But of the town walls only the gatehouse – "Hotspur Tower" – now remains, and the leaden warriors on the castle battlements are symbolic only. Like the fortifications of Berwick, they never frightened the Scots. They were put there in the 19th century.

Northumberland in 1603 might no longer be a military zone, but the long wars had left it a poor county, sadly declined from Saxon times. Then it had been the core of a kingdom, containing its own two bishoprics. Now it was the tag-end of the bishopric of Durham, itself much weakened since the Reformation. One great noble family, the Percies, had dominated it in the past; but by now they too were in eclipse, and would soon retreat to Sussex. Meanwhile castles fell into decay, law and order had collapsed, banditry was endemic – Camden could not visit a Roman fort because of the "rank thieves and robbers everywhere" – and the main local industry in the Tyne valley was the manufacture of stirrups, bits and harness. However, even now a new force was arising which, once again, would transform the county: coal.

Coal had long been mined in the Tyne valley, for local use, but in the reign of Elizabeth it acquired a new importance. The change was caused by the growth of London and the use of "sea-coals" – that is, coal brought by sea – for heating it. The trade was a monopoly of the incorporated merchants of Newcastle, a close family group which soon controlled the whole industry. Already by 1640 Newcastle supplied the kingdom, and "coals to Newcastle" was a proverb. On that base, the industry of the valley "took off". Railways followed coal – George Stephenson began his career in a Newcastle colliery – and then shipping; and the wealth thus generated spread gradually through the county as Newcastle industrialists established or inserted themselves into rural dynasties and their capital financed agricultural improvement.

Thus upstart merchants moved into the county; ancient families were refreshed by mercantile fortunes; and crumbling castles were repaired, extended, replaced. Sir William Blackett, a great coal-magnate, built the fine house at Wallington which would pass, by marriage, to the Cornish Trevelyans. Coal enabled the Delavals to hire Vanbrugh and build Seaton Delaval, now engulfed by their own former collieries. In restoration, the heirs of the Percies set the example. Now become great coal-lords, they returned to the North, resumed the old name, and rebuilt their castle, with gothic frills. The gentry followed their lead. Even the bishops entered the game, for they too, as landlords, had acquired vast wealth from coal, some of which they even spent in Northumberland. Lord Crewe, a turncoat bishop who backed the wrong horse in politics, showed the way: he sweetened his reputation by founding the lifeboat at Bamburgh and laying out one of the most perfect of planned villages at Blanchland – and is commemorated by eponymous hotels in both places. In this great renewal, the fashionable architects saw their chance. They alit like bees on those tempting castle-sites, classicising or gothicising as the taste changed: Robert Adam at Alnwick and Ford, Wyatt *alias* Wyatville at Chillingham, the Northumbrian Dobson at Beaufront, Belsay, indeed everywhere. So did the great landscape-gardener "Capability" Brown, another Northumbrian, who laid out the parks and gardens at Alnwick, Wallington and Capheaton.

So began that re-feudalisation of rural Northumberland which is still so obvious in its social structure and physical pattern: its country houses and parks, its large farms, its nine packs of hounds. Socially, the county falls into three parts. "Hexhamshire" is to Newcastle as Sussex to London: there the industrial money gives itself the grandest gentry airs. North of the Wansbeck it is different: a world of its own (I am prejudiced in its favour, having been born in the village of Glanton, on the edge of the Cheviot hills). The third part is Tyneside and its industrial sprawl reaching up to its new satellite, Ashington: the disowned base on which the whole archaic edifice so comfortably reclines.

Still, it is a very agreeable edifice, full of quaint survivals, fossils of history untouched by intervening time. Think of the Chillingham wild cattle. How long have they been there? Nobody seems to know. As native Northumbrians they have naturally stayed put, in their private park, for centuries. They too have a strange social system, dominated by a King Bull, a kind of hereditary duke. They too are difficult to know and flee on sight – unless, of course, one meets them out hunting, when they take one for granted: I have ridden straight through the herd and not an animal moved – they merely nodded a kind of Northumbrian recognition. Or think of those sea-birds on the Farne islands – guillemots, puffins, terns, all settled for centuries in their distinct colonies. I have known some splendid human eccentrics too, tucked away in rural corners, on whom I would gladly expatiate; but not here, to the profane: they might not understand.

A figure of a soldier on the battlements of Alnwick Castle.

ANTHONY BURTON'S
Yorkshire

Photographs by Tim Mercer

Yorkshire, it seems, no longer exists: the bureaucrats have had their way. The county, like Caesar's Gaul, has been divided into three parts and large chunks have been hacked off and handed to newly created bodies, Cleveland and Humberside. The absurdity of giving the address "Humberside" to, for example, Bridlington, which stands a full 30 miles from that river, seems to have occurred to no one at Whitehall. And, worst indignity of all, parts have even been pushed across the border into Lancashire.

Yet all is not quite lost, and when I speak of Yorkshire I mean the old Yorkshire, the area still recognized by at least one official body. The Yorkshire County Cricket Club sent word to all those unfortunates so untimely ripped from the body of the mother county to the effect that as far as the club was concerned they were still children of Yorkshire. This was no point of mere academic concern, for Yorkshire alone among the cricketing counties still insists that only those born in the county can play for the county. The ruling might be regarded by some as rather quaint, out of touch with the realities of modern sport, but then cricket has always been something more than a sport to the true Yorkshireman. Indeed, anyone wanting to understand the character of the natives could do far worse than turn up for the Roses match against the old enemy, Lancashire.

Numerous stories surround the annual Roses encounters, of which the best loved and most often repeated tells of a match during which one spectator punctuated proceedings with cries of "Oh, I say, well played," and "Good shot, sir." This flippancy at a solemn occasion proved too much for the Tyke at his side. "Art tha' Lancashire?" he inquired and, on receiving a negative, asked in disbelief, "Tha's never Yorkshire?" On again being answered in the negative the Yorkshireman became quite angry. "Then shut up," he ordered. "This has got nowt to do wi' thee."

The story illustrates the insularity of Yorkshire folk, which can so infuriate outsiders, and a well-known distrust of southerners. It also shows a local pride, a feeling of being different from the rest of the world, and a proper sense of seriousness for an occasion at which the honour of the county is at stake. And if asked about what some might see as arrogance, the Yorkshireman would probably have replied that there was quite simply nowhere else in the world that could offer the native more in which he could take a pride.

Where should you go to try to capture the unique appeal and character of Yorkshire? This is a difficult question to answer. There are, of course, the five-star attractions, starting with the great city of York. Here is a spot where history can be read in tangible form, in the remains left by Roman and Norseman and in the splendid Minster surrounded by its huddle of medieval streets. The religious theme can be followed up to the famous monasteries in their superb and beautiful settings, Bolton, Rievaulx and, perhaps the most glorious of them all, Fountains Abbey. Those on the hunt for grand scenery can turn to the magnificent coastline with high, dramatic cliffs under the shade of which sit little fishing villages, such as Staithes and Robin Hood's Bay, as picturesque as any to be found in Cornwall. And there are the dales, well known and well loved even before James Herriot revealed their beauties to millions through his books and television.

The Leeds and Liverpool Canal passes through Skipton, "the gateway to the dales".

I would be the last to deny the merits of any of these, yet if I were asked what image comes first to mind when I think of Yorkshire, what places most clearly express the character of the place, then I would turn elsewhere. For me much of Yorkshire's unique appeal lies in a fascinating conjunction of opposites – of town and country, the noise and clatter of industry with the peace and beauty of the moors no more than a brisk walk away.

As a child I lived near and went to school in the popular tourist town of Knaresborough. It is an undeniably picturesque spot where the town seems to tumble down the slopes from the castle towards the River Nidd. The martial theme is taken up and repeated in the tall railway viaduct, castellated in the best tradition of Victorian Gothic. Along the banks can be seen the petrifying well with gloves and teddy bears suspended forever in stony immobility. Here, too, is Mother Shipton's cave, home of a prophetess who looked into the future and saw little to encourage her successors. It seems the complete tourist town, with little else to justify its existence.

Yet it is also a busy market town, and there are reminders of another way of life in the linen mill down by the weir. And 30 and more years ago when I was a schoolboy there were other reminders that the busy life of the textile mills was being carried on just over the horizon. On summer days coach loads of mill girls used to descend on Knaresborough, all, in memory at least, fat and jolly women, characters from McGill postcards come to life. A trip on the river was an essential part of the day's excitement, and they would be rowed in one large boat powered by a perspiring oarsman. On one memorable day they all decided to sit on the same side of the boat with the inevitable result. The ladies were hauled out to lie in rows like stranded whales, but laughing uproariously at the absurd comedy in which they had been unwilling actors. They seemed a world away from the gentility of neighbouring Harrogate, yet geographically they were not that far. The factories, too, were just over the next hill.

Yorkshire is dominated by the spine of the Pennines, and along the ribs and in the valleys in between are the settlements that helped to make the county rich. A fine place to start on a hunt for my essential Yorkshire is Skipton, described in today's tourist brochures as "the gateway to the dales" which indeed it is, but it is also a great deal more. It is the meeting place of two worlds.

To the north and west lie the moors where for generations the human population has been far outnumbered by the sheep that roam and graze there. It is wonderful country, where that hard, rocky spine keeps poking through to provide a sudden hard edge to the soft swelling of the moor. There is no shortage of "beauty spots", but they tend to have little of the conventionally pretty about them. Drama rather than serenity is the overwhelming impression. There is the huge gash in the escarpment of Gordale Scar or the falling away of the hillside into the overhanging limestone cliff at Malham Cove. And those with a strong appetite for the open spaces and possessed of suitably sturdy legs can set out for the western edge of the moors to tackle the three peaks of Whernside, Ingleborough and Pen-y-Ghent – preferably all in the one day. But wherever you walk in this region you are never far from the sight of sheep, trundling like grey, woollen, mobile boulders over the lower slopes.

To the south and east of Skipton lies the world of factory and mill, where once the

High cliffs mark the coastline near the fishing village of Staithes.

workers were busy turning the wool from the sheep's backs into yarn and cloth. And Skipton partakes of both worlds. At first glance it is no more than another attractive market town, its stone houses sitting easily in a stony landscape, with just the one imposing feature in the shape of a splendid castle. But the other world exists in Skipton as well. Along the Leeds and Liverpool Canal are the warehouses and mills of the woollen trade. Skipton marks the boundary between rural and industrial Yorkshire. The tourist who dashes away from the latter to enjoy the former is doing what most of us are trying to do on holiday – escaping the rush and noise of the modern world for a few moments of tranquillity. But along the way he could be missing a great deal.

The old villages where men and women worked at spinning wool into yarn, then weaving the yarn into cloth, often have immense character and charm. The best-known example is Haworth, but the wool-working sites are not what the visitors come to see. The Keighley and Worth Valley steam railway is the attraction for some, but for rather more it is the parsonage, home of the Brontë family. Haworth is an undeniably attractive spot, but much of its original character has been all but swamped by the Brontë connexion. Even those characteristics which so strongly influenced the Brontës have tended to disappear under the floods of trinkets and souvenirs.

If I wanted to show a visitor the kind of world that gave the novelists their inspiration, I would travel a few miles south to the village of Heptonstall. This is a closed-up community of narrow streets turning back on each other to form a tight little knot of a village. Here are the old weavers' cottages built out of local stone and

245

Golcar boasts one of the best fish and chip shops in Yorkshire.

a small 18th-century octagonal chapel erected on the spot where John Wesley preached. Snaking away over the surrounding hills are the tracks where the trains of pack horses made their way, laden with cloth and yarn. It seems far closer to the real world portrayed in, say, *Shirley* than does commercialized Haworth. And from the hill one can look down on the new world of industrialization that supplanted the old world of cottage workers.

Down in the valley, below Heptonstall, sits Hebden Bridge. River and canal are lined with the mills of the Industrial Revolution, while the houses range around them, piling in terraces up the hillside. Now Hebden, too, has been left behind by newer inventions, improved industries. Hand crafts have come back to the area, though some see the change in some way affecting the essential toughness of the region, reducing its impact. I would disagree, seeing the new generation of potters and weavers as a revitalizing force for a region which was steadily decaying.

But if you want the reality without the "prettification", move south again to the Colne Valley, a long finger pointing westward from the tightly clenched fist of Huddersfield. Villages straggle out along the valley. High on the northern rim is Golcar, where the Colne Valley Museum at Cliffe Ash has brought the old weaving cottages back to life. Golcar can also boast a fish and chip shop which is among the best in Yorkshire – which, of course, means the best anywhere – and which richly repays the customer who joins the inevitable queue. In the valley bottom are the small towns such as Slaithwaite (pronounced "Slowit") and Marsden. They contain no very great buildings, no architectural splendours, but they do have a wealth of character. These are the places I would come to for the real heart of Yorkshire. They are honest, no-nonsense places, and they possess one great virtue: walk out of the town and in minutes you are on the open moorland, as isolated and alone as if you were on a polar expedition. And when limbs are weary and the sun is setting it is back to the town and the local speciality – hot pie swimming in mushy peas, washed down with a pint of good real ale.

There will always be those who regard the true heart of Yorkshire as lying in the great industrial cities – in Leeds, Bradford, Huddersfield, Halifax or Sheffield. Certainly the cities have their splendours. Look, for example, at the Piece Hall in Halifax, the old trading centre of the woollen industry and as handsome a set of Georgian buildings as you would find in a fashionable square in Bath. Yet, for me, they are less characteristic than the small towns: they are merely the same experience multiplied several times over. But they have this in common: however the city might have grown, whatever the developers might have perpetrated, it is still possible to get away. Around the cities is that same wild countryside that encroaches so nearly on the smaller towns, and for those of us who love this part of the world there is no finer scenery to be had.

I no longer live in Yorkshire but when I think of it, as I often do, this is the image that remains: sitting alone among the bracken and heather below a skyline ruled straight by an outcrop of black, lumpy gritstone. The lower slopes will be patterned by a network of dry-stone walls, leading the eye down to the factory chimney poking out from a cluster of houses. The stone of the town is the stone of the crags above, and there is a sense of peace and of unity between nature and man, even industrial man, that is quite unique.

Arden Great Moor in the North Riding.